The Study of
the Past in the Victorian Age

Edited by Vanessa Brand

Oxbow Monograph 73
1998

Published by
Oxbow Books, Park End Place, Oxford OX1 1HN
for
The British Archaeological Association and
The Royal Archaeological Institute

ISBN 1 900188 28 7

This book is available direct from
Oxbow Books, Park End Place, Oxford OX1 1HN
(Phone: 01865–241249; Fax: 01865–794449)

and

The David Brown Book Company
PO Box 5111, Oakville, CT 06779, USA
(Phone: 860–945–9329; Fax: 860–945–9468

Printed in Great Britain at
The Short Run Press, Exeter

Contents

Preface

THE PAPERS PRINTED in this volume were delivered at a one-day seminar entitled 'The Study of the Past in the Victorian Age', held in the rooms of the Society of Antiquaries of London, Burlington House, on Saturday 25 September 1993. Attended by over one hundred people, many of whom participated in a reception held afterwards, the seminar was a joint event arranged by the British Archaeological Association and the Royal Archaeological Institute to celebrate the 150th anniversary of the foundation of the original Association in 1843.

In 1991 the British Archaeological Association's Council started to consider suitable events that should mark this special landmark in its history. From the outset the Council was unanimous in the view that the Institute should be jointly involved. Two proposals were not able to be pursued. It was thought impractical to join forces for a summer conference at Canterbury in 1994, the location in 1844 of the Association's first congress. In the event the British Archaeological Association celebrated its 150th year with a conference held in Utrecht in July 1993. The idea of a joint Anniversary Reception in St James's Palace in the presence of Her Majesty the Queen, the Institute's Patron, was abandoned because the Institute was to develop its own plans for such a reception in 1994. That the two bodies came together for this joint seminar is, however, in itself a source of great pleasure and a notable event.

It is appropriate that the seminar examined the contributions made by our Victorian predecessors to the study of the past, for it was that interest in the 1840s that lay behind the Association's origins: at a county level new antiquarian societies were springing to life, many as the direct result of railway construction that threatened so many monuments and uncovered so many sites; at the national level it was felt that the Society of Antiquaries was in stagnation and was not then concerned with the preservation of medieval buildings and the monuments daily threatened with destruction in an increasingly industrial age. The formation of a new national organisation was thought necessary. It was to be independent of the Society of Antiquaries yet aligned to its activities: its protestation was that 'No kind of rivalry or interference with the recognised province and professed objects of that Society is contemplated'. In bringing the Association into being three gentlemen played key roles, Albert Way, Director of the Society of Antiquaries, Thomas Joseph Pettigrew, a surgeon, and Charles Roach Smith, a London chemist and passionate collector whose acquisitions were to form the nucleus of the British Museum's Romano-British collections. Thomas Wright, a friend of Roach Smith was also a major figure.

With Lord Conyngham as President, the British Archaeological Association was launched by the end of 1843. The first volumes of the *Archaeological Journal* were published in 1844 and the first congress was held in September 1844 at Canterbury, copious descriptions of which were published in provincial and many national publications. Divisions in the membership were apparent at the very end of 1844 and an ever-widening chasm opened throughout 1845, with two rival factions headed by Albert Way and Thomas Wright respectively. So absurd was the rivalry that both factions decided to meet separately, but within a month of each other, at Winchester in 1845.

The split is part of the folklore and history of British archaeology and is ably chronicled in detail by Joan Evans and David Wetherall.[1] Suffice it to say here that reconciliation was there none. In September 1845 the Way faction adopted rules and regulations for a new organisation and in February 1846 this group adopted the title The Archaeological Institute of Great Britain and Ireland taking with it, as dowry, the *Archaeological Journal*.

In the course of our histories the British Archaeological Association and the Royal Archaeological Institute have developed their own special areas of interest and inevitably, their activities have changed: neither body, for instance, any longer unwraps mummies, as demonstrated at the 1844 congress in Canterbury. The original disagreements have faded and very amicable contacts have been maintained. Indeed, there is a large number of people who belong to both organisations.

The friendly atmosphere was evident at the seminar. For its success a debt of gratitude is owed to the members of the joint Working Party: Vanessa Brand, John Cherry, Jonathan Coad, Martin Henig, Kenneth Painter, Caroline Raison, Andrew Saunders (Chairman), and the late Hugh Chapman. Special thanks must go to Caroline Raison who shouldered the burden of administration and organised a splendid lunch for the speakers, and to Kenneth Painter, who made all the arrangements with the speakers. To the speakers themselves, whose papers are printed here, and to Chris Brooks who has since supplied an Introduction, we owe particular thanks. John Cherry, Secretary of the Society of Antiquaries, made it possible for us to meet at Burlington House and we are especially grateful to him for arranging this. It was an appropriate

---

[1] Evans, 'RAI', Wetherall, 'Foundation'.

venue since it was from the Society that we sprang and, over the years, the Society has kept an eye on us and encouraged its offspring.

The Noviomagian Society, one of the Society's offshoot dining clubs, in March 1845 minuted its amusement at the unfortunate division in the Association and the ineffectiveness of those concerned in resolving differences:

> It was proposed that as a cure for squabbling, or fussy, or overbearing dispositions, the parties should be compelled to join the British Archaeological Association, where nothing is eaten but honey, and nothing drunk but the milk of human kindness. A premium was offered for a new pun, on the names of the rival disputants, and a fresh Way to set all Wright was anxiously worked for, but not found.[2]

Let us all hope that the Anniversary seminar and this volume will point the way for closer collaboration and even more amicable contacts in the future.

Laurence Keen
President, British Archaeological Association

---

[2] Wetherall, op. cit.

Introduction:
Historicism and the Nineteenth Century

Chris Brooks

HISTORICISM AND MODERNITY

The idea of the century as a category of the historical imagination and as a unit of historical investigation seems to have been invented in the second half of the eighteenth century. It was taken up with a vengeance by Victorian writers, and the century they were primarily concerned to invent was their own. The nineteenth century seems, indeed, to have been the first in which contemporary commentators consistently used the label of the hundred-years slice of time to which they belonged in a way previously reserved for the act of historical retrospection. The pamphleteers of the Great Civil War, though in no doubt as to the historic magnitude of the events in which they were participating, never located those events within a temporal unit called 'the seventeenth century'. Augustan men of letters, though highly conscious of their own cultural historicity by virtue of the gap that separated ancients and moderns, spoke of 'the present age' as the defining category of contemporaneity far more readily than they spoke of 'the eighteenth century'. But the nineteenth century knew its own name, and used it with unprecedented self-consciousness.[1] Appropriately, it became the title of that most heavyweight of Victorian reviews, J. T. Knowles's *The Nineteenth Century*, which began publication in 1877. In taking such a name the journal constituted its historical moment as that of the whole century to which it belonged, and constructed that century not only as the object of review but also as the agent. In the pages of *The Nineteenth Century* the nineteenth century reviewed itself and, through itself, the world.

---

[1] I am grateful to my colleague Dr Nick Groom for discussion on some of the issues raised in these opening sentences.

1

Such reflexivity is at the heart of nineteenth-century historicism, and it is unsurprising to find that the title of the review was suggested to Knowles by Alfred Tennyson.[2] Tennyson is a key figure in understanding historicism, for a large part of his output was occupied with reoriginating the narrative stuff of the past, from the Elizabethan sea-doggery of 'The Revenge: a Ballad of the Fleet' to the chivalric ambiguities of *Idylls of the King*. Such a fixation with the past was enough to exasperate Barrett Browning's Aurora Leigh.

> I do distrust the poet who discerns
> No character or glory in his times,
> And trundles back his soul five hundred years,
> Past moat and drawbridge, into a castle-court,
> To sing ...
> ... of some black chief, half knight, half sheep-lifter,
> Some beauteous dame, half chattel and half queen,
> As dead as must be, for the greater part,
> The poems made on their chivalric bones ...
>
> Nay, if there's room for poets in this world
> A little overgrown (I think there is),
> Their sole work is to represent the age,
> Their age, not Charlemagne's ...[3]

Vigorous as this is, it largely misses the point. Tennyson's assiduous remaking of the past — and it is surely Tennyson who is the target of Aurora's irritation — was not a block to his engagement with the present: it was precisely his historicism, and the precise historicism he exemplified, that were so characteristically contemporary, that made him modern.

HISTORICISM AND DISCONTINUITY

Tennyson's historicism, and that of the nineteenth century generally, was derived from the historical relativism that emerged towards the end of the previous century, and that found its most popular and perhaps most influential expression in the novels of Walter Scott. Scott understood the past as another country, not merely as a concoction of chain-mail and whimples or of periwigs and patches, but as a domain distinct in place and time shaped by its own social, cultural, and political stresses. In *Ivanhoe*, destined to have such an impact upon nineteenth-century medievalism, the tournament-ground heroics are conditioned by the wider context of the Anglo-Norman struggle

[2] Metcalf, *Knowles*, 276.
[3] Browning, *Aurora Leigh*, V, 11. 189–203.

for ascendancy, and by Scott's acute sense of the instability of early thirteenth-century England. In *Waverley* even so recent a drama as the '45 is historicised, Charlie and his entourage figuring not as romantic icons but as representatives of a hopelessly outmoded economic and social order. It does not matter how wide of the mark we may now think Scott's history to have been; what matters is the model of historical understanding his fictions embodied. That model was essentially one of reconstruction, for it was based in the acceptance of a scission between the present and the past. It is discontinuity not continuity that brings historical consciousness into being. And discontinuity is the precondition for imaginative reconstruction, for inventing the past in the sense both of making it up and of discovering it. Once invented, the past becomes available for deployment in terms of the now: as caution or inspiration, as contrast or analogy, as a measure of how far we have advanced, or how far we have declined. So this piece of history I am putting together here, my location of a historical period in which historical disjunction happened, is itself, necessarily, an act of invention, a construction that I deploy out of a sense of where I am writing from now. In a much larger way, the nineteenth century's unprecedented historicism was the corollary of its unprecedented consciousness of its own present.

The process of disjunction for which I am arguing had a long history of its own with origins at least as far back as the seventeenth century. From the second half of the eighteenth century, however, that process accelerated towards the moment of scission as the generative forces of economic change themselves accelerated. Feeding those forces, and fed by them, was rapid demographic growth. Although it is difficult to be sure of precise figures for the eighteenth century, it would seem that the population of England and Wales in 1750 was around 6,500,000, an estimated increase of a little over a million since 1700. By the year of the first census in 1801 that population had leapt to more than 9,000,000; in the half century that followed it virtually doubled. At the same time the pace of change in the national economy increased. In the eighteenth century agrarian capitalism had become the dominant mode of production, and the capitalisation of the agricultural sector was complete in all its essentials by 1800. But its preeminence was already being challenged by the emergent power of manufacturing, and industrial capitalism would replace agrarian as the dominant mode of production in the course of the nineteenth century. As part of the process Britain became the first urban nation in the modern world. Although populations increased everywhere up to about 1850, the second half of the nineteenth century saw a sharp demographic differentiation between town and country. In rural areas throughout the kingdom people left the land, particularly after the onset of the Great Agrarian Depression in the 1870s. Some, particularly in Scotland, Wales, and famine-racked Ireland, emigrated to the Empire or the Americas; most left for London and the industrial centres. By the end of the nineteenth century Britain had been urbanised, with 75% of its people living in cities or urban concentrations compared to only about 20% a hundred years earlier. Whereas in 1801 there had been no city other than London with a population of more than 100,000, by 1851 there were nine, and by 1901 eighteen, with Glasgow, Liverpool, Manchester, and Birmingham all totalling more than half a million inhabitants.

The triumph first of agrarian then of industrial capitalism profoundly changed the traditional relations of production, and with them all relationships between the social groups that comprised the rapidly growing population. It is here, in the lived experience of British men and women, more than in the statistics of industrial expansion and urban proliferation, astonishing as they are, that I want to locate the moment of historical disjunction – or perhaps, considering the millions of people involved, the moments. In the eighteenth and early nineteenth centuries the conversion of agricultural production to capitalism established a class system in the British countryside. At different speeds in different places, the social relations that had typified the old economic order of the rural community, the vertical ties of responsibility and deference in terms of which the rural hierarchy had been structured, were replaced by the horizontal cleavages of class. Common lands were enclosed; inherited working practices were supplanted; contractual agreement replaced customary obligation. Landowners remained on top of the social heap but came to occupy that position as a *rentier* upper class; farmers and an increasingly diverse body of agrarian entrepreneurs and technical specialists joined the old professions, often uneasily, in an expanded middle class; agricultural workers became a rural proletariat, though the stuttering history of agrarian trade unionism is an indicator of how long they took to realise the new situation. In the roaring industrial centres of the Midlands and the North, by contrast, the old economic and social order vanished more quickly and more totally. Aristocracy and gentry, the traditional leaders of society, hardly existed in the new cities – although leases, mines, and mineral rights could swell their rent rolls. Malthus, laissez-faire, and the exigencies of the factory system dictated the relations between the owners and the hands. When trade boomed the mills worked night and day; when it slumped whole labour forces were laid off *en masse*. And just as the nature of work had changed utterly, so also had the material setting of existence itself. For the urban workers the hastily thrown up streets and closes of the proletarian districts bore scarcely a vestige, either physical or psychological, of the rural societies in which many of them had been born.

SOCIAL CONFLICT AND THE INVENTION OF THE PAST

For better or worse the Agrarian and Industrial Revolutions made Britain anew, and in the process severed the lived historical continuity that was the condition of precapitalist, preindustrial, preurban community. Across the Channel the French Revolution had effected a rather different severance from the past, and though a semblance of the old European order was patched together at Versailles the rumble of the tumbrils would continue to haunt ruling elites, as the ideals of the revolutionaries would continue to inspire radicals. If the transformation of the British economy was the disjunctive moment that brought the nineteenth century's self-consciousness into being, and that threw the uncoupled past into sharp and distinct relief, then it was the spectre of popular insurrection that gave urgency to historicism and self-consciousness alike. After all, had not the *sansculottes* abolished history itself and begun the world again with Year 1 of the Revolution? Certainly, in the trade slump that followed the end of the Napoleonic War, there seemed every reason for the British governing classes to fear revolution. Luddites smashed machines in the textile mills; incendiarism flared across the countryside; the Blanketeers marched on London in the winter of 1816–17; in 1819 the notorious Peterloo Massacre saw yeomanry sabre a peaceful mass meeting in Manchester – and receive the congratulations of Lord Liverpool's government for so doing. Although improved trade conditions gave a measure of nervous peace to the 1820s, the end of the decade brought popular violence on an even larger scale. Across southern and eastern England in 1830–1 agricultural workers rose in revolt, breaking machines and firing ricks in the name of Captain Swing; in 1831–2 agitation in support of the Reform Bill occasioned widespread urban rioting that achieved its most sensational result in the burning of the centre of Bristol; the continuing struggles of trade unionism elicited a vindictive response in the sentences handed down to the Tolpuddle Martyrs in 1836; and the last years of the decade saw the first gathering of the forces of Chartism. In fact, very few of the disturbances in the quarter-century after Waterloo seem to have been directly impelled by any revolutionary example that derived from France – whatever the British ruling elite might have thought to the contrary. Rather, they can be seen as attempts, frequently desperate, to negotiate the disjunction between the past and the present that had been effected, or was being effected, by the triumph of capital: by seeking to abolish change and restore previous working conditions, as, most obviously, in the case of industrial and agrarian machine-breaking; by seeking a defensive formation in which to confront the new economic order, as in the case of trade unionism. It would be to trivialise the distress of working people in these years merely to theorise their struggles into so many instances of a new, enforced historical awareness. Nevertheless, some such awareness did lay near the heart of their experience, for history is not merely a matter of books and archives, but a vital part of the lives and memories and traditions of ordinary men and women.

Of course, it was not only the proletariat that had to find means of negotiating disjunction. Because fundamental change had occurred in the relations of production, all classes needed strategies of accommodation and explanation – though with the vital, if obvious, difference that it was members of the middle and upper classes who had been the primary beneficiaries of that change. Differences notwithstanding, it seems to me clear that because the unrest of the early nineteenth century was one of the consequences of a radical break with the past, the construction of history – the present's invention of its past – became a central project for British culture at every level. And it was a project that was enabled by the very fact of the break, by the way in which, as I have argued, self-consciousness brought historicism into being.

I do not have the room here to attempt even a summary account of the complex nature and development of nineteenth-century historicism; nor to do anything more than acknowledge the perils that such an attempt would involve, starting, as it would have to, from the embattled terrain of historicism in the late twentieth century. Nevertheless, some specific characteristics of the historicism that emerged in the late Georgian and early Victorian periods are worth picking out and discussing in greater detail: first, its emphasis upon narratives of causation, upon telling stories about why the past – and thus the present – happened as it did; second, its concern with measuring the present against the cultural practices and products of the past, and of the social formations to which they belonged; third, a fascination with the material artefacts, the buildings and objects, of earlier societies, and with the possibilities of stylistic revival. Of course, I am not claiming that any of these three was new: all three can be traced back, in part at least, to the seventeenth century, and were developing as major features of historical engagement by the second half of the eighteenth. What was new, however, was the kind of emphasis the nineteenth century placed upon them and the synthesis between them that evolved.

NARRATIVES OF CAUSATION

The nineteenth century was the great age of narrative history. In the simple identification of history, particularly History with a capital aitch, with a narrative sequence, there is nothing remarkable. Xenophon, Tacitus, and Josephus provided ready precedents from antiquity. Hume and Gibbon were exemplars from the eighteenth century, when narrative histories devoted to specific cultural fields also began to emerge: for example, Thomas Warton's *The History of English Poetry, from the Close of the Eleventh to the Commencement of the Eighteenth Century*, published in 1774. But the range of narrative history written as the nineteenth century developed, and the scale upon which so much of it was conceived, are remarkable. So also is the extent to which its concerns are aetiological. The model provided by empirical science encouraged a historical methodology centred in the analysis of the processes of cause and effect. As the historian's nearest equivalent to experimental data, original documents were increasingly widely used as the starting-point for such analysis. The end in view was a scientific history, alluring in its promise of delivering the authority and objectivity that science seemed able to command. Analogous processes affected the novel, as the episodic structure of picaresque fiction was relinquished in favour of the tightly plotted causality that typifies literary realism. In 1836 Mr Pickwick may still have been able to meander through the world like a middle-class Don Quixote, but a quarter century later the career of Pip Pirrip was shaped by harder, more deterministic hands. From my point of view, such narratives of causation were a response to the reality of historical disjunction – and the narrative I am constructing at this moment is another such. The enterprise of aetiology is to tie phenomena to causes, and though an aetiological history cannot reconstitute a lived continuity, it may offer a causal logic to explicate phenomena experienced as discontinuous. Such a history would thus provide a conceptual recoupling of the present and the past as a substitute for the organic relationship that had been lost: and as such would necessarily be an invention, in both the senses I have already indicated.

In the Introduction to John Wade's *History of the Middle and Working Classes* of 1833, for example, Wade explains that he must write the history of his two classes, 'their origin and progress', to show 'the chief circumstances by which their social condition, up to this time, has been determined'.[4] Tailored to a bourgeois audience, this history turns out to be a smooth record of industrious advance towards the present happy state, and Luddites, Blanketeers, and Captain Swing are not part of the story: disjunction? what disjunction? In Wade, the upheaval of the present is managed through a causal narrative that maintains reassurance by eliding inconvenient evidence.[5] Wade's invention of the past was directed at the immediately contemporary situation. Most writings of history in the first half of the nineteenth century were not; but a significant number were concerned with earlier periods of major social change – periods that, after the manner of historicist thinking, could provide analogies to the present. Their political stance was very varied, as a few examples will indicate. Henry Hallam's *The State of Europe during the Middle Ages*, published in 1818, is very much the work of the professional historian and was celebrated for its extensive use of original source material. But its scientific method is used to demonstrate a causal link between medieval institutions and the development of post-medieval constitutional government, and Hallam particularly engaged those aspects of medieval society in which he read the signs of the coming upheaval of the Reformation. That upheaval itself was dealt with directly in William Cobbett's 1824 *History of the Protestant Reformation*. Gloriously prejudiced, Cobbett inverted the smug establishment version of the Reformation, retelling it as a history of systematic pillage that enriched an unscrupulous *arriviste* aristocracy at the expense not merely of the Church, but of the common people of England and Ireland. And here was the point, for Cobbett saw a link, both by cause and analogy, between the pauperism created by the rapacity of the Reformers and the endemic poverty of the rural England of his own day, brought about – as the snarling pages of *Rural Rides* continually insist – by the tax-eaters and fund-holders of the all-devouring Wen. Radical in quite a different way was Thomas Carlyle's *The French Revolution* of 1837, written with a Messianic eye on the increasingly bitter class conflict of the late 1830s. Far from seeing the Revolution as an outbreak of national insanity – a view derived from Burke – Carlyle tied its events to a highly determined pattern of cause and effect, historical in its agency but apocalyptic in its nature. At the opposite pole to such Tartarean broodings,

---

[4] Wade, *Middle and Working Classes*, V.

[5] Wade's complacency is surprising in that he had been the editor of the great radical compendium of establishment abuses, *The Black Book*, which first appeared in 1820.

Thomas Macaulay's *History of England* dwelt minutely on that very English uprising, the Glorious Revolution, the decisive moment, for Macaulay, in the establishment of constitutional liberty and the foundation of national prosperity.[6] The opening paragraph not only announces the Whig view of history with which Macaulay has become identified, but also epitomises the narrative of causation at its most ambitious – and most triumphalist.

> I shall trace the course of that revolution which terminated the long struggle between our sovreigns and their parliaments, and bound up together the rights of the people and the tide of the reigning dynasty. I shall relate how ... the authority of law and the security of property were found to be compatible with a liberty of discussion and of individual action never before known; how, from the auspicious union of order and freedom, sprang a prosperity of which the annals of human affairs had furnished no example; how our country...rapidly rose to the place of umpire among European powers; how her opulence and her martial glory grew together; how, by a wise and resolute good faith, was gradually established a public credit fruitful of marvels which to the statesmen of any former age would have seemed incredible; how a gigantic commerce gave birth to a maritime power, compared with which every other maritime power, ancient or modern, sinks into insignificance ...

Ultimately, the narrative of causation changed the whole way in which relationships between past and present were perceived, and did so most dramatically – some would say cataclysmically – through its two greatest works, those metanarratives of causation that we know as Darwinism and Marxism.

CONTRASTING PAST AND PRESENT

The invention of the past, as I remarked earlier, makes it available for comparison and contrast with the present: such a process is implicit in the analogous nature of the various narratives of causation discussed above. But measuring contemporary society against earlier societies and cultures was also an explicit strategy of nineteenth-century historicism. Perhaps the best known example, and surely the most polemical, was Augustus Welby Pugin's *Contrasts*, first published in 1836. Dedicated, by way of calculated insult, to the architectural 'Trade', *Contrasts*'s plates set richly textured examples of medieval buildings next to the starved modern equivalents erected by the architects of Georgian England (figs 1a and 1b). Pugin's concern was more than a matter of stylistic preference or competence of design, however. His accompanying text located the source of aesthetic decline in the Reformation schism from the Catholic Church, with the consequent abandonment of Gothic – for Pugin the only architectural language possible for Christianity – and the debauching of taste and morality alike in the pagan

---

[6] Macaulay began writing his *History* in 1839, in the midst of the economic slump that created 'the hungry forties' and with Chartist agitation intensifying. He intended to bring the work down to the present day; in the event he only got as far as the death of William III.

Catholic town in 1440.

1a

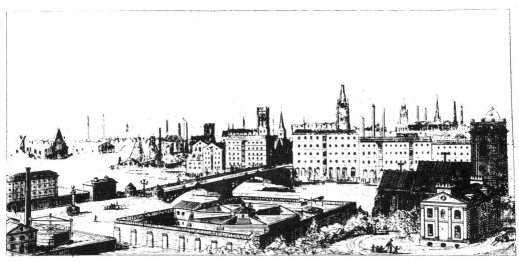

THE SAME TOWN IN 1840

1b

Figs. 1a and 1b. Medieval versus *Modern: 'Contrasted Towns: Catholic Town in 1440 and The same Town in 1840'. (Pugin,* Contrasts*)*

riot of Neoclassicism. His concern, that is, was with architecture as the articulation of a whole social formation – its culture, its institutions, its faith. The contrasted plates make the same point: the medieval wayfarer pauses for refreshment at the Gothic conduit of West Cheap, while lounging Peelers drive a street urchin away from the padlocked pump of St Anne's, Soho; liveried bedesmen reverently bury their departed brother at the medieval hospital of St Cross, while hirelings of the Benthamite workhouse box up dead paupers for dissection; a pilgrim kneels in prayer at the cross outside Bishop Skirlaw's chapel in Yorkshire, while an unseemly crowd jostles in the bleak streets around the newly-built chapel of St Pancras. Most telling are the two plates added to the second edition of 1841 (figs 1a and 1b), contrasting an imaginary 'Catholic town in 1440' with 'The same town in 1840'. In the first spires and towers rise above gabled houses that cluster safely within the castellated walls of the town, and a tree-lined river curves past some great abbey and on towards rural England, spreading into the distance. In the second, wharves and bottle-kilns crowd the river bank, the churches are maimed or demolished to make way for warehouses, spires are replaced on the skyline by factory chimneys, instead of a chapel on the bridge there is a toll-gate, and a gaol squats on the foreground fields where the children of the middle ages played. Nineteenth-century industrialisation and urbanisation have replaced the worship of God with the worship of Mammon. It is not just an architectural style that has gone, it is a whole world.

Other writers followed Pugin in invoking a carefully mythologised middle ages to critique the Britain that had been made by the Agrarian and Industrial Revolutions. Few followed the Roman Catholic agenda that he had set, however: by its very nature, historicism's invention of the past allowed for more than one way of putting it together. In *Past and Present* of 1843, Carlyle quarried the then recently published *Chronicle of Jocelin of Brakelond*[7] for his construction of medieval England. He was considerably more interested in power than in piety, and in the *Chronicle*'s account of Abbot Samson's authoritarian reform of the thirteenth-century abbey of St Edmundsbury he found an exemplary tale of the Carlylean strong-man at his work. Against it, in the rest of the book, he set a nineteenth-century England drifting in the directionless thrall of laissez-faire, its working class destitute or depraved, its upper class active only in preserving game, its complacent middle class interested only in the heroics of making money. In John Ruskin's *The Stones of Venice*, the first volume of which appeared in the same year as the Great Exhibition, the parallel between a medieval society and that of the nineteenth century is more covert. But medieval Venice, like Victorian Britain, was a state built on trading interests, the centre of a mercantile empire that relied upon seapower for its maintenance; and the tripartite division of Ruskin's text into 'The Foundations', 'Sea Stories', and 'The Fall', may be read as paradigmatic, not only

---

[12] *Jocelini de Brakelonda*. Such was the impact of Carlyle's *Past and Present* that an English translation of the Chronicle, by Thomas Edlyne Tomlins, was published in 1844.

descriptive but also predictive. Pugin, Carlyle, and, to an extent, Ruskin found in their own versions of the middle ages a model of social cohesion founded on hierarchy.[8] But their historicism engaged the whole nature of the social formation, whether medieval or modern, and in so doing attacked the very basis of a world in which the values of capitalism were increasingly hegemonic. The possibilities that opened up as a result went far beyond a reactionary desire for a preexisting order. In 'The Nature of Gothic' in *Stones of Venice*, for example, Ruskin's celebration of the individual creative freedom he thought characteristic of Gothic was angrily mobilised against the division of labour that is a key component of capitalist modes of production.

> Men were not intended to work with the accuracy of tools, to be precise and perfect in all their actions. If you will have that precision out of them, and make their fingers measure degrees like cog-wheels, and their arms strike curves like compasses you must unhumanize them ... Men might be beaten, chained, tormented, yoked like cattle, slaughtered like summer flies, and yet remain in one sense, and the best sense, free. But to smother their souls within them, to blight and hew into rotting pollards the suckling branches of their human intelligence, to make the flesh and skin which, after the worm's work on it, is to see God, into leathern thongs to yoke machinery with, – this is to be slave-masters indeed ...[9]

In the carving of a medieval cathedral, by contrast, Ruskin found proof of 'the life and liberty of every workman who struck the stone', and concluded that 'it must be the first aim of all Europe at this day to regain [these] for her children'.[10] Here was a revolutionary demand, one that ultimately proposed dismantling the economic organisation upon which Victorian manufacturing was based. After *Stones of Venice*, seeking to work out how such a social transformation could be effected, Ruskin turned increasingly to questions of the political economy of art and production. His inability fully to jettison hierarchical modes of thinking wrecked his attempts, and helped to wreck the man himself. It was William Morris, the self-confessed disciple of Ruskin who called 'The Nature of Gothic' 'one of the few essential texts of the nineteenth century',[11] who took the radical path forward: the 'life and liberty of every workman', he concluded, could only be achieved by the revolutionary overthrow of capitalism itself. In his utopian novel, *News from Nowhere*, written in 1890, Morris dreamed of England after the revolution as a loose federation of communes, industry abolished, religion abandoned, money redundant; an England in which there were no masters and hands, but free men and women working for the love of craft and making buildings, clothes and artefacts that, though independent of any particular historical style, breathed

---

[8] This is essentially the reading of Victorian medievalism put forward by Alice Chandler in *Dream*.
[9] Ruskin *Stones*, II, Chap. 6, Ss 12–13.
[10] Ibid., S. 14.
[11] He did so in his Preface to *The Nature of Gothic. A chapter of 'The Stones of Venice'* (Hammersmith, 1892), which was the fourth publication of the Kelmscott Press.

the creative spirit of the fourteenth century.[12] It is Ruskin understood through Marx, or perhaps Marx re-read through Ruskin: whichever, *News from Nowhere* is one of the most extraordinary products of nineteenth-century historicism.

REVIVALISM AND IDEOLOGY

Morris's love of the historical traditions of craft, Ruskin's passion for medieval architecture and the glories of Gothic, Pugin's position as not only one of the great polemicists of the Gothic Revival but also one of its greatest designers, all bring us to the third aspect of nineteenth-century historicism: its fascination with the material products of earlier cultures and with the creative possibilities of stylistic revival. The languages of Victorian architecture and design were pre-eminently historicist, and their sources were international. It takes a long list to check off the major stylistic revivals in architecture alone: Greek and Neoclassical; Romanesque and Gothic, with precedents drawn from France, Italy, and northern Europe as well as from Britain; Elizabethan and Jacobean; Renaissance, inspired by buildings that ranged from fifteenth-century Italy to seventeenth-century Holland; Wren and the English Baroque; Queen Anne; and the English vernacular tradition as well, from Cotswold manor houses, to Cheshire timber framing, to West Country thatch. And this is not to mention the exotics: the Egyptian mausolea, the Moorish factories, the Swiss cottages, the Indian bungalows. The long building boom of the nineteenth century and its plethora of styles were, of course, determined ultimately by economics. Not only in the obvious sense that it was British economic power that enabled everything, but also that the pattern and type of building activity were determined by the distribution of wealth – whether it be a country squire in the Golden Age of High Farming deciding to rebuild the family house, or a northern manufacturing centre converting commercial strength to civic pride by erecting a town hall. Ruskin saw this with great clarity, and told the good burghers of Bradford as much in 1864 when they asked for his advice on the style of their new wool exchange.[13] But within this economic determination, all the architectural styles of the nineteenth century were, I believe, ideological in their inception. I would stress 'in their inception' because the sheer extent of building activity in the nineteenth century gave style a determining life of its own. Ruskin, again, understood this, and lived both to deplore Victorian architecture's enthusiasm for stylistic pot-pourri and to lament his own role in engendering it: culturally, it was a long way from *The Seven Lamps of Architecture* or *The Stones of Venice* to the spicy Gothic details of the speculative builder.

Nevertheless, it was the understanding and aspirations of classes, class segments,

---

[12] Morris, *News from Nowhere*; the story first appeared in the socialist journal *Commonweal* in 1890.

[13] Ruskin's Bradford address was published under the title 'Traffic' in *The Crown of Wild Olive*. Asserting that the real deity worshipped by the nation was 'the "Goddess of Getting-on", or "Britannia of the Market"', Ruskin told his audience that 'it is quite vain to ask me to tell you how to build to her; you know far better than I' (S. 73). For discussion of Ruskin's relationship to Bradford see Hardman, *Ruskin and Bradford*.

and individuals, of and for themselves and their society, that informed the origins of stylistic choice. That is, to select consciously one style rather than another was to make a choice that was ideological. The turn taken by the ecclesiastical Gothic Revival after the mid-1830s is an obvious case in point. By combining the Puginian crusade for Gothic as the only Christian style with the renascent High Anglican theology of the Oxford Movement, the young men who set up the Cambridge Camden Society invested church-building with a new set of meanings. The architectural features insisted upon by the Camdenians in *The Ecclesiologist* of the 1840s – historically correct English Decorated, a developed chancel, interior alignment on the sanctuary and altar, the subordination of the pulpit, the replacement of box pews by open benches – all functioned semantically to denote High Church doctrine. To build an ecclesiologically correct church was to assert the catholicity of Anglicanism, the primacy of the sacraments, and the sacerdotal nature of the clergy. Here were style and design as ideological statement. And it was an ideology that was specific to the time and place of Victorian Britain. Most buildings of the preVictorian Gothic Revival had been domestic rather than religious, and the meanings they generated were quite different from those prescribed by the Camdenians – who, in any case, thought Georgian architecture 'the *nec plus ultra* of wretchedness'.[14] Nor was the ecclesiological semantic to be found in the mediéval churches the Camdenians claimed as their source. Of course, they insisted that it was, and in 1843 John Mason Neale and Benjamin Webb, the founders of the Society, published a hefty translation of the first book of Durandus's *Rationale Divinorum Officiorum* to demonstrate the fact. But Durandus's treatise on symbolism is essentially a work of scholastic ingenuity, characteristic of the educated clerical elite to which he belonged. There is no evidence that its reading of the emblematism of the church fabric, its fine-spun system of allegories and equivalences, ever influenced the way churches were actually designed and built in the middle ages. Ecclesiological symbolism, sacramentalism as Neale and Webb called it, was read into the fabric and planning of medieval churches from the here and now of High Anglicanism in the 1840s. To use a term I have used several times before, it was an invention: discovered, in that it claimed to be based on the forgotten practices of a historical culture; made up, in that it was constructed to answer specific contemporary needs. Sacramentality and the kind of Gothic it produced typify the Janus-like nature of nineteenth-century historicism itself: leaning on the past yet speaking to the present; affirming continuity but, by the very fact of being revivalist, discontinuous.

The whole phenomenon of ecclesiology also exemplifies the powerful interaction between historicism and ideology at this period. If we define ideology in a limited sense as being a system of ideas held by a particular group of people at a specific time, then we can see that it was historicism that gave shape to, that articulated, Camdenian ideology. But ecclesiological practice – the building of particular sorts of churches and

---

[14] Neale and Webb, *Durandus*, cxxvii.

the particular sorts of social ritual that went on in them – was also an ideological form, a cultural text that constituted a specific way of reading the world. That reading claimed a transhistorical authority for the central role of the priesthood in a paternalist and hierarchical society – a traditional social model that was directly pitched against the 'liberalism' of the new economic order. In this sense, ideology was determinant upon historicism. But, as I have already argued, historicism was itself brought into being by fundamental economic change, and was a key conceptual response to it. In the end the nexus between historicism and ideology in the nineteenth century was so close as to be interpenetrative: ideologies emerged as historicist constructs; historicism was an ideological formation.

Something of the same complex relationship between ideology and historicism seems to me to be evident in all the major Victorian architectural styles. Though rarely as overt and self-conscious as in ecclesiastical Gothic, it was the social and cultural basis for the establishment of what Henry-Russell Hitchcock many years ago identified as stylistic paradigms for certain nineteenth-century building types.[15] The tradition of the eighteenth-century Grand Tour, the esteem that classical learning enjoyed, its aristocratic pedigree, the dominance of the classics in public schools and the universities, all combined to make neo-Greek paradigmatic for museums, galleries, and similar cultural institutions in the late Georgian and early Victorian periods: W. H. Playfair's Scottish Royal Academy in Edinburgh (1822–6), University College, London by William Wilkins and J. P. Gandy-Deering (1827–8), Wilkins's National Gallery in Trafalgar Square (1834–8), the Fitzwilliam Museum in Cambridge designed by George Basevi (begun 1837), Charles Robert Cockerell's Ashmolean Museum in Oxford (1841–5)(fig.2), and, of course, the British Museum by Sir Robert Smirke, eventually completed in 1847. The iconic status historicism afforded to the traditional manor house, nostalgic versions of preindustrial rural society, evocations of hospitality and chivalry in the manner of Sir Walter Scott, the mythologising of the bluff old squire and the loyal English peasant, all informed the Tudor and Jacobethan paradigm for the country houses designed by Edward Blore, William Burn, and, preeminently, Anthony Salvin. Later in the nineteenth century the Old English style of Ernest George – and a hundred less original imitators – played to much the same cluster of concepts, though the client was now likely to be an aspirant landed gent bankrolled by trade, while the houses of the English Vernacular Revival tastefully promoted their own version of pastoral in the leafier reaches of the Home Counties. Other conceptual sets, variously historicist and ideological, fixed the paradigmatic relationship between style and building type: versions of the Renaissance for commerce, the palazzo model for clubs, Queen Anne for Board Schools, and so forth. But I have said enough to indicate the nature of their construction. Significantly, paradigms could be challenged and were subject to change. Thus the use of Gothic in Deane and Woodward's Oxford University Museum

---

[15] See Hitchcock, *Early Victorian Architecture*.

(1855–60) contested the secularisation of learning that was inherent in the neo-Greek paradigm, while the classicism employed for late Victorian and Edwardian museums and galleries – for example, Sidney R. J. Smith's Tate Gallery of 1897 – was engaged in a rhetoric of imperialism largely absent from the classicism of the early decades of the century.

THE AUDIENCE FOR THE PAST

By the very nature of historicism, the stylistic principles and practices of nineteenth-century architecture involved issues that were determinant upon the whole shape of contemporary culture and society. Historicism also ensured that those issues would bear upon every aspect of the century's engagement with the material remains of the past – buildings, artefacts, objects of all sorts, from armour to archaeopteryx, from Bellinis to bench-ends, from castles to cuneiform tablets. History was, and is, contested ground, and the things of the past were, and are, at the heart of the conflict. Questions about how those things should be dealt with confronted the culturally-empowered at every turn: the art gallery director trying to decide how paintings should be grouped and displayed; the museum curator seeking a taxonomic structure for his catalogue; the parson and his architect deciding how to restore a parish church; the municipal corporation contemplating a civic improvement that would cost their town its medieval gates. Because of the social context in which such problems emerged both questions and answers were contingent upon the developing shape of nineteenth-century society, and thus, ultimately, upon the power relations of its economic base. Those relations generated a still larger set of questions. For whose benefit were the material remains of the past to be safeguarded? Who decided which buildings, artefacts, objects were to be kept, and why? Was their keeping a matter of private interest or public responsibility? Who would have access to them, and on what terms? Above all – Whose history was it anyway?

Fig. 2. The classical paradigm: the Ashmolean Museum, Oxford, 1841–5, by Charles Robert Cockerell. (The Builder, 24 October 1846)

However the people of the nineteenth century may have responded to this last question – and there was, and is, more than one answer – a reply from the standpoint of 1901 would have been very different from one given a hundred years earlier. By the beginning of the twentieth century the past, and the things of the past, engaged the interest not only of more people than ever before, but also, crucially, of people from a broader social spectrum. In part this was a consequence of the steady expansion of state provision in education; in part a result of art galleries and museums in every major city, and of opening times that made them accessible to working people – in particular, the Sunday opening that had been won, after a long battle, in 1896. There had also been a remarkable growth in locally-based amateur societies whose principal interests were archaeology, antiquities, and natural history. The earliest, the Berkshire Ashmolean Society, was founded in 1840; by the end of the century there were at least forty such bodies in England and Wales. Like schools and museums, these societies were very much in the hands of Victorian cultural elites, distributing the past to the populace, as it were. Organisations like Mechanics' Institutes, Working Men's Associations, and Working Men's Clubs, though usually subject to middle-class monitoring, may have been less paternalistic; and, to judge from such of their libraries as survive, they too often fostered an interest in historical studies of one sort or another. Even so, and not underestimating any of these provisions, it seems to me that it was changes in society as a whole that were critical in creating a wider constituency for the past.

By the end of the century the railway system had made the cities accessible to country dwellers, and the countryside and coast accessible to the townspeople who, by now, made up some three-quarters of the population. Between 1870 and 1900 improvements in timetabling so reduced journey times that the size of England, Scotland, and Wales was effectively shrunk by a third. The cheap trains that central government required companies to run every day, special rates for excursions, and third-class travel brought the railway system within reach of the proletariat. In a closely related process the industrial system settled into a pattern that included regular provision for time away from work. The adoption of 'the English weekend', the gradual relaxation of sabbatarianism, annual holidays for the lower middle class and upper working class, and bank holidays for the masses, created the novel phenomenon of popular leisure. Day-trippers to London visited the Tower, admired the Houses of Parliament, gazed at the tombs in Westminster Abbey, and perhaps found their way to South Kensington to look at the dinosaurs. Trams and omnibuses took Londoners out to the edges of the metropolis, to discover villages that would soon become suburbs. Trains took them further afield, to the sea and the deeper countryside. And if it was public transport that carried city dwellers to parts of Britain they may never otherwise have known, it was the bicycle that gave men and women alike the freedom to explore for themselves. Contemporary writers bemoaned the cockneyfied resorts, the vulgarisation of pretty Thames-side villages, the excursionists who broke the calm of country towns. *Punch* sneered at 'Arry and 'Arriet on their 'olidays and joked about the spread

UNHAPPY INFLUENCE OF MODERN MUSIC-HALL MELODIES.

"THERE LIES THE BRAVE KNIGHT, DARLING, WITH HIS FAITHFUL DOG AT HIS FEET, AND HIS WIFE BY HIS SIDE!"
"AND HAS SHE GOT A DOG, TOO, MUMMY?"   "NO, DARLING, ONLY A CUSHION!"
"AH, I SUPPOSE HER DADDY *WOULDN'T* BUY HER A BOW-WOW-WOW!"

*Fig. 3. Historic culture meets popular culture. (*Punch*, 30 September 1893)*

of mass popular culture(fig.3). Yet guide books to popular tourist centres make it quite clear that working people found more to interest them than just the pierrot shows and the beer gardens. *Picnic: the Illustrated Guide to Ilfracombe and North Devon* is representative (fig.4).[16] Late Victorian Ilfracombe boomed as a resort and *Picnic*, published in boards at one shilling, was priced for a popular readership. Alongside information about trains, steamers, and hotels, and a eulogy on the salubrity of the climate, there is a wealth of history: potted histories of Ilfracombe, of the medieval parish church, of local worthies and famous visitors, of nearby towns and villages, of neighbouring churches and buildings of interest. The first words of the Introduction read 'North Devon, celebrated in history as the home of the sea-dogs of England...' Among the thousands of people who, each year, thronged Ilfracombe, and scores of towns like it, were the new audience for the past. They came, by and large, as strangers among the remains of that other country, divorced from whatever lived traditions had once constituted its history, even though many of them must have been visiting parts of Britain that their families had left only a few generations before. What had been the

---

[16] *Picnic*. Significantly, the guidebook is dedicated to that key figure in the commercial development of popular culture, George Newnes, proprietor of *Tit-Bits* and the *Strand Magazine*. Newnes paid for the building of the Lynmouth-Lynton cliff railway and subsequently built himself a large house in Lynton.

TEMPLE BAR, CLOVELLY.   THE STAIRCASE, CLOVELLY.

Fig. 4. Historic Britain for the cultural mass market: illustrations of Clovelly. (Picnic)

material fabric of a historical culture had become for them just something that was old. But what was old was also undeniably interesting, and could be advertised as an attraction by the promoters of towns like Ilfracombe. For the new audience for the past would come to constitute the cultural mass market of the twentieth century: Historic Britain was being born.

THE PRESENT BOOK

The essays in this collection celebrate the 150th anniversaries of the British Archaeological Association and the Royal Archaeological Institute, and consider the cultural products of nineteenth-century historicism from many different angles. The variety of topics and approaches mirrors the diversity of nineteenth-century historicism itself.

The fact that there are two anniversaries to celebrate is a demonstration of the contentiousness that was inherent in much of the nineteenth century's response to the past. Within a year of its foundation in 1843 the British Archaeological Association had split following a bitter wrangle. David Wetherall's essay discusses the early years of the British Archaeological Association and the Archaeological Institute of Great Britain and Ireland in the context of the remarkable growth of such societies in the late Georgian and early Victorian periods. Underlying the quarrel in the Archaeological Association were some of the questions I raised earlier, questions about what the past meant, what it was for, and how it was to be used. The terms upon which the nineteenth century started to ask such questions crossed what were to become fixed boundaries between the sciences and the humanities. Hugh Torrens's paper stresses the interdisciplinary nature of the nineteenth-century historical project by exploring the vital relationship between geology and archaeology in the first half of the century. The historical painters discussed by William Vaughan also demonstrate how smoothly the matter of the past could be manoeuvred for contemporary purposes. As he shows, a painting like Poynter's *Faithful Unto Death* was able to call upon recent archaeological discoveries, literary sources, and imperial parallels to create a particularly potent image of Victorian heroic aspirations. The case was very different for the architect George Aitchison, the subject of Jo Mordaunt-Crook's essay. In the lectures and writings that were so important a part of his long career, Aitchison unhappily pursued the idea of a contemporary style that would somehow be an alternative to historicism: the pursuit, like the idea, was largely chimerical. What Aitchison could never recognise was the way in which Victorian historicism, far from replicating the past, constantly converted it into the present. The enthusiastic eclecticism that emerged was often underpinned by the kind of interdisciplinarity evident in the career of Robert Willis, whose life and work are discussed by Thomas Cocke. He shows how the problematics of the past were resolved, or at least negotiated, by Willis's sensible combination of practical expertise and antiquarian learning – though his falling-out with the young zealots of the Cambridge Camden Society nicely illustrates the limitations of common sense when confronted by a crusade. As I argued earlier, the Gothic crusade stemmed from a paradoxical play between continuity and discontinuity, and for all its insistence on archaeological precedent it necessarily involved invention. Chris Miele's essay on architectural restoration shows very clearly the extent to which the Victorians constructed the architectural past that they wanted, turning the ambiguous evidences of medieval buildings into an ideal paradigm. As storehouses of the material remains of the past, museums assisted in these processes of invention, which included the manufacture of what I have called narratives of causation as means of bridging the gap of historical discontinuity. Arthur MacGregor's paper examines the role played by museum collections of so-called 'national antiquities' in constructing one of the most crucial of such narratives, that of national historical identity. Finally, Brian Cook's essay on British archaeologists in the Aegean not only reveals the pioneering nature of the British contribution to the archaeology of the Mediterranean, but also reminds us that the Victorians' sense of their historical identity was grounded in an understanding of the whole of the Western cultural past, and of the classical inheritance as a seminal influence within that.

The Growth of Archaeological Societies

David Westherall

INTRODUCTION

> Never, perhaps, in the history of learning, have more rapid and essential changes taken place
> in any one branch of knowledge than the last few years have produced in the study of
> antiquities. By the exertions of the modern school of antiquaries, a new face has been put on
> archaeology; and its professors, for a long while the ridicule of a majority, have taken their
> deserved station amongst the real scholars of the day.[1]

The Archaeologist and Journal of Antiquarian Science enthusiastically proclaimed these
confident words in the opening address of its first number in 1841: a time of
unprecedented interest in antiquity. The 1830s and 1840s saw a great proliferation of
printing clubs and learned societies that radically altered the study of the past in
Britain and that formed the basis of an extensive antiquarian community. These
organisations varied in size and influence and spanned a wide number of disciplines;
but, despite their differences, they all shared a common passion for the past. This
climate of growing popularity for history, and a corresponding growth of antiquarian
societies, helped foster the birth of the British Archaeological Association 150 years
ago.

My purpose is to investigate the nature of some antiquarian societies of the early
Victorian period and explore how their development can be seen as part of wider
changes beyond the bounds of the antiquarian community alone. This will involve
discussing the growth of printing clubs and their fields of interest; exploring some
parallels with the organisation of the scientific community; and briefly considering the
influence of the Gothic Revival and the Ecclesiological movement on the development

---

[1] *Archaeologist* 1, (1841), 2.

of architectural and archaeological societies. These themes help illuminate the early years of the British Archaeological Association and the Archaeological Institute and lead to a greater understanding both of the climate within which these and other societies flourished, and of the people who made up their membership. Involvement in learned societies reflected the Victorians' obsession with employing their leisure-time productively, whether as interested, but relatively passive observers, or as more active workers within an intellectual discipline.

INTELLECTUAL COMMUNITIES – THE MEMBERS OF SOCIETIES

Since I will use the term 'community' extensively some definition of it may be useful. At its broadest I use it to include all those who who saw themselves as connected, even if only loosely, with a general body of knowledge. More narrowly it consists of those who published in specific fields and/or were active in relevant societies. In an analysis of collective biography as a research tool for the history of science, Shapin and Thackray have identified three categories for inclusion within the British scientific community from 1700 to 1900, and these can be modified to fit the antiquarian community:

> [Those] who published a scientific paper, book or pamphlet
>
> Those who formally and actively associated themselves with a scientifically-orientated society or institution, or themselves taught or disseminated scientific knowledge
>
> A large body of cultivators of science who patronized, applied or disseminated scientific knowledge and principles, but who themselves neither published science, taught science, nor actively associated themselves with scientifically-orientated institutions.[2]

The phrase 'cultivators of science', originally Francis Bacon's, was used by contemporaries to refer to the wide body of people associated with scientific matters in the first half of the nineteenth century. Similarly, the antiquarian community can be seen to consist of 'cultivators of antiquity', which group includes the antiquarian equivalents of Shapin and Thackray's categories, together with collectors of manuscripts and antiquities, and those working with records or archives and in museums.[3]

Within the large body of cultivators, was a smaller number of the most active workers. In his *On the Constitution of the Church and State*, Coleridge had seen their role to be: 'at the fountainheads of the humanities, in cultivating and enlarging the knowledge already possessed and in watching over the interests of physical and moral science'.[4] Coleridge had envisaged a 'clerisy' of the intelligentsia, forming a 'national church of intellect'. The clerisy consisted of both the larger body of cultivators and the smaller

---

[2] Shapin & Thackray, 'Prosography', 1–28.
[3] For an invaluable analysis of the antiquarian community in Victorian times see Levine, *Amateur*
[4] Coleridge, *Constitution*, 46.

body of those at the fountainheads. Although Coleridge's idea of a learned order directing the nation's knowledge never really existed as a conscious class, it was a popular concept and there were bodies that aspired to the role of a clerisy.[5] Many of those actively involved in antiquarian societies felt a responsibility to help safeguard antiquities and direct researches for the benefit of a wider antiquarian community. In my discussion of the development of various societies and printing clubs, it will be apparent that certain key people frequently appear in close association with a number of related organisations.

A look at the *Archaeologist and Journal of Antiquarian Science* and its editors can help illustrate the state of the antiquarian community in the early Victorian period. The journal only lasted until June 1842 – perhaps because of its over-ambitious monthly publication schedule – but in its ten issues it covered a wealth of subjects and helped prepare the ground for the British Archaeological Association that would later follow much the same aims. The aims of the journal were: to review new archaeological publications; to report on the proceedings of antiquarian societies, including foreign ones 'which have not hitherto appeared in any English Journal'; to review little-known curious old books; and to publish original essays. The editors wished their journal 'to become a depository for the preservation of notices of antiquarian studies'. The journal took particularly seriously the task of reporting on antiquarian societies and printing clubs, publishing long articles on the Oxford Ashmolean Society, the Cambridge Antiquarian Society, and the Cambridge Camden Society; and short notices on the Percy, Camden, Oxford Architectural, and Anglo-Saxon Societies.

The editors of the journal were James Orchard Halliwell and Thomas Wright, both of whom were actively involved in a number of antiquarian societies and printing clubs, including the short-lived Historical Society of Science which they founded in 1840. Halliwell (later Halliwell-Phillips) was a mathematician by origin, but had become interested in antiquity at Cambridge where, like Wright, he was an undergraduate at Trinity. He had been elected both a Fellow of the Society of Antiquaries and a Fellow of the Royal Society in 1839 at the age of only eighteen, being sponsored to the latter by Charles Barnwell of the British Museum and supported by such distinguished names as William Whewell, George Peacock, Adam Sedgwick, Edward Hawkins, and Sir Henry Ellis.[6] Halliwell had been the original mover behind the Cambridge Antiquarian Society, and later also contributed to the creation of the British Archaeological Association. In 1844, however, he was to fall into disrepute when it transpired that he had stolen papers from Trinity College library.

---

[5] These ideas are explored further in Knights, *Clerisy*; and in Morrell & Thackray, *Gentlemen*, 17–29.

[6] Whewell, Peacock and Sedgwick each served as Presidents of the British Association for the Advancement of Science and were all Fellows of Trinity College, Cambridge. Whewell later became Master of Trinity and Professor of Moral Philosophy; Peacock was Dean of Ely; Sedgwick was Professor of Geology. Hawkins was Keeper of Antiquities at the British Museum, where Ellis was the Principal Librarian. Ellis was also Secretary of the Society of Antiquaries.

Thomas Wright, who was elected a Fellow of the Society of Antiquaries in 1837, was one of the few Victorian antiquarians who supported himself through his antiquarian researches. He contributed many papers to archaeological periodicals and the British Library catalogue contains 129 entries of his works. He also held a number of offices in printing clubs, such as Secretary of the Camden Society, and Secretary and Treasurer of the Percy Society. In 1843 Wright drew on his experiences of antiquarian societies and, together with Charles Roach Smith, founded the British Archaeological Association. A year later it was the publication of his *Archaeological Album* that provoked the rift that would split the Association in two and lead to the formation of the Archaeological Institute.[7]

PRINTING CLUBS

I have mentioned Wright and Halliwell's involvement in printing clubs because these organisations were vital in sowing the seeds from which archaeological societies later blossomed. Printing clubs began flourishing in the 1830s and 1840s by making available relatively inexpensive editions of manuscripts and rare books. The clubs consisted of members voluntarily associated together as subscribers, thus guaranteeing the circulation of works whose publication might otherwise be too risky. Initially they tended to concentrate on publications of an antiquarian nature. As this means of publication became established, the number of clubs proliferated and their fields widened. By the end of the 1840s there were clubs devoted to such subjects as ancient music, early medical literature, and chemistry. However, the printing clubs devoted to scientific concerns were far less common than those on antiquarian subjects.

The models for these popular societies were the Bannatyne Club (founded by Sir Walter Scott in 1823) and the Maitland Club (founded in 1828), which aimed to print works 'illustrative of the History, Literature and Antiquities of Scotland'. These were followed in 1834 by the Surtees Society which concentrated on manuscripts relating to the area constituting the ancient Kingdom of Northumberland. The society was based in Durham, and more than half of its original 101 members were resident in the north-east of England. Its first two publications were typical of those to be produced by the new printing clubs in the coming years. The first was a collection of legends relating to St Cuthbert's miracles, taken from a thirteenth-century transcript of a twelfth-century work by Reginald of Durham. The second was a selection of 'Wills and Inventories Illustrative of the History, Manners, Language, Statistics, &c. of the Northern Counties of England, from the Eleventh Century downwards.'[8]

---

[7] Some of the British Archaeological Association's Central Committee believed that Wright had abused his position as acting editor of the *Archaeological Journal* by only including in it a 'mere skeleton of a report' of the 1844 Canterbury Congress, thus increasing the appeal of his privately published *Archaeological Album* which contained a far more detailed report of the proceedings. For more about the split, see Wetherall, 'Foundation'.

[8] Thompson, *Surtees*, 101.

One of the larger and most active clubs was the Camden Society, formed in 1838 by Thomas Gough Nichols, John Bruce, and Thomas Wright. The Camden Society drew much of its support from members of the Society of Antiquaries: of the 547 members listed at the end of its first volume, 150 were Fellows. There was also a significant number of lawyers (at least 58) which reflects the legal interest in the publication of records. The membership was not, however, confined to these groups or to London, and the bulk of the provincial members were introduced to the Society by a network of local secretaries. A few years later, both the British Archaeological Association and the Archaeological Institute were to find local secretaries invaluable in recruiting and retaining their members.[9]

Several of the clubs were, like the Surtees Society, intentionally regional in nature. For instance, the Chetham Society was concerned with the Counties Palatine of Chester and Lancaster, and drew 91% of its members from the immediate locality. Other clubs were more nationally orientated, though normally the bulk of their membership came from London and the South-East. For example, 74% of the Percy Society were from London, and 62% of the Hakluyt Society came from London and the South-East. This is similar to the significant support that the British Archaeological Association and Archaeological Institute later drew from the region.

The early Victorian printing clubs varied in the number of subscribers from fifty to several thousand members. Unlike the Camden Society, many of them placed a ceiling on the number of members. This was normally for practical reasons in order to minimise logistical difficulties, although others kept their membership down to increase their selectiveness. In his 1847 study of learned societies and printing clubs, Hume suggests that in total about 15,000 individuals subscribed to one or more printing clubs in 1847, and that between them the clubs had published about 600 different volumes.[10]

The Parker Society, with over 7,000 members, was the most prominent of a number of clubs specifically concerned with the publication of ecclesiastical texts. The constitution required that at least sixteen out of the Council of twenty-four should be Anglican clergy. Before finishing its publications in 1853, it issued fifty-four volumes to erect 'a bulwark against Popish Error'. Many Victorian churchmen were at this time concerned about the Tractarian movement in the Church of England and also about moves towards Roman Catholic emancipation. Unhappy with the climate of reform, some churchmen felt the need to assert more consciously their Anglican roots. Although not their primary purpose, the Parker Society and newly formed diocesan architectural societies provided a means of reaffirming tenets of the Church of England.

Normally the only contacts between members of printing clubs were at the annual meetings when the councils were elected. Frequently the same antiquarians sat on the

---

[9] For more on the Camden Society see Levy, 'Camden'.
[10] Hume, *Societies*.

councils of several clubs. For instance, in 1842 Thomas Amyot, Treasurer of the Society of Antiquaries, and Thomas Wright were on the Councils of each of the Camden, Percy, and Shakespeare Societies. Even more prominent was Lord Braybrooke, the editor of Pepys, who in 1842 was on the Councils of the Society of Antiquaries and the Camden Society, a Vice-President of the Shakespeare Society, and President of both the Percy and Surtees Societies. He became President of the Camden Society as well the following year. The anniversary meetings of the Camden and Percy Societies occurred on the same day, and no less than six men were elected to both Councils.

This involvement with printing clubs bound together some of the most active members of the British Archaeological Association's first Central Committee. Amyot and Wright were both on the British Archaeological Association's Central Committee as were Thomas Crofton Croker, Frederick Madden, and Thomas Pettigrew who each sat on the Councils of two of the Camden, Percy, and Shakespeare Societies.

Printing clubs differed significantly from the local and national societies that were appearing, in that contact with the membership extended no further than the paying of subscriptions and the receiving of texts. The societies that were beginning to develop depended upon a more active and participatory membership that would meet face-to-face. The pattern had been set in the 1820s and 1830s by local literary and philosophical societies, which had a broad interest in the sciences and were later to contribute to the success of the British Association for the Advancement of Science. Many people interested in the sciences also shared an interest in antiquity and their local area; thus societies straddling these interests began to appear in the 1830s. The Maidstone Scientific and Antiquarian Society was founded in 1834 and soon followed by Natural History and Antiquarian Societies for Shropshire and North Wales (1835), Warwickshire (1836), and Penzance (1839).

PARALLELS BETWEEN SCIENTIFIC AND ANTIQUARIAN SOCIETIES

There had long been considerable similarities between the antiquarian and scientific communities. Changes in how natural philosophers saw themselves and structured their disciplines were often followed by analogous developments in the antiquarian community. This was true for metropolitan and national societies as well as for provincial local societies. In part this was due to the overlap in key figures between the different cultures, especially in the Royal Society and the Society of Antiquaries. Ever since its foundation in the seventeenth century the Royal Society had taken an interest in antiquarian matters as well as in natural philosophy and in 1707 it had provided a model for the establishment of the Society of Antiquaries. In 1843, the year of the foundation of the British Archaeological Association, twelve of the twenty-one members of the Council of the Antiquaries were Fellows of the Royal Society (including the Earl of Aberdeen, the Antiquaries' president). By the time of Aberdeen's resignation in 1846, the Antiquaries' Council was less dominated by the Royal Society (only seven members of the Council were also Fellows) although the two societies still had seventy-nine Fellows in common.[11]

The Royal Society and the Antiquaries both faced growing criticism of their lack of vitality. Critics urged reform, seeing the two prestigious bodies as moribund and unable to keep up with changes in their disciplines.[12] Their inability to offer leadership in developing fields eventually led to the setting up of new bodies.

The Geological Society, formed as an offshoot from the Royal Society in 1807, had begun as a London dining club for those interested in mineralogy and geology to meet one another and discuss their interests. It soon took on the status of a learned society with the aim of 'inducing [geologists] to adopt one nomenclature, of facilitating the communication of new facts, and of ascertaining what is known of their science and what yet remains to be discovered'.[13] In doing so it widened its membership to geologists all over the country, and produced a booklet entitled *Geological Inquiries*. Leaders of the Royal Society initially opposed the Geological Society's development, seeing its publications as a threat to their own *Philosophical Transactions*. However, the Geological Society survived and was the spur for a number of others: the Astronomical (1820), the Zoological (1826), and the Geographical (1830).

Just as the Royal Society was unable to cater to the specialist interests of geologists, so too the Society of Antiquaries failed to provide an adequate forum for those interested in numismatics; thus, in 1836 the Numismatic Society of London was formed. Its first president was Dr John Lee, who had been involved in the foundation of the Astronomical Society and later became a Vice-President of the British Archaeological Association. Charles Roach Smith, one of the Numismatic Society's original members, recalls in his *Retrospections* that the society owed its origin, at least in part, to the lethargy of the Society of Antiquaries which had ignored growing interest in numismatics amongst some of its members and refused to establish a research committee for the subject.[14] By contrast, the Numismatic Society actively pursued its interests, gaining 132 members by the end of its first year, and keeping them informed through publication of its *Proceedings* and John Yonge Akerman's *Numismatic Journal*, which were later combined and replaced by the *Numismatic Chronicle*.[15] The unwillingness on the part of the Antiquaries to sanction the creation of active subsidiary bodies, such as a numismatic committee, was repeated in 1843 when the Council refused to sponsor directly the creation of a committee of its active antiquarians to promote the preservation of national antiquities. As a result, the British Archaeological Association,

---

[11] Evans, *Antiquaries*, 227.
[12] Prominent critics of the Royal Society included: Sir Humphrey Davy *(Consolations,*1829); Charles Babbage *(Science,* 1830); John Herschel, probably the most eminent natural philospher of the period; and David Brewster, editor of the *Edinburgh Journal of Science*. The most vocal critic of the Society of Antiquaries was Sir Nicholas Harris Nicolas.
[13] Rudwick, 'Foundation', 329.
[14] Smith, *Retrospections*, 277.
[15] Carson, *Numismatic Soc.*

like the Numismatic Society before it, was formed as a separate body from the Antiquaries. Although the British Archaeological Association had far wider interests, many of the Numismatic Society's most active members were to form the core of the new Association's membership, including Lord Albert Conyngham who was already President of the Numismatic Society when asked to become the British Archaeological Association's first President.

The British Archaeological Association's development echoed the establishment of the British Association for the Advancement of Science, which had first met at York in 1831. It aimed to promote science in a more active way than the Royal Society was capable of doing, and soon found great public support for its annual summer meetings. The similarity in name between the two associations is no coincidence, for the British Archaeological Association also sought to promote popular interest in its subject and hoped to emulate the success of the British Association for the Advancement of Science's congresses. These congresses were great public displays, bringing pomp and ceremony to science, as well as acting as a forum for leaders of the scientific community to meet together and pursue research. Although smaller in scale, the annual congresses of the British Archaeological Association and Archaeological Institute helped increase the visibility of archaeology, and influenced the foundation of many new provincial societies in the same way that the British Association for the Advancement of Science had fostered local natural philosophical societies.[16]

The British Archaeological Association's membership rapidly increased, passing a thousand members by September 1844, although at this stage there was no charge for membership. Analysis of the membership lists gives an indication of the composition of the antiquarian community (table 1); particularly notable is the prominence of the clergy who comprised more than a third of the membership; this, too, is comparable to the British Association for the Advancement of Science which was supported by large numbers of clergy. Following the dispute that gave rise to the Archaeological Institute, both the British Archaeological Association and the Institute soon imposed subscriptions, but continued to see a steady increase in subscribers over the following years (table 2). Meanwhile, other local societies were growing up all over the country, some as a direct result of the activities of the British Archaeological Association and Archaeological Institute, but others the result of different causes which had preceded the British Archaeological Association's foundation.

ARCHITECTURAL SOCIETIES AND ECCLESIOLOGY

By the 1840s there were other influences in addition to that of the scientific community

---

[16] For a more detailed consideration of parallels between the BAA and BAAS see Wetherall, Durham thesis, 55–70. The BAAS is comprehensively surveyed in Morrell & Thackray, *Gentlemen*; Macleod and Collins, *Science*; and Orange, 'BAAS'.

leading to the formation of local antiquarian societies. This was reflected in the founding of many new societies that had an interest in architecture and that were often associated with Anglican dioceses. Early examples were Durham, Lichfield, Exeter, and Bristol Architectural Societies which were all founded in 1841. When, in 1850, six 'Associated Architectural Societies' began publishing their reports and papers in a single volume, a further seventeen other similar societies were listed as being 'in union' with them. Although their prime focus was architecture, many of these societies were also involved with archaeology or natural history. Driving influences behind the creation of these architectural societies were the Gothic Revival and the Ecclesiological movement led by the Cambridge Camden Society.[17]

A taste for Gothic architecture had grown out of the glorification of the Middle Ages by the Romantic Movement. Romanticism, although essentially a literary movement, touched all branches of art, and not least architecture. Most prominent among the Romantics who influenced architecture was Sir Walter Scott, whose poetry and historic novels abound with allusions to the military and ecclesiastical architecture of earlier periods. A detailed assessment of Scott's influence on architecture cannot be included here, but without doubt he was a great inspiration to many antiquarians.

The Cambridge Camden Society was founded in 1839 by John Mason Neale and Benjamin Webb, then undergraduates who both went on to become Anglican clergymen. It took the name 'Camden' from the famous sixteenth-century antiquary, and 'Cambridge' was added to distinguish it from the Camden Society printing club. The underlying interest of the society was 'ecclesiology' – the 'science' of church architecture. Its first law states: 'The object of the Society shall be to promote the study of Ecclesiastical Architecture and Antiquities, and the restoration of mutilated architectural remains.'[18]

In addition to these stated architectural aims, the founders were also interested in restoring reverence and dignity to worship and promoting their concerns over Church ritual. As a result the society eventually became associated with the Tractarian movement.

From the very start the Cambridge Camden Society grew rapidly, soon expanding beyond the university. By May 1841 it had about 300 members and by 1843 its membership had risen to over 700, including both archbishops and sixteen bishops. Its influence was even wider than its large membership suggests. This was largely due to its highly popular pamphlets. For instance, *A Few Words to Churchwardens on Churches and Church Ornaments* sold about 5,000 copies within six weeks of its initial publication in 1841, necessitating ten editions in its first year and a further three by 1843 when it was reported that 13,000 copies had been circulated.[19]

---

[17] For a Victorian view on these subjects see Eastlake, 'Revival'.
[18] *The Ecclesiologist* 1, (1843).
[19] White, *Cambridge Movement*, 115.

Prior to the Ecclesiological movement, there was little reverence for church buildings or their contents and many medieval churches were in very poor repair. A paper read at the Exeter Diocesan Architectural Society in 1842 described the neglect and lack of respect for churches of which people were suddenly becoming aware:

> we may now see in most of our rural churches a rabble of boors and boys seated on the very steps and rails of the altar, and the altar itself is used to place their hats on... This extreme irreverence, and shocking desecration of holy things is capable of no excuse.[20]

Other publications of the period recorded instances of servants bringing luncheon to the squire during sermons, and even of a churchwarden climbing on the altar to open windows during a service. However, the reforms initiated by the Cambridge Camden Society were rapidly adopted almost universally across the country, leading to greater reverence in worship, and more respect for church buildings and religious antiquities.

The Ecclesiological movement, exemplified by the Cambridge Camden Society, was a major force behind the widespread establishment of local architectural societies, almost all of which show a number of distinct characteristics. Generally, either the local bishop or the lord lieutenant of the county was the president, and the other would almost invariably be a patron. The councils of these societies tended to involve local peers, baronets, and MPs, as well as large numbers of clergymen — a similar composition to the British Archaeological Association's membership (table 1). For example, the Yorkshire Architectural Society had the Archbishop of York and the Bishop of Ripon as patrons, and the Lord Lieutenants of the North and East Ridings as presidents. The vice-presidents included nine peers, five baronets, five MPs, six 'the honourables', four archdeacons, one dean, and seven other clergymen. The Yorkshire Society was one of the larger ones with over 300 members, but even smaller societies such as the Lincolnshire Architectural Society were dominated by the clergy. Thirteen out of its nineteen vice-presidents were clergymen, as were 64% of its 112 members in 1850. Similarly, clergy made up 77% of the original 120 members of the Architectural Society of the Archdeaconry of Northampton which was founded in 1844.[21] The objects of this society mirrored those of the Cambridge Camden Society, being:

> to promote the study of ecclesiastical architecture, antiquities and design, and the restoration of mutilated architectural remains within the archdeaconry; and to furnish suggestions, as far as may be within its province, for improving the character of ecclesiatical edifices hereafter to be erected.[22]

A general distinction can be drawn between the societies that concentrated exclusively on architecture and maintained Ecclesiological principles, and those that combined

---

[20] Quoted in White, ibid., 4.
[21] Levine, *Amateur*, 48.
[22] Associated Architectural Societies – Reports and Papers, 1, (1850–1).

their architectural interests with archaeological ones in a more secular manner.[23] Those that remained Ecclesiological in nature tended to restrict their membership to Anglicans and drew most of their officers from the clergy. The second class, archaeological and architectural societies, were generally founded slightly later than the purely architectural societies and, to judge by their aims and objects, were influenced as much by the British Archaeological Association as by the Cambridge Camden Society. The objects of the later societies tended to be broader, speaking of 'examining, preserving, and illustrating all Ancient Monuments and Remains'.[24] Although they were interested in the restoration of ancient remains, they were less concerned with advising architects about the building of contemporary structures, which had been a key component of the Ecclesiological movement.

An example of a local antiquarian society that was not involved with Ecclesiological concerns was the Cambridge Antiquarian Society (not to be confused with the Cambridge Camden Society). This was founded in May 1840: 'for the encouragement of the study of the History, Architecture and Antiquities of the University, County, and Town of Cambridge...[and] to collect and print information relative to the above-mentioned subjects'.[25]

The only non-graduate among the founders of the Cambridge Antiquarian Society was Halliwell, who appears to have envisaged the Society as primarily a printing club and was responsible for publishing lists of manuscript sources in the first annual reports. Despite his enthusiasm for the Society, he was forced to resign as secretary after leaving Cambridge for London in 1841 due to financial difficulties. The Society originally aimed to meet three times a term. Although this proved to be too ambitious, sufficient communications were made to the Society to enable it to publish fifteen 'miscellaneous tracts' from 1840–9.

The Cambridge Antiquarian Society differed from most local antiquarian societies in that it was dominated by the University. By 1846 it had 106 members, of whom 58 were dons, 7 were Heads of Houses, and 5 were professors.[26] As with so many other societies of the period, the most active members were involved in the organisation of other societies, and could draw on their experience; in particular, there was a definite overlap between the Cambridge Camden Society and the Cambridge Antiquarian Society. For instance, Reverend J. J. Smith, a founder of the Cambridge Antiquarian Society, was a vice-president of the Cambridge Camden Society, and Professor Willis, president of the Cambridge Antiquarian Society 1845–6 and 1850–1, had also been a vice-president of the Cambridge Camden Society until he withrew from both in 1841 due to their theological stance.[27] Both J. J. Smith and Cardale Babington, who helped

[23] Levine, *Amateur* 47.
[24] This wording is based on the Cambrian Archaeological Association, founded in 1846.
[25] Report of the Cambridge Antiquarian Society, (1851), 13.
[26] Thompson, *Cambridge Antiquarian.*
[27] See Page 98 below: Cocke, *Robert Willis: the Religious Revival and its Impact on Architecture.*

found the Cambridge Antiquarian Society, had been involved in establishing the Cambridge Ray Society in 1837 – a small exclusive club for scientists. Babington and Willis also both held office within the Cambridge Philosophical Society. Thus, in typical Victorian fashion, the key figures within the Cambridge Antiquarian Society were involved in other learned societies.

CONCLUSION

The Victorians often displayed a conscious desire to use their leisure time fruitfully. Involvement in scientific and/or antiquarian organisations helped meet this aim by providing opportunities through which an understanding of the past could be advanced by the meeting of like-minded individuals. For many:

> Recreation needed to include the Victorian attributes of being purposeful, utilitarian, fortifying and efficacious....the true gentleman...could not be seen to idle away his leisure hours but must add to his respectability by...undertaking some form of earnest, self-improving education. Archaeology was just such a respectable pursuit.[28]

Although the meetings and activities of archaeological societies and associations were recreational in nature, antiquarians were confident that their subject was not a mere intellectual pastime. The practitioners of nineteenth-century archaeology believed that, like the physical sciences, their studies provided 'useful knowledge' that could help maintain the fabric of society. Roach Smith wrote:

> it must ever be borne in mind, that the science which these collections [of antiquities] promote is one of the highest consideration, that it might be made of great public utility, and without which every system of education must be incomplete.[29]

Like other disciplines in this period, archaeology aspired to the status of an exact science. Antiquarians believed their methods could become sufficiently rigorous to join the body of organised knowledge headed by the natural sciences. The desire to increase knowledge through careful observation using a scientific, inductivist approach was particularly prevalent amongst numismatists and ecclesiologists. Others in the antiquarian community followed suit and, as I have explained, the structure of antiquarian societies reflected the organisation of scientific learned societies. A rigorous scientific methodology was never achieved, but the development of printing clubs and the establishment of archaeological societies and associations enabled the antiquarian community to increase in size dramatically in the early Victorian period. This can be clearly seen in the first few years of the British Archaeological Association and the

---

[28] Brookes, 'Establishment'.
[29] Preface to Smith, *Coll.*, I, vii.

Archaeological Institute. The growth of these and other societies, both in numbers and activities, helped lay the foundations for the discipline of archaeology as we know it today.

Acknowledgements

Much of this paper derives from my MA thesis (Durham University, 1991). I am grateful to Dr Colin Haselgrove, Dr Martin Millett, and Professor Martin Jones for help and advice during my research at Durham. I am also deeply indebted to Professor David Knight whose knowledge and enthusiasm about the history of science has been a great inspiration to me.

Table 1. The British Archaeological Association Membership, September 1844

Total membership	1024
Includes:	
Fellows of the Society of Antiquaries	167
Fellows of the Royal Society	68
University academics	30
British Museum employees	14
Nobles	23
Baronets	18
Knights	19
Members of Parliament	23
Officers in learned or provincial antiquarian societies	33
Foreign members	27
Clergy (Total)	368
Bishops	12
Deans	12
Archdeacons	16
Rural Deans	16

Table 2. *Subscribers to the British Archaeological Association
and the Arcaheological Institute, 1845–9*

BRITISH ARCHAEOLOGICAL ASSSOCIATION

| | Subscribers | | | | | |
	Annual	Life	Total	Clergy	F.S.A.	Nobles
April 1845	177	15	192	29 (15%)	37 (19%)	4 (2%)
July 1845	240	13	253	27 (11%)	46 (18%)	4 (2%)
Sep. 1847	468	17	485	32 (7%)	72 (15%)	25 (5%)
1848/49	456	14	470	40 (9%)	69 (15%)	22 (5%)
1849/50	436	20	456	37 (8%)	76 (17%)	20 (4%)

ARCHAEOLOGICAL INSTITUTE

| | Subscribers | | | | | |
	Annual	Life	Total	Clergy	F.S.A.	Nobles
March 1845	143	8	151	35 (23%)	? ?	3 (2%)
Sep. 1845	621	23	644	197 (31%)	62 (10%)	19 (3%)
June 1848	886	37	923	254 (28%)	86 (9%)	36 (4%)
June 1849	933	55	988	274 (28%)	83 (8%)	38 (4%)

Geology and the Natural Sciences: Some Contributions to Archaeology in Britain 1780–1850

H. S. Torrens

INTRODUCTION

> 9 April 1847: went to the monthly meeting of the Archaeological Institute; Dean of Westminster [the geologist William Buckland] in the chair; a very poor attendance and still worse affair; a mere twaddle on tumuli, barrows, etc[1]
>
> *Diary entry by the geologist Gideon Mantell,*
> *recording his first attendance at a meeting of the Royal Archaeological Institute.*

In the Autumn of 1845 Hugh Miller (1802–56), the Scottish geologist and writer, visited England and was profoundly affected by the industrialisation he saw. The first English city he visited was Newcastle-on-Tyne and in its Town Museum he noted that its geological collections were superior in extent and arrangement to any he had previously seen in Scotland. Its Anglo-Roman antiquities moreover were 'greatly more numerous than in any other museum I ever saw'. Miller here gives a vital insight into one major contribution that geology and archaeology could then give to each other; the encouragement to *collect* them both; the fruitful results of which are still to be seen in our – often sadly neglected – museums.

Miller then made a further significant observation on the relationship between these two subjects, as he then saw them;

> as I passed, in the geologic department, from the older Silurian to the newer Tertiary, and then on from the newer Tertiary to the votive tablets, sacrificial altars and sepulchral memorials of the Anglo-Roman gallery, I could not help regarding them as all belonging to one department. The antiquities piece on in natural *sequence* [italics added] to the geology; and it

---

[1] Curwen, *Gideon Mantell*, 215.

seems but rational to indulge in the same sort of reasonings regarding them. They are the fossils of an extinct order of things, newer than the Tertiary – of an extinct race – of an extinct religion – of a state of society and a class of enterprises which the world saw once but will never see again.[2]

This attitude to the then continuous, and equally past, worlds of geology and archaeology is now extinct. In their ever more specialised worlds, today's archaeology and geology have drifted apart to join the opposing continents on either side of C. P. Snow's 'Two Cultures' ocean; the one human, the other scientific. The growth in North America of the new – and to me divisive – discipline of 'geo-archaeology' or 'archaeological geology' has only widened this division so that the two subjects are now studied across this divide and the gulf between them seems to be reflected in the limited historiography of their links. Those few explorations that have been made seem superficial[3] or, in the particular case of the new 'archaeological geology' or 'geoarchaeology', only start their (North American) history with the publication of Charles Lyell's influential *The Antiquity of Man* in 1863.[4] I believe the links between the subjects were greater than history has allowed. For instance, Beriah Botfield and Sir Philip Egerton, the only geo-archaeologists I could note in Philippa Levine's book,[5] do not seem adequately to reflect those links. The fact that Levine's book is on such a 'rare' subject, to me provides further proof of the width of the present gulf.

This paper considers how geology might have helped the new archaeology of the 1840s to have had such confident beginnings. In an area which seems so little explored, this superficial attempt is very much one as viewed from only one, the geological, side of the fence. But links between the subjects can still be seen all around us. For example, anyone visiting quite uninhabited areas to study geology can be offended by the highly human, and thus 'archaeological', pollution found all along the shores in such areas, brought there simply by the natural agency of ocean currents. The visitor to the archaeological Egyptian Museum in Turin can equally today ask whether the Eocene fossil echinoid preserved there (with its Egyptian hieroglyphic inscription) is not also a geological artefact.[6] Obvious ways to help foster the links are the study of the geology of graveyards and their contained monuments or the archaeology of building materials.

HUMAN PETRIFICATION

An early topic which united the two subjects was the late eighteenth-century interest in the problems of human petrification. A fascinating correspondence started in the

---

[2] Miller, *Impressions*, 10–11.
[3] Daniel, *Origins*. I except Stuart Piggott's most stimulating essay 'Origins Arch. Socs'.
[4] Gifford and Rapp, 'Arch. Geology', Rapp, 'Geoarchaeology', and Thorson and Holliday, 'Geoarchaeology'.
[5] Levine, *Amateur*.
[6] Scamuzzi, 'Fossile', Socin, 'Fossile'.

Gentleman's Magazine in 1787 by a 'Constant Reader'.[7] Contributors were concerned with separating petrification (which implied antiquity) from 'mere' incrustation (which did not). They were drawn from all over England and referred other correspondents and readers to examples from Yorkshire, Dublin, Switzerland, Rome, Gibraltar, and farther afield. But their problems were not merely concerned with human antiquity and whether such petrifications were or were not 'antediluvian'. Scientific experiments were urged in the Peak district, 'whose waters produce such beautiful petrifactions', to see how human bone would be changed with time. In 1788 the artist and antiquary, James Douglas (1753–1819), produced a notably scientific appraisal of the Gibraltar human fossil of 1742, in which he doubted that any 'human skeleton petrified' had been found up to that time. In particular he criticised the chronology of 'a thousand years' as the duration that one writer had assigned for proper petrification to be effected. Douglas noted that the establishment of a chronology for petrification was now 'the great *desideratum* on these enquiries'.

The accurate identification of human anatomy, whether in geological or archaeological records, was equally important, as the famous earlier case of Scheuchzer's *Homo diluvii testis* of 1726 demonstrates.[8] The non-human origin of this famous fossil was only published in 1790, over sixty years later, by the anatomist Petrus Camper, who claimed it as a lizard, although, again, James Douglas had already noted that the specimen 'has no resemblance whatever to a human skeleton' in 1788. Greater truth had to wait for another famous anatomist, Georges Cuvier, who demonstrated in 1812 that it was a fossil salamander.[9] Other problems in petrifactional interpretation emerged as merely bibliographic in origin in this correspondence. One correspondent, for example, found it hard to countenance the 'petrified human body Sir Richard Fanshaw had seen in Rome in 1693', since Sir Richard had died in 1666, never been in Italy (or Rome), and the bibliographic source quoted for this 'petrification', *Fanshaw's Travels*, was not his.[10] Such problems remind us of the real difficulties facing scholars in days before good libraries were widely available.

WHAT ANTIQUITY FOR MAN AND THE EARTH?

Some solution to the controversy about the 'age of the earth' was vital if James Douglas's wish for a chronology of petrification was to be answered. This was a question which certainly brought geology and archaeology together. A good survey up

---

[7] *Gentleman's Magazine*, vol. 57 (1787), 463 and continued ibid., 578, 593–4 (the latter by Philip Thicknesse), 781–21, 793 (the latter by Thomas Parsons of Bath – a member of the former Philosophical Society set up there in 1779), 968–9, 1071–2; vol. 58 (1788), 31–2, 383–4 (by James Douglas), 694–5 and 951–2 (by James Douglas). It was concluded in vol. 62 (1792), 25–6 by an anonymous correspondent.

[8] Jahn, 'Scheuchzer'.

[9] Grayson, *Human Antiquity*, 88–9.

[10] *Gentleman's Magazine*, (1787), 968–9, 1071–2.

to 1788, and of the well-known work of James Hutton (1726–97), is given by Dean, who notes how the debate had by then become increasingly focused on geological rather than theological evidence.[11] Important estimates of the antiquity for the earth from the geological, as opposed to the biblical, record include that of 1778 by Georges-Louis Leclerc, Comte de Buffon (1707–88), in France. He then claimed figures of up to 75,000 years.[12] Dean has noted how deviant Hutton was in endorsing soon afterwards such 'vague but daring lengths of geological time' and in showing how limited the human record was in geological terms.[13] But support for such vague time scales was not what students of human antiquity most needed.

A forgotten English contributor to this debate was an English land surveyor and steward, John Middleton (1751–1833), who published two notes in the *Monthly Magazine* in 1816.[14] In the first he claimed a sea level rise of '40 or 50 feet...in the next 4 or 5 thousand years'. In the second he extended this idea to suggest that the 7,700 feet of recorded strata in England, which he and other 'mineral surveyors' had largely helped to elucidate by then, must represent a duration of 770,000 years. But, since the Slate Stratum below was now known to be of a similar kind, he thought this estimate should now be further extended to one of 'upwards of a million years' in duration. He calculated that these two miles of sedimentary sequence had taken 1,056,000 years to form. Critics were not slow to point out some problems with this analysis[15] but Middleton deserves credit for an early attempt to apply the methodology that John Phillips (1800–74) was later to popularise in 1860, after Charles Darwin had set his cat among the pigeons of the earth's chronology.[16]

In 1817 Charles Hall I (1751–1831) from Ansty, Dorset published his agreement with Middleton's figure for the duration of the stratigraphic record, as then interpreted in England.[17] Hall asked that some additional allowance should be made for the Granite Stratum and earlier rocks which he still envisaged as lying below the main sequence. He also called attention to an earlier estimate, by Sir George Staunton (1737–1801), of the rate of infilling by the Yellow River which Staunton had seen on the Macartney Embassy journey to China in 1793. This river they found took to the sea 'a volume of 17,520,000,000 solid feet a year'. If a mean depth of 120 feet deep was assumed for the Yellow Sea, it would be filled in 24,000 years. The accuracy of

---

[11] Dean, 'Age of the Earth'.

[12] Roger, *Buffon* and see Evans, 'Prehistory', 15–16 .

[13] Dean, *Hutton*, 275.

[14] Middleton, 'Rise of Ocean' and 'Gradual Rise of Ocean'. Middleton had considered these questions of antiquity in an earlier paper (Middleton, 'Planet').

[15] See articles in *Mon. Mag.*, 41 (1816), 217–18 (Jennings, 'Earth Surface'), 310 (Nicholson, 'Increase or Decrease'), and 311. William Nicholson, the engineer and editor, called Middleton's first piece 'a dismal piece of intelligence'. Middleton's second paper was criticised in vol. 42 (1817), 518–9 by James Jennings who there acknowledged his authorship of the earlier piece.

[16] See Burchfield, *Kelvin*, 59–60.

[17] Hall, 'Depositories'.

such calculations is not of real interest here. The fact that such calculations were now being attempted at all is the important point. The vital advance had been that the English stratigraphic sequence was now starting to be known and with some approximation to completeness.

By the last years of the eighteenth century, others were also busy on other, often non-chronological, aspects of the links between geology and archaeology. In 1797 Samuel Lysons (1763–1819) published his work on the Roman Antiquities of Woodchester in Gloucestershire.[18] In this he speculated with remarkable accuracy on the geological origins of the tesserae of which the pavements there were composed.[19] In the same year John Frere MP (1740–1807) read his famous 'Account of Flint Weapons discovered at Hoxne in Suffolk' to the Society of Antiquaries in London on 22 June 1797, first published in 1800.[20] This reported the finding of weapons of war, fabricated by a people who had not the use of metal, at a 'very remote period indeed; even beyond that of the present world'. Frere, like Hutton, made no attempt to quantify the remoteness.

Soon afterwards in 1799, that remarkable polymath Robert Townson (1762–1827) privately published his observations on the lithological variations of rocks used at Stonehenge.[21] Townson noted that the great sarsen stone pillars were of fine grained sandstone that did not effervesce with acid. The other, Bluestones, he carefully separated as of fine grained Grünstein. He also noted two other lithologies among the second inner row of stones; one of 'blackish siliceous shistus' and the other of 'argillaceous shistus'.

STRATIGRAPHIC SEQUENCE AND THE PLACE OF 'THE DELUGE'

The advance of stratigraphic knowledge was crucial to the realisation that there had to have been a long pre-Diluvial history recorded in rocks. This yielded the first real debt that archaeology could owe to geology. This was, as Hugh Miller later pointed out, in the elucidation of *sequence* and of stratigraphic methodology.[22]

The beginnings of the study of sequence are lost in the largely papyrophobic world of mining. Here quarrymen and miners became aware of the sequential orders of rocks as soon as they penetrated them to uncover and exploit mineral deposits. The first such sequences to be written down included attempts made all over Europe, like that in a Dudley coal mine in 1712.[23] Later attempts in England, like those of John Player (1725–1808) of Tockington, Gloucestershire to elucidate the sequence of rocks

---

[18] Lysons, *Woodchester*
[19] See Torrens, 'Cirencester', 78.
[20] See Daniel, *Origins*, 46–8.
[21] Townson, *Natural History*, 227–8.
[22] Miller, *Impressions*, 10–11.
[23] Bellers, 'Description'.

exposed between London and Cornwall in 1765, or of John Michell (1724–93) in 1788 to do the same for the Eastern Counties, both suffered from not being published.[24] Some of these records were made by people who attempted to explore both archaeology and geology, like the antiquary John Strange (1732–99) in 1779.[25] His 'curious Remains of Antiquity' were *Gryphites* fossil oysters. He used them to trace the geological outcrop of the Lias formation with some success across England and Wales. His attempt was then criticised as insufficiently accurate by one of the pioneers in stratigraphic method who soon provided the new precision needed: John Farey senior (1766–1826).[26]

One of the *Gentleman's Magazine* contributors to the human petrification debate in 1787 had referred to 'this our exploring age' as an important contributory factor that had supplied many fossils now newly available in England from its new mines, pits, canals, and housing developments. This feature of the Industrial Revolution was clearly vital in helping the major advance which was soon to come. This was to achieve a first and accurate *sequential* chronicle of rocks against which a measure of the antiquity of other rocks could be made. But the history of humankind and its possible relation to the chronology of this older earth were still seen in terms of the scriptural record. The date of Creation was accepted as recent; many still accepting Archbishop Ussher's famous date of 4004 B.C. Creation still took only six days with Adam created on the sixth. He was created perfect but soon fell into sin, for which his descendants suffered through the Universal Deluge that wiped out the entire world, save the few human and animal species gathered together into Noah's Ark. The geological record was merely seen as likely to confirm this.

SMITH AND FAREY AND A DILUVIAL OR ALLUVIAL RECORD

The English pioneer in unravelling the geological record was William Smith (1769–1839), whose canal surveying and engineering work from 1791 while he was based in Somerset led to his major discoveries.[27] It was Smith who first documented the near complete sequence of rocks found in England (fig.5). This could then be used as an ever-improvable standard against which to place other rocks elsewhere in their correct orders. Smith also provided the key to identifying many rocks against that sequential standard, by showing that strata could often be identified by their 'contained fossils'. But such sequential science had no direct chronological significance until it could be connected with some other historical record.

It was while excavating canals in Somerset in the 1790s that Smith had realised

---

[24] John Player's important observations remain in manuscript and J. Michell's observations were only published by John Farey in 1810 ('List ', 102).
[25] Strange, 'Glamorganshire'.
[26] Farey, 'Strange'.
[27] Eyles, 'Smith', 149–54.

Order of the Strata in the Vicinity of Bath ;—drawn up by Mr. WILLIAM SMITH *in* 1799.
[From the Original in the possession of the Geological Society.]

Strata.	Thick-ness.	Springs.	Fossils, Petrifactions. &c, &c.	Descriptive Characters and Situations.
1. Chalk	300	Intermitting on the Downs.	Echinites, Pyrites, Mytilites, Dentalia, funnel-shaped Corals, and Madrepores, Nautilites, Strombites, Cochliæ, Ostreæ, Serpulæ ...	Strata of Silex, imbedded.
2. Sand	70	.....	....	The fertile vales intersecting Salisbury Plain and the Downs.
3. Clay	30	Between the Black Dog and Berkley.		
4. Sand and Stone	30			
5. Clay	15	Hinton, Norton, Woolverton, Bradford Leigh.	....	Imbedded is a thin stratum of calcareous Grit. The stones flat, smooth, and rounded at the edges.
6. Forest Marble	10	.....	A mass of Anomiæ and high-waved Cockles, with calcareous Cement...............	The cover of the upper bed of Freestone, or Oolyte.
7. Freestone	60	.....	Scarcely any Fossils besides the Coral	Oolyte, resting on a thin bed of Coral.—Prior Park, Southstoke, Twinny, Winsley, Farley Castle, Westwood, Berfield, Conkwell, Monkton Farley, Coldhorn, Marshfield, Coldashton.
8. Blue Clay......	6	Above Bath		
9. Yellow Clay..	8			
10. Fuller's Earth	6	.....	....	Visible at a distance, by the slips on the declivities of the hills round Bath.
11. Bastard ditto, and Sundries	80	.....	Striated Cardia, Mytilites, Anomiæ, Pundibs, and Duck-muscles.	
12. Freestone	30	.....	Top-covering Anomiæ with calcareous Cement, Strombites, Ammonites, Nautilites, Cochliæ, Hippocephaloides, fibrous Shell resembling Amianth, Cardia, prickly Cockle Mytilites, lower Stratum of Coral, large Scollop, Nidus of the Muscle with its Cables	Lincombe, Devonshire Buildings, Englishcombe, Englishbatch, Wilmerton, Dunkerton, Coomhay, Monkton Combe, Wellow, Mitford, Stoke, Freshford, Claverton, Bathford, Batheaston, and Hampton, Charlcombe, Swainswick, Tadwick, Langridge.
13. Sand	30	.....	Ammonites, Belemnites	Sand Burs.
14. Marl Blue	40	Round Bath .	Pectenites, Belemnites, Gryphites, highly-waved Cockles..........................	Ochre Balls.—Mineral springs of Lincombe, Middle Hill, Cheltenham.
15. Lias Blue	25	.....	Same as the Marl with Nautilites, Ammonites, Dentalia, and Fragments of the Enchrini	The fertile Marl lands of Somersetshire. Twerton, Newton, Preston, Clutton, Stanton Prior, Timsbury, Paulton, Marksbury, Farmborough, Corston, Hunstreet, Burnet, Keynsham, Whitchurch, Salford, Kelston, Weston, Pucklechurch, Queencharlton, Norton-malreward, Knowle, Charlton, Kilmersdon, Babington.
16. Ditto White ...	15			
17. Marl Stone, Indigo and Black Marl	15	.....	Pyrites and Ochre	A rich manure.
18. Red-ground...	180	.....	No Fossil known......................	Pits of Ruddle. Beneath this bed no fossil shells, or animal remains are found : above it no vegetable impressions. The waters of this stratum petrify in the trunks in which they are conveyed, so as to fill them, in about fifteen years, with red Watricle, which takes a fine polish.—High-Littleton.
19. Millstone.				
20. Pennant Stone	...	.....	Impressions of unknown Plants resembling Equisetum.	
21. Grays	...	.....	....	Fragments of Coal and Iron Nodules.—Hanham, Brislington, Mangotsfield, Downend, Winterbourn, Forest of Dean, Pensford, Publow, Chelwood, Cumptondando, Hallatrow near Stratford-on-Avon, Stonebench on-the-Severn, four miles from Gloucester.
22. Cliff	...	.....	Impressions of Ferns, Olive, stellate Plants, Threnax-parviflora, or Dwarf Fan Palm of Jamaica	Stourbridge, or Fire-clay.
23. Coal	...			

Fig. 5. Smith's Standard Sequence of 1799. (Fitton, Notes*)*

the necessity of separating the 'alluvial ruins of strata' above, from the 'regular and undisturbed strata' below; according to the *Claims* drawn up early in 1818 for him by Farey, with Sir Joseph Banks's encouragement. This breakthrough had come in 1795 or earlier, at 'a time when almost all observers and writers on the subject, were confounding the alluvia with the strata'. In John Farey's opinion, this discovery was 'quite fundamental to any progress in acquiring a knowledge of the British strata as without which discrimination, no progress whatever could have been made'.[28] He had already emphasised this point when, in 1806, he published the 'Rules' by which 'the relative position of each stratum with regard to those above and below it in the series' in Britain could be elucidated.[29] In 1813 Farey again noted that this separation was the 'first and most important principle of the Smithian School'.[30] Farey's own part in publicising, disseminating, and advancing Smith's results has been too long ignored.

In all of these discussions, written by Farey between 1806 and 1818, Smith is represented as having referred neutrally to 'alluvia', a word with no attached chronology. But when John Phillips, Smith's nephew, later came to write Smith's only biography in 1844, he claimed that his uncle had, by 1797–8, assigned such alluvial deposits to Diluvial action. Later he claimed that the word Diluvial had been first employed by Smith.[31] This had given Smith's early work an archaeological significance by placing geology in a directly human, if only biblical, context. Smith can certainly be shown to have held his Diluvial opinion in 1799.[32]

The most important contact between Smith and the world of Diluvial archaeology comes from the work of William Cunnington (1754–1810), in Wiltshire; one of the true fathers of scientific archaeological excavation in England, and also a significant geologist.[33] Smith and Cunnington were in contact by 1797, according to John Britton (1771–1857), another important figure in the development of British archaeology.[34] In 1804, the historian of Wiltshire, Sir Richard Colt Hoare (1758–1838) had agreed to fund Cunnington's future researches. By 1807 Cunnington was busy writing up his investigations of Stonehenge and seeking advice on the different lithologies found among the stones there, but by this time Smith had moved to distant East Anglia and Smith and Cunnington had been out of direct contact for some years. Cunnington's work, and Smith's part in it, is recorded by Hoare[35] and others. The two major types of stone used at Stonehenge were in part confirmed by Smith. These identifications

[28] Farey, 'Smith', 175.
[29] Farey, 'Stratification'.
[30] Farey, 'Bakewell', 105.
[31] Phillips, *Manual of Geology*, 420.
[32] Cox, 'Smith', 89–90.
[33] See Cunnington, *Antiquary*.
[34] Britton, *Auto-biography*, I, 461–73.
[35] Hoare, *South Wiltshire*, I, 151–2.

allowed Cunnington to suggest Stonehenge must have had its own chronology, with the local sarsen stones used first before the foreign Bluestones. Cunnington had a high opinion of Smith's originality and he also recorded Smith's intriguing hypothesis to explain the origin of the sarsen stones, then still lying on the Wiltshire Downs.[36] Smith 'supposed that a stratum of sand containing these stones once covered the chalk land and at the Deluge this stratum was washed off from the surface and the stones left behind'.[37] To call this hypothesis merely 'an interesting confusion'[38] is hardly fair to Smith. This same hypothesis of their origin was still being promoted in 1852 as one 'still held by our leading geologists'. It was merely that Smith's suggestion that the Deluge was the erosive agent was then no longer supported.[39] At the time Smith formulated the idea, Diluvial distribution was an ingenious attempt to reconcile what would soon after be viewed as irreconcilable by friends of his such as Farey.

The change from Smith's according such rocks a Diluvial, to Farey's granting to them a 'merely' alluvial origin, seems to have been a direct and original contribution to the debate by Farey made between 1806 and 1812. In this last year Farey discussed the issue of the Deluge and its geological record with Jean Andre De Luc (1727–1817) the British-based biblical geologist of Swiss origin.[40] In this Farey correctly noted, as James Douglas had before him, the vital point that in the gravel or alluvial deposits of England there were no known remains of man or his 'works of art', except in the most recent deposits. This was in direct opposition to inferences to be drawn from the biblical account. Farey thus conceived that the 'effects of the deluge would scarcely remain visible on the earth for a single age, much less can we see anything of its effects'. The Deluge in Farey's view was 'known only through a revelation to Moses...and must be received as articles of *faith*, and seem incapable of any *natural proof*. In a letter written to the new president of the Geological Society in London, G. B. Greenough, in 1813 Farey similarly commented of Joseph Townsend's new book[41]

> poor Moses...of whom so a ridiculous a parade is made in his Title etc, seems after all most unfairly dealt by: the primitive waters, under which the Strata were formed, & dislocated, etc are confounded with the Deluge which Moses describes, as happening long after this, and after Men & all our present races of Beings had long existed on the earth, the such confounding is in violation of every sentence that is handed to us *as Moses' description* of his *Deluge*, which I maintain to be an object of faith or belief only and incapable of [the] least philosophical proof.

[36] See Anon, 'Salisbury Plain', 623 and Hoare, 'Oct. 1807'.
[37] Cunnington, *Antiquary* 33, 109–110, 119 and 141.
[38] Woodbridge, *Landscape*, 221.
[39] Long, 'Sarsen Stones'.
[40] Ellenberger and Gohau, 'Stratigraphie'.
[41] Townsend, *Moses* and Farey's letter 12 March 1813 in G. B. Greenough archive: University College, London.

Farey deserves credit for his early advocacy of the need for careful study of the most recent fossil record and for his realisation that it now proved impossible to reconcile geology with the previously undisputed biblical record (fig.6).

Fig. 6. The only known portrait of Farey. (Silhouette of John Farey senior (1766–1826) by White Watson (c. 1806–7) (Derby Public Library collection))

It is probably through his very important contacts with Farey and his highly original views that Smith was turned from seeing his record as Diluvial to viewing it (apparently at least in part) as a merely alluvial record, some time between 1799 and 1806.[42] But by 1826, after William Buckland (1784–1856) had advocated the view that remains of the Deluge could be found in the fossil record, John Phillips, Smith's nephew, is found studying 'the Direction of Diluvial Currents' in Yorkshire.[43] By the later 1830s it is clear that Smith himself had reverted to separating alluvial and Diluvial geological records, again through the lingering influence of William Buckland.[44]

By 1809 Smith's work, with Farey's vital input, was becoming well-known among the academic and 'gentlemanly' figures of English Geology, then centred on the new Geological Society[45] and the Royal Society in London. One of them, W. D. Conybeare (1787–1857) wrote later that 'the general fact of the successive distribution of these ancient genera [of fossils] when first laid down as an admitted fact in the progress of geology,...was...about this time, 1809'.[46] At the same time it was also becoming known among some of the better informed industrialists in England like the Mushet family, one of whom later wrote that it was 'the persevering intelligence of Dr Wm Smith...[who] clearly established the succession of the sedimentary rocks..., this nucleus of the science of geology was pretty well established and received by the year 1810'.[47] Such comments show that Smith's sequential ordering of the strata of England, and his additional discovery of the means to identify many of them by their contained fossils, was well known before his famous *Geological Map* was published in 1815 with its accompanying sequential *Table of Strata*. These crucial debts which William Buckland owed to Smith have been neglected by some recent workers on Buckland.[48]

---

[42] Torrens and Ford, 'Farey'.
[43] See Phillips, 'Diluvial Currents'.
[44] Cox, 'Smith', 69.
[45] For the founding of the Geological Society see p.27 above and Rudwick, 'Foundation'.
[46] Conybeare, *Letters*, 137.
[47] Mushet, 'Geologists'.
[48] Eg Rupke, *Chain*, 191–3.

It is notable at this time how well geologists and antiquarians could still collaborate. The revival of the Society of Antiquaries of Scotland from 1813 by Scottish geologists is a case in point.[49] But exclusion from much of the European continent from 1793 with the onset of the Napoleonic Wars had meant that much of this work remained insular. The Grand Tour was now no longer possible, except for brief intervals,[50] and many of the normal scientific contacts with Europe were no longer possible until 1815.[51] Those in search of 'The Romantic' had to stay at home, to the advantage of British geology and archaeology. But news of the major advance made by Georges Cuvier and Alexandre Brongniart in elucidating the stratigraphical sequence in the Paris basin *above* the Chalk did soon penetrate the walls of war. This work was particularly important in an 'archaeological' sense, as it brought the well-established English sequence upwards to a position closer to any human record. Their work was well publicised in England by John Farey in 1810.[52]

A New Problem with 'Fossil' Man

Another interlude of much archaeological significance gained notoriety because of these wars. This concerned 'Guadaloupe Man'. By 1810 collectors and scientists were alerted to the need to reconcile the sequential fossil record, as elaborated by Smith and Farey in England and Cuvier and Brongniart in France, with that of fossil man. As we have seen, Farey was already of the opinion that no true fossil men had yet been found and felt strongly that it was not possible to reconcile the biblical with the geological record. But many were now hunting for evidence. In October 1813 an announcement that ten petrified human skeletons had been found at Pansey Llyn near Llandebie in Wales caused much interest; the skulls were 'of great size and thickness and the bones were of larger calibre'.[53] Sir Joseph Banks, President of the Royal Society, asked Lewis Weston Dillwyn (1778–1855) who lived nearby, to investigate. Banks had recently received a skeleton imbedded in limestone from Guadeloupe in the West Indies, and wanted further details of petrified humans. Dillwyn was soon able to put Banks's mind at rest since the Welsh skeletons proved to be from reburials and neither fossilised nor petrified.[54] News of the Guadeloupe skeleton, which had been captured from the French, was soon released to the public in January 1814[55] after Charles Konig (1774–1851), Keeper of Natural History at the British Museum, had read his paper on the skeleton to the Royal Society on 20 December 1813.[56] Konig recorded that although

---

[49] Stevenson, 'Museum'.
[50] Evans, *Antiquaries*, 198.
[51] Challinor, 'Webster' 148; Lyell, *Life*, II, 48; Simpson, *Yorkshire Lias*, iv; and Rupke, *Chain*, 11.
[52] Farey, 'Cuvier'.
[53] *Mon. Mag.*, 36 (1 October 1813), 285.
[54] Dawson, *Banks*, 268.
[55] *Mon. Mag.*, 36 (January 1814), 528.
[56] Konig, 'Guadaloupe', pl. III.

*Fig. 7. Konig's illustration of the specimen of Guadeloupe Man.
(Konig, 'Guadaloupe', pl. 3, drawn by William Alexander)*

the skeleton was imbedded in limestone its skull was lacking. He concluded that 'the calcareous rock in which these bones are imbedded is an aggregate...of zoophytic [i.e. coral] particles and the detritus of compact limestone' which was not stalactitic. The age of the skeleton was assigned to 'a late period', which was, however, 'not of very recent origin'. Konig hoped that 'the attention of geologists now being directed towards this object... will not fail ere long to fix its age and assign to it the place it is to occupy in the series of rocks' (fig.7).

Farey wrote to the *Monthly Magazine* in January 1814 complaining that the first, earlier notice of its discovery in that magazine had claimed to 'disturb the many fine-spun theories, relative to the comparatively recent formation of the human species'. This, Farey said, was designed 'to call into question the Mosaic account of the origin and date of our species'. In Farey's view the evidence was still far too limited to allow this. He noted having read that the site from which this Guadeloupe skeleton had come had been a burial ground and asked for further evidence on this point. In June, De Luc also joined the debate.[57] He, too, agreed that the discovery did not call into question the Mosaic account. He noted that Guadeloupe was a volcanic island and that, when settled by Europeans in 1635, it had been found to be inhabited by native people. De Luc said it was probably these natives who had been enveloped by the coral growth that grew so fast there and in the Red Sea, and that now surrounded the

---

[57] De Luc, 'Guadaloupe'.

London skeleton. De Luc said this must mean 'it did not require much time to envelop them completely'. The 'human species could still be of comparatively recent formation' despite the evidence of its being surrounded by coral rock. With the end of the Napoleonic Wars, Banks was able to receive a French Report made earlier in 1806, on the 'nature and formation of the Stone encrusting these skeletons' from Guadeloupe. This he read to the Linnean Society in 1815.[58] It also confirmed their recent origin, but the question is still debated.[59]

DILUVIAL GEOLOGY RE-EMERGES

Some others were busy defending the Mosaic account; in 1815 William Blake's close friend, George Cumberland (1752–1848),[60] knew of no account 'more probable'. The Reverend Stephen Weston, whom the Antiquaries' historian[61] called 'the Society's chartered bore of the moment', published a note in 1817 on the site of the Ark in an attempt to document its archaeology.[62] Others were soon introduced to the Diluvial debate by the work of the geologist the Reverend William Buckland at Oxford University. In 1819 Buckland was confidently seeking evidence for human remains in the Diluvial gravel to support the idea that human fossils would turn up there in the fossil record.[63] Buckland ventured into some rather heterodox speculations in support of his Diluvial theory. In 1819 he gave his inaugural lecture as Reader in Geology at Oxford. It was published in 1820.[64] This contained an added four page Appendix, 'containing a brief summary of the proofs afforded by Geology of the Mosaic Deluge'. Buckland demonstrated his enthusiasm for reconciling the Mosaic and geological records by the geomorphology of hills and valleys, by the occurrence of outliers, by the immense deposits of gravel and their nature when found on hills, 'to which no torrents or rivers could ever have drifted them', and by the nature of the organic remains found in such gravels. In a recent commentary, James Edmonds has studied the gestation of Buckland's lecture.[65] The fact that his Readership was financially supported by the Royal Family may have made Buckland feel he must reconcile the geological and Mosaic accounts. In this he received the crucial encouragement of W. D. Conybeare. As Edmonds notes, 'some of Buckland's "proofs" [of the Deluge] appear so obviously contradictory that it is difficult to believe that Buckland had considered the problem sufficiently carefully'. One of Buckland's critics who read his lecture in 1820 was again John Farey, who commented specifically that there was still little evidence for any 'Mosaic Deluge' in

[58] Banks, 'Guadaloupe'.
[59] *New Scientist*, 29 March 1984, 44–5 and Tyler, 'Guadeloupe'.
[60] Cumberland, 'Mosaic System', 'Effects of Deluge', 'Deluge'.
[61] Evans, *Antiquaries*, 199.
[62] Weston, 'The Ark'.
[63] Rupke, *Chain*, 91.
[64] Buckland, *Vind.Geologiae*.
[65] Edmonds, 'Buckland'.

Fig. 8. Kirkdale Cave, Yorkshire 1823 (Buckland, Reliquiae Diluvianae, pl. 2, fig. 1)

the geological record, and noted how 'rare' Buckland's attempt at reconciliation was among modern authors on geology.[66]

A third camp, more biblically literalist in persuasion, was also opposed to Buckland. This included George Cumberland, who also commented on Buckland's lecture.[67] In particular, Cumberland found fault with Buckland's conciliatory claim that the stratigraphical column had been formed slowly and gradually. Cumberland wanted biblical days to be literal and considered cystallisation to have been a major cause for the 'sudden production of a thick sequence of rocks'. Farey again replied, denying the claim.[68]

Buckland's influence on English geology was then considerable and despite, or maybe because of, Farey's opposition, Buckland's theory of Diluvialism became popular in the 1820s in Britain, especially after Buckland's book *Reliquiae Diluvianae* was published in 1823.[69] This followed the discovery of ante-Diluvial caves at Kirkdale in Yorkshire in 1821 (fig.8) and Paviland in Gower in 1822.[70] Buckland broke new ground on the palaeoecological front with his careful analyses of caves and their former inhabitants.[71]

---

[66] Farey, 'Deluge'. Farey's authorship is acknowledged by him in 'Cumberland', 302.

[67] Cumberland, 'Buckland'.

[68] Farey, 'Cumberland'.

[69] As Page's fine review demonstrates (Page, 'Diluvialism').

[70] North, 'Paviland'.

[71] See Rupke, *Chain* and Boylan 'Buckland'. The most recent reviews are Boylan, 'Buckland' (thesis), chaps 4.2 'Fossil man' and 5.1 'Diluvialism': 'The Quaternary Dilemma'; and Shortland, 'Darkness Visible'. See also Dart, 'Hyena', for a fascinating illustration of how to misuse history to support science.

In 1825 Adam Sedgwick (1785–1873) working at Cambridge University wrote in support of Buckland's ideas. He noted that Buckland had been the first to adopt the separate terms *diluvium* and *alluvium*[72] though, in fact, the first to do so seems to have been one of Buckland's earliest pupils, William T. H. Fox-Strangways (1795–1865).[73] Fox-Strangways had also been influenced by William Smith (who had been employed by both his father and his half-brother). In his paper Strangways carefully separated post-Diluvial, Diluvial, and ante-Diluvial formations. This was the stratigraphic classification that Buckland then followed in *Reliquiae Diluvianae*.[74]

In a fascinating book Boyd Hilton[75] discusses how the post-Malthusian cultural climate of the 1820s still favoured catastrophic and apocalyptic visions of the past. 'Shipwreck' and 'oceans of debt' were common metaphors and Hilton suggests that enthusiasms for the biblical Deluge then current among geologists encouraged such figures of speech. Geological metaphors that saw business crashes as commercial 'earthquakes' were even more persuasive. The science then most closely connected with political economy was certainly geology and Buckland seems to have been riding a wave of popular appeal with his attempts between 1820 and 1828 to reconcile the Mosaic and biblical records with geology. The extinction of biblical geology between 1828 and 1836, which followed, was to prove a major break in the English cultural climate.

SOME 'ARCHAEO-GEOLOGISTS' 1810–30

The decade 1810 to 1820 saw others moving easily between what we today distinguish as geology and archaeology. Sir Henry Charles Englefield (1752–1822), who had earlier worked on both antiquities and geology, provided crucial patronage for Thomas Webster's work on the newer rocks of Hampshire, Dorset, and the Isle of Wight, which he published in 1816.[76] 1811 saw the first appearance in print of a significant scholar who bridged the two disciplines; Gideon Algernon Mantell (1790–1852). This 1811 publication on archaeology was his first, before he had published anything on geology, the field in which he was later to become famous. The paper announced the 'Fine Roman Pavement discovered at Bignor' in Sussex.[77] Mantell became one of the first to make contributions to both the new geology and the new archaeology. Another, active at the same time, who made perceptive contributions to both Mesozoic and recent geology was Henry Shorto III (1778–1864) of Salisbury: an area with a later proud record in archaeology, which he helped directly to inspire through his children.[78]

---

[72] Sedgwick, 'Origin'.
[73] Fox-Strangways, 'St Petersburgh'.
[74] Buckland, *Reliquiae Diluvianae*.
[75] Hilton, *Atonement*, 147–55.
[76] Englefield, *Isle of Wight*.
[77] Mantell, 'Bignor'.
[78] Torrens, 'Shorto'.

The letters that passed between John Hawkins (1758–1841) and the Lysons brothers, Daniel (1762–1834) and Samuel (1763–1819), from 1812 to 1830 similarly record the contributions of three men all of whom happily crossed today's divide.[79] Others include the Cambridge mineralogist and traveller Edward Daniel Clarke (1769–1822) who published a total of five archaeological papers in *Archaeologia* between 1817 and his death in 1822. It is difficult to think of these men as anything other than scholars fascinated by a still undivided past.

The next decade, the 1820s, saw the continuation of this tradition. Samuel Woodward (1790–1838) of Norwich, who published nine papers in the same journal between 1829 and the year of his death in 1838, was one. Another was Richard Cowling Taylor (1789–1851), the Norfolk-based pupil of William Smith who emigrated to Philadelphia in 1830. He published on monastic architecture as well as on the stratigraphy and palaeontology of East Anglia before his emigration and he continued his dual interests after his move to the New World. Joseph Harrison Fryer (1777–1855), a forgotten pioneer of the geology of Cumbria from 1808, went out to Peru in 1826 to superintend mining operations. On his return he published on South American archaeology.[80]

DOUBTS ON THE GEOLOGICAL STANDARD SEQUENCE

By 1823 Farey could accurately write of the known sequence of English rocks having become 'the standards for comparing and classifying the strata of other countries'.[81] But these standards still needed continual improvement. Doubts about the geological position of supposedly 'old' rocks at Stonesfield near Oxford were voiced from France, in 1825. These had yielded the monstrous fossil reptile *Megalosaurus* and the inconveniently ancient fossil mammal *Didelphis*.[82] Such doubts were answered in England, when the horizon of the Stonesfield Slates was again confirmed in 1828.[83] French doubts also concerned the correct geological position of the strata in the Tilgate Forest in Sussex that had yielded the equally monstrous new reptile *Iguanodon* to Mantell. In 1826 Mantell published his response as 'Remarks on the Geological Position of the Strata of the Tilgate Forest'.[84] He argued that doubts over the geological position of these beds were now unjustified. But doubts there had been. They demonstrate that the euphoria of English stratigraphers in having helped 'lead the way' would need to die down before the complete sequence of rocks, linking geology to archaeology, could be correctly placed in order.

---

[79] See Steer, 'Hawkins and Lysons'.
[80] Torrens, 'Fryer'.
[81] Farey, 'Notice'.
[82] Prevost, 'Schistes calcaires'.
[83] Broderip, 'Stonesfield Slate' and Fitton 'Strata', pl. 11.
[84] Mantell, 'Tilgate Forest'.

THE EXTINCTION OF THE DELUGE

New excitement followed in the late 1820s when Charles Lyell (1797–1875) and Roderick Murchison (1792–1871) returned from their continental tour with news that the rivers that flowed through the volcanic country of the Auvergne, had excavated their own valleys. This was a challenge to Buckland who had contended from 1820 that such valleys owed their form and origin to Diluvial action. Lyell wrote of their conversion[85] in powerful terms. By 1829 Sedgwick had similarly changed his mind over the Diluvial origin of such phenomena and he publicly recanted in 1831.[86] It is clear that this 'revelation' was the reason that Buckland abandoned his intended second volume to *Reliquiae Diluvianae*.[87] The debate was a fascinating, if complex one before Buckland finally abandoned Diluvialism in 1836.[88]

The debate about the actual rate of geological processes was, however, still unresolved. In 1830 Thomas Bird read a paper to the Antiquaries on a Roman Pavement at Bishopstone in Herefordshire.[89] He argued, using notes that the rector there, the Reverend Adam John Walker, had provided, that the depth of its burial could be used as a chronometer. Walker reported Humphrey Davy's (1778–1829) opinion that 'the surface of England was being raised by natural causes, *about an inch in a century*'. Davy had earlier acquired some reputation as a geologist while based at the Royal Institution and the fact that the Roman army had left the Bishopstone area sixteen centuries before was taken as 'remarkable confirmation' of his opinion. This case shows how archaeologists were now trying to apply earlier geological opinions to the rates of archaeological processes. Charles Lyell's attempt to use more recent fossil faunas as chronometers from 1833 was also of major significance, even if his project soon failed.[90]

THE 'CULTURE' OF FOSSILS

Anothe major factor which must have had its effect on archaeology was the new 'palaeoecology' movement. This can be said to have started with the 1830 drawing by Henry De la Beche (1796–1855) of *Duria Antiquior* (fig. 9).[91] It provided a novel way of looking at the fossils found in rocks and of interpreting how they had lived and interacted together whilst they were alive at any one 'period'. In an archaeological sense, geology could now reveal the 'culture' of fossils, whose chronology had already

---

[85] Lyell, *Life*, I, 253–8.
[86] Clark and Hughes, *Sedgwick*, I, 357–70.
[87] Lyell, *Life*, I, 253.
[88] A good review is by Rupke, *Chain*, chap.7.
[89] See *Archaeologia*, 23 (1831), 417–18.
[90] Rudwick, 'Lyell'.
[91] The subject of the pictorial representations of geological pasts is well covered by Secord, 'Survey' and by Rudwick, *Deep Time*.

Fig. 9. Duria Antiquior (Ancient Dorsetshire). Scharf's 1830s lithograph from Henry T. De La Beche's original of 1830 – inspired by the discoveries of Mary Anning (1799–1847).

been established. It gave an exciting second dimension to the study of the past. This work culminated in the impressive reconstructions of past biotas by William Buckland in his popular 'Bridgwater Treatise' *Geology and Mineralogy considered with reference to Natural Theology* which went through four editions between 1836 and 1869.[92] But exactly how and when this work achieved a precisely archaeological dimension still remains to be investigated.

PROVINCIAL SOCIETIES

Equally significant for archaeology was the development signalled by Lyell in his review of provincial societies' publications in the *Quarterly Review* in 1826.[93] Lyell pointed out the valuable work being done by many of the newly emerging Literary and

---

[92] Rupke, *Chain*, chap.11; Jacobs, 'Cephalopod Shells', demonstrates Buckland's remarkable ability to understand the function of ammonite shells.
[93] Lyell, [Review].

Philosophical Societies in the provinces. Some, like that at Bath, were set up with great enthusiasm in areas where antiquities and geological material were both abundant. But Bath's early euphoria soon waned and by 1829 the Bath Royal Literary and Scientific Institution was reported as 'chiefly sought as a place for Newspapers and Pamphlets and Easy Chairs and heated air. In addition to this misfortune, that Bath itself cannot support such an establishment, this has the ill-luck to be placed where no one can reach it'.[94] The situation of the several such societies in nearby Cheltenham, where again both antiquity and geology were of interest, was equally complex and evanescent.[95]

Lyell and the *Principles*

The publication of Lyell's *Principles of Geology* in 1830 caused a major change in the climate of geology. Uniform change was now accepted as a causative agent replacing the catastrophic change which biblical geology had encouraged in the previous decade. While Lyell's place in history is still intensely debated,[96] as one of his reviewers so correctly noted, now 'TIME is, in truth, the master key to the problems of geology'.[97] Lyell's influence is clearly seen in the new ease with which geologists start to talk of 'millions of years' for the production of the geological record.[98] But the scriptural geologists were still active and perhaps the most significant were those who, in the following decade, attempted to persuade the new 'parliament of science' as the new British Association for the Advancement of Science was known, of the literal truth of Genesis.[99] The most remarkable attempt was that of 1840 by the geologist and presbyterian minister in Whitby, Reverend George Young (1777–1848) (fig.10). He tried to persuade the British Association for the Advancement of Science that 'attempts made by some geologists, to reconcile the system of pre-adamite formations with the Mosaic account of creation and the deluge have signally failed'. Young argued, using the example of the Yorkshire rocks with which he was so familiar and which had inspired so much of the detailed stratigraphic work done up to that time, that rates of deposition of up to 900 feet a month by wave action, would allow a reconciliation between Scripture and geology.[100] It was Buckland's recantation of 1836 that had, once again, opened up this debate.

The 1830s saw geologists still easily crossing the archaeological divide. One was William Pengelly (1812–94) whose proper induction to geology occurred in this decade

[94] Torrens, 'Bath', 185.
[95] Torrens and Taylor, 'Cheltenham'.
[96] See Flinn, 'Essay Review'.
[97] Scrope, 'Lyell', 410.
[98] De La Beche, 'Theoretical Geology', 371.
[99] Morrell and Thackray, *Gentlemen*, 234–405.
[100] Young, *Scriptural Geology*, 8, 40 .
[101] Warren and Rose, *Pengelly*.

SCRIPTURAL GEOLOGY,

OR

AN ESSAY

ON THE

High antiquity ascribed to the Organic Remains imbedded
in Stratified Rocks;

Communicated, in Abstract, to the Geological
Section of the British Association, at the
Annual Meeting held in Newcastle:

IN TWO PARTS.

*Part I.—Proving that the Strata, instead of requiring myriads
of ages for their formation, may have been deposited nearly about
one period.*

*Part II.— Shewing that the Deluge was the period, when all the
Secondary and Tertiary Rocks were formed.*

SECOND EDITION:

*With an APPENDIX, containing strictures on some passages in
the Rev. Dr. J. Pye Smith's Lectures, entitled*

SCRIPTURE AND GEOLOGY;

Particularly his theory of a local Creation, and local Deluge.

BY

THE REV. GEORGE YOUNG, D.D.;

M. W. S.; &c.; &c.;

Author of a Geological Survey of the Yorkshire Coast; &c.

LONDON:

SIMPKIN, MARSHALL, AND CO.:

OLIPHANT AND SON, AND M. PATERSON, EDINBURGH :

M'LEOD, GLASGOW: AND ALL OTHER BOOKSELLERS.

1840.

Fig. 10. The title page of Rev. George Young's 1840 ultimately literal Scriptural Geology of 1840.

and who later made major contributions to archaeology.[101] Another young geologist, Louis Hunton (1814–38), had about the same time started his remarkable, if sadly curtailed, work on discriminating detailed stratigraphies *within* individual lithological units. William C. Williamson (1816–95), of Scarborough, a geologist of later distinction working in the same area as Hunton was also involved in this newly detailed geological work. His contribution to this geology may have been less novel,[102] but it was Williamson who, as a young man of only seventeen and encouraged by both William Smith and William Buckland, became involved in archaeological researches as well as geological studies in this area.[103] In York the Yorkshire Philosophical Society, set up with much geological intent in 1822, established its Antiquarian Committee in 1831 and a separate interest in archaeology then seems to have been taken up with some enthusiasm in Yorkshire.[104] The 'folly [soon] to be lamented, [of] the tacit, and often the expressed, ridicule of one class of naturalists for the pursuits of another' noted in 1837[105] had not yet struck this part of England.

But tensions were starting to come to the surface. On 10 December 1838 *The Times* noticed the recent archaeological discovery at Pangbourne in Berkshire of a new Roman mosaic pavement by labourers on the new Great Western Railway. 'The discovery had excited much interest... and orders have been given by Mr [Isambard Kingdom] Brunel [1806–59] the engineer, for the whole to be preserved entire'. The *Civil Engineers and Architects Journal* soon recorded the sad outcome.[106]

> It is with regret that we learn that Mr Brunel has directed this interesting relic to be broken up...we are sorry to see this disrespect for objects which are of universal interest to every man of education and refinement. Such deeds of barbarism have been but too frequent, and geologists have repeatedly complained of the ravages which have been committed through the negligence of engineers.

Disasters of this type had more fruitful consequences. They clearly encouraged the establishment of archaeological societies – including the British Archaeological Association and the Royal Archaeological Institute – and in 1839 William Sharp (1805–96) urged the British Association for the Advancement of Science, with some success, to support the formation of local Museums.[107] But the tensions between antiquarians and naturalists observed by David Allen even in party politics, helped to draw the two sides further apart in the 1840s.[108]

---

[102] Torrens and Getty, 'Hunton'.
[103] Williamson, *Reminiscences*, 43–8.
[104] See Morrell, 'Perpetual Excitement'.
[105] Macauley, *Introductory Address*.
[106] vol. 2 (1839), 29.
[107] Sharp, 'Local museums'.
[108] Allen, *Naturalist*, 143–4.

Glaciation 'The Grand Key to Diluvial Phenomena'

The vacuum left by the lack of any Diluvial theory to explain the distribution of erratic rocks and land forms was soon filled by the realisation that glaciation had left an important imprint on the geological record. It became the 'Grand Key' to explain Diluvial phenomena (fig.11).[109] In this way, the geological record was further distanced

Fig. 11. William Buckland satirised in his new 'Diluvial' costume in about 1840 by Thomas Sopwith. (Thomas Sopwith, engraved cartoon showing Buckland's conversion to 'glacialism', c. 1840, author's collection).

---

[109] See North, 'Centenary'; Rupke, *Chain*, chapter 9, 96–107 and Davies, *Earth In Decay*.

from scriptural and human records. Ironically, this helped the drifting apart that has led to the present separation between archaeology and geology.

A FINAL LEGACY FROM THE NATURAL SCIENCES

A vital additional contribution that biology and geology made to the work of archaeologists was in providing a system by which taxonomy and natural classifications could be 'policed'. The need had arisen as the work of palaeontologists and biologists uncovered the enormous wealths and diversities, in both space and time, of the natural and fossil worlds. The main stimulus for this had come from a group who attended the 1841 meeting of the British Association for the Advancement of Science at Plymouth led by Hugh Strickland (1811–53). Strickland had written in July 1841, just before this meeting: 'I have some thoughts of moving in the Zoological Section at Plymouth for the appointment of a Committee to prepare a set of regulations with a view of establishing a permanent system of zoological nomenclature'.[110] His initiative succeeded and the subject was properly set in motion at Plymouth. A Committee of geologists and naturalists was set up early in 1842 and their 'Report' was issued in the printed *Reports* of the 1842 meeting of the British Association for the Advancement of Science published in 1843. This vital work provided the bases for today's *Codes of Zoological and Botanical Nomenclature* but more importantly in this context, it was in place in time to allow the new archaeological movement of the 1840s to be guided by its deliberations. Strickland's critical papers to this debate are reprinted by Jardine.[111] As Chippindale has noted[112] such advances in biological taxonomy were vital parts, with the stratigraphic knowledge from geology, of the paradigm shift which brought scientific archaeology into being.

THE LAST DECADE 1840–50

Distinct paths for the two subjects now start to be discernable. One vital element that undoubtedly helped to separate geology more from archaeology was clearly observed and pointed out by Hugh Miller in his best seller *The Old Red Sandstone* first published in 1841. 'Geology in a peculiar manner supplies to the intellect an exercise of [an] ennobling character. But it also has its cash value'.[113] The public's interest in its own human past was also soon stimulated by some fascinating 'public relations' exercises which imaginative archaeologists set up. By 1842 the country's provincial societies seem to have become wrapped up in mummy-unrolling exercises. That at Shrewsbury took place on 15 September 1842.[114] The committee had at first invited William

---

[110] Jardine, *Strickland*, clxxv-cxcv.
[111] Ibid., 366–417, covering 1835–43.
[112] Chippindale, 'Bicknell', 190–1.
[113] Miller, *Sandstone*, 196.
[114] The archives of the Shropshire and North Wales Natural History and Antiquarian Society (Public Library, Shrewsbury) give the full story with many ephemeral items.

Buckland to unroll their mummy. Buckland declined on the grounds that 'I could have rendered no aid to the operation of opening your Mummy having never assisted on any similar occasion. Dr [Augustus Bozzi] Granville [1783–1872] and Mr [Thomas Joseph] Pettigrew [1791–1865] are the persons whose names appear most frequently in the papers on such occasions in London'.[115] The important point was that Buckland had been approached first, a clear indication of his prestige in the world of archaeology. Mummy-unrolling soon followed at the Cheltenham Literary and Philosophical Society in 1842.[116] Members here had heard of the success of the Shrewsbury enterprise in both attracting a large audience and some badly needed funds. We should also note that there was a real crisis of confidence in both the Mechanics Institutes and the Literary and Philosophical Societies in England in the 1840s.[117] The opposing explosion of the 'entertainment value of science' in the 1840s noted by Inkster[118] may have helped the new archaeology into being. But the revival which Field Clubs also brought about, assisted by the new railways, again shows how well geologists and archaeologists could still collaborate. When the railway came to Dorset in 1845, William Barnes (1801–86) took the opportunity it gave to expose his pupils to both subjects and help found the Dorset County Museum, designed to save mutually relevant objects from the depredations of railway diggers.[119] The unity between the two groups is still notable.

But there were other astonishing developments in this decade. Some resolution of the problem of the actual rate of geological processes came in sight with J. Middleton's paper of 1844, *On Fluorine in Bones, its source and its application to the determination of the geological age of Fossil Bones*.[120] Middleton is an unsung figure, elected a Fellow of the Geological Society of London on 6 March 1844. He was then Principal of the College at Agra, Bengal. From an editorial note to this paper Middleton seems to have trained as a chemist at University College, London under Thomas Graham (1805–69).

On a more negative front the problem of archaeological forgery seems to have reared its head in this decade, again inspired by geology. The career of 'Flint Jack' from Yorkshire, where he had been introduced to geology by the literal Biblicist, the Reverend George Young in the 1830s, is notable. By 1843 he was successfully both forging flints and selling fossils.[121] Other dealers, like Thomas Jenkins (*c*.1793–1868) at Cheltenham, were also now busy dealing (but more honestly) in both geological and archaeological objects in this decade.[122]

[115]Shrewsbury Public Library MSS 133, p 170 (his letter dated 4 August [1842]).
[116]Torrens and Taylor, 'Cheltenham', 179.
[117]Cardwell, *Organisation of Science*, 70–3 and Torrens and Cooper, 'Richardson', 262.
[118]Inkster, 'Mechanics Institutes', 296–8.
[119]Hearl, *Barnes*, 211–13.
[120]Middleton, 'Fluorine'.
[121]Credland, 'Flint Jack'.
[122]Torrens and Taylor, 'Cheltenham', 186–7.

In our final year 1850, the *Archaeological Journal* provides two fine and final examples of the unity still possible between what we now separate as geology and archaeology. In volume seven are papers by two well-known geologists: James Buckman (1814–84), 'On the substances employed in forming the Tessellae of the Cirencester Pavements..';[123] and, more significant, that by Gideon Mantell on 'The remains of Man, and works of Art imbedded in Rocks and Strata'.[124] The latter attempted to show, from a geological viewpoint, how closely the two subjects were related. It forms a fitting conclusion to this attempt to survey a history of the relationship. That Mantell was inspired to write by 'perusal of the treatise of M. Boucher de Perthes, entitled, *Antiquités Celtiques et Antédiluviennes*; in which the author has deteriorated the value of his antiquarian labours by vague and erroneous conclusions' only shows how very soon the relationship was to change for good. But it was science that was to change it.

ACKNOWLEDGEMENTS

In venturing into unfamiliar territory I gratefully thank Francis Celoria for his ever ready encouragement. The staff of the Library of the Institute of Archaeology, at University College, London were really helpful. Christopher Chippindale and Andrew Grout kindly read and commented on an earlier draft.

---

[123] Buckman, 'Tessellae'.
[124] Mantell, 'Rocks and Strata'.

Picturing the Past:
Art and Architecture in Victorian England

W. Vaughan

ARCHAEOLOGY AND HISTORY PAINTING

Nowadays we recognise the period in which the two archaeological societies celebrated in this book were founded, as being a time when archaeology made great strides, not only in the development of more exacting methods for extracting and analysing the artefacts of the past, but also in introducing new perceptions of history. Indeed, it has been remarked on many occasions that archaeology, together with geology – that other excavatory science – did more than any other discipline in changing notions of the past in the nineteenth century. This was accomplished largely through the usage of first-hand material evidence to question traditional textual accounts. Through direct study of the earth's surface the geologist mapped out unprecedented eons of time. The archaeologist – through a similar close analysis of human products – brought into focus civilisations that were only dimly recorded in legend, and gave a new and vivid account of daily life from early times, to lay beside the traditional verbal accounts of heroic exploits of leaders.

In providing different accounts of the nature and extent of the past, archaeology threw into question the way history was being used and narrated by others. Here I will be looking at the works of one particular group that experienced this challenge; the visual artist.

As an agent for providing clear records of the appearance of artefacts and making reconstructions, the draughtsman retains, of course, a valued position in archaeological practice to this day. But this is not the kind of artist I am talking about here. I am talking about the 'fine' artist, the one who sets store on his idealising and imaginative capacities. It might seem strange, nowadays, to think of such an artist as a historian. We are so familiar with 'fine' art as a vehicle of self-expression, that we no longer think of it as a means of making authoritative statements about the past. Yet in the mid-Victorian period – before the advent of impressionists, aesthetes and abstractionists – its tasks was still primarily understood as those of description and narration.

In the traditional hierarchies of art – those that had pertained in Europe since the Renaissance and that had their origins in the practices of Ancient Greece – 'History Painting' was in fact the highest activity in which an artist could be involved. History painting was concerned with the narration of the past. But it was a form of narration that we would hardly call history nowadays – rather poetry, or myth. History painting was in fact closely based on literary models, in particular on epic poetry. It told stories not about the past in general, but of heroic deeds, of great men in great places.

As with epic poetry, history painting demanded a high and ideal style in order to convey the grandeur of its subject-matter. It was this that was essential for its primary position in the visual arts, for it was held to provide the place where the ideal could take on visual form. In line with this view, there was a clear understanding that history painting should not be confined to the vulgar facts of appearance. It could and should improve where necessary.

'The artist...' as Sir Joshua Reynolds, first President of the Royal Academy put it in the fourth of his *Discourses* in 1771 '... must sometimes deviate from vulgar and strict historical truth, in pursuing the grandeur of his design'.[1] And he added, by way of illustration '... Alexander is said to have been of a low stature; a painter ought not so to represent him'.

Although such a practice flew in the face of factual evidence, it was understood to be a necessary licence to allow the visual artist to represent the grandeur of important historical personages and events. But with the growth of archaeology as a discipline there came a new perception of history, that emphasised the mundane as much as the exceptional. History was no longer just about famous people. Furthermore, as archaeology presented material that was visual, it was likely to contradict the reconstructions of the pictorial artist in a manner that was far more direct than anything that came from verbal accounts.

At first this challenge did not appear to be too great. Since the sixteenth century there had been sporadic excavation of artefacts from classical antiquity. But these essentially antiquarian exercises had tended to provide details that could be incorporated into existing historical schema. It was only in the nineteenth century when the excavation of whole sites began to suggest alternative readings of complete civilisations that the trouble really began.

John Martin's Historical Landscapes

The trouble first occurred, not in history painting proper, but in that sub-category

---

[1] Reynolds, *Discourses*, 57.

known as 'historical landscape'. For historical landscape implied a representation of subjects from the past in actual places, factually accurate settings. Historical landscape experienced a huge critical and popular success in the early nineteenth century. It fed on the Romantic interest in exotic nature, and also seemed to provide an immediacy of contact with the past; something that was in itself a product of the new interest in materially-based historical evidence.

No one negotiated this field more successfully than John Martin. Born in 1789, this Newcastle artist came to London early in life, and soon established a reputation for pictures that combined every kind of dramatic scenic effect with assurances of their scientific accuracy. Like the producers of historical and science fiction today, he made the extraordinary seem believable. In a fundamentalist age, he had little trouble in presenting accounts from the Bible as literal historical fact. Painting such scenes as *Joshua Commanding the Sun to Stand Still upon Gideon*.[2] Martin traded on a cunning mix of biblical narrative, fantasy and observational fact. Spectators of the day were staggered, frightened, by the display of storm and violence, of nature beyond human power. But they were consoled by the fact that this nature was still controlled by God, who was on the side of the righteous. As with the modern disaster movie, only the wicked are punished in the catastrophes he displays.

Hard though it is for us to believe this now, Martin traded on the fact that he was representing actual historical events, more or less as they happened. He therefore took a great interest in new evidence as it occurred. He was an ardent student of contemporary geological and archaeological studies, and tried where possible to incorporate their findings into his representation of the natural world.

In 1822 he exhibited The Destruction of Pompeii (fig.12), at the Egyptian Hall – a place then used for popular exhibitions. In the descriptive catalogue that accompanied the work he claimed to have 'sedulously consulted every source of information within his reach' .[3] He paid particular attention, he claimed, to Sir William Gell's account in his *Pompeiana* of 1817–19. The result was one of the least inspiring of Martin's compositions. Perhaps, as has frequently been suggested, the fault lay in the fact that Martin had too much evidence to hand to allow him to embellish it with his usual level of fantasy.

The site of Pompeii was too well known to allow Martin to indulge in the usual multiplications of mountain ranges to suggest staggering extensions of space. Furthermore the actual immolation of the city, while dramatic enough as an event, was disappointing in having failed to bring about the deaths of a sufficient number of the wicked – or indeed of any humans. Martin had to content himself with focusing upon an incident – recorded by Pliny the Younger and repeated by Gell – of those fugitives

[2] *Joshua Commanding the Sun to Stand Still Upon Gideon*, oil, 149.9 × 231.1 cm, exh. 1816, United Grand Lodge of England, London.
[3] Martin, *Herculaneum and Pompeii*, 3–4.

Fig. 12. The Destruction of Herculaneum and Pompeii, engraving, 1821, 20 × 26 cm.
(Frontispiece to Descriptive Catalogue, BM)

from the city who had hoped to escape by sea, and who found themselves trapped by the violent waves that had been whipped up by the vibrations of the eruption of Vesuvius. As Gell put it ...

> ...now was heard the shrieks of women, screams of children, clamours of men, all accusing their fate, and (the deliverance they feared) imploring death with outstretchedhands to the Gods, whom many thought together with themselves about to be involved in the last eternal night.[4]

It is widely held by students of Martin's work that Gell's account provided sufficient factual evidence about Pompeii in the public domain to hinder the artist from indulging in his wilder fantasies. Significantly, he did not attempt again to produce a historical drama about a site whose features were so well-known.

Whatever problems Martin may have had with peddling his vision of Pompeii, these did not occur with his dramatic rendering of the *Fall of Nineveh*, exhibited in 1828. The mezzotint after the work (fig.13) was dedicated to Charles X of France, the monarch who had awarded him a gold medal for other historical fantasias. This added

---

[4] Gell, *Pompeiana*, I, 50.

Fig. 13. The Fall of Nineveh, Mezzotint coloured by hand, 1829, 66.9 × 91.1 cm.
(Victoria and Albert Museum, London)

an ironic poignancy to the subject – for within a month of its publication Charles X had been overthrown by the July revolution of 1830. This picture of the demise of the Assyrian tyrant Sardanapalus (Ashurbanipal) had been dedicated to a monarch who had fallen victim to an uprising in modern times – albeit with a less violent outcome. The theme of Sardanapalus's death through self-immolation as the rebels closed around him had already been treated in a well-known play by Byron, and had been the occasion of a scandalous scene of debauch by the French painter Eugene Delacroix a few years before. In his dramatic perspectives Martin played to the Romantic imagination, in particular its perception of the Sublime. But he also laid claim to historical accuracy in his rendering of the actual site. He had examined architectural studies of the region – notably those by Daniell, and had drawn on the Reverend Thomas Maurice's History of Hindustan. His contemporaries, too, appear to have been convinced that they were seeing an authentic reconstruction of the fabled city of Nineveh. No less a severe critic than the German art historian Gustav Waagen remarked that the work was marked by 'topographic and historical naturalism and truth'.[5]

---

[5] Waagen, *Kunstwerke* II, 430.

Martin's main strength here lay in the fact that Nineveh was at the time unexcavated. While there had been some intriguing accounts of the site published – notably that by Rich – nobody knew what the city actually looked like.

Undoubtedly the main attraction of the subject was the great scope for mayhem and violence that it provided, alongside the potential for huge exaggerations of scale in depicting a city legendary for its strength and magnificence but as yet virtually unknown. As the subsequent excavator of Nineveh, A. H. Layard, put it:

> The architecture of Nineveh and Babylon was a matter of speculation, and the poet or painter restored their palaces and temples as best suited his theme or his subject.[6]

It was Martin's bad luck that Layard should have published his account of his excavations at Nineveh in *Nineveh and Its Remains* in 1849. For Layard gave a detailed and factual account of the site that completely undermined Martin's imaginative reconstruction.

As the quotation above suggests, Layard had no time for the fantasies of poets and painters, and put his trust instead in careful measured drawings. It might seem that with his work a new scientific view of ancient remains had been made available. Certainly William Feaver, in his biography of John Martin, cites Layard's publication as one of the reasons for the dramatic decline in Martin's reputation in the 1850s. And even if this is an exaggeration, it is true to say that Martin's mixture of romantic fantasy and detail no longer stood up to the new standards that people like Layard were making public.

It would be a mistake, I think, however, to claim that this was the end of the use of romance and fantasy in the popularising of ancient sites. For a start, there was the drama of the present day location of the sites. Layard may have been scrupulous in his measurements of Nineveh. But the popularity of his account depended less on the accuracy of his measurements than on the tales in the book of his personal struggles in trying to recover the relics of an ancient civilisation. Layard spared few details in his description of the carnage and corruption that marked the part of the Turkish empire in which he was working.

His colourful narrative was accompanied by views of the ruins in their present state – such as the one of the so-called Tomb of Jonah (fig.14). Worked up from his own sketches by the topographer George Scharf, they gave the appropriate moody and threatening tone to the landscape. It was as though the menage that Martin had represented in ancient times had been transferred to the modern topography. And not without purpose. For part of Layard's claim – a claim habitually made by Victorians appropriating parts of the heritage of other lands – was that he was rescuing these priceless historical treasures from the hands of the unprincipled vandals into which they had fallen in modern times.

---

[6] Layard, *Nineveh*, I, xxv–xxvi.

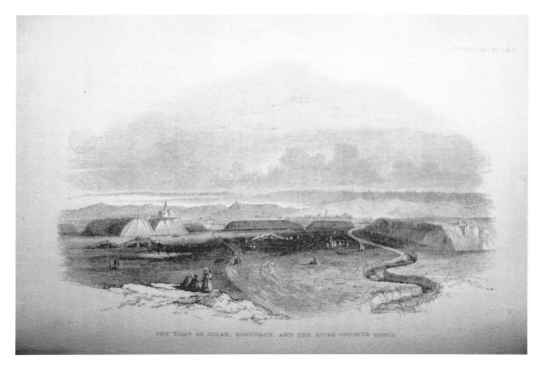

Fig. 14. The Tomb of Jonah, engraving (Layard, Nineveh, vol.I, opp. p. 131)

The use of George Scharf to smarten up Layard's own sketches – a role that Layard acknowledges with characteristic fairness in his preface – raises another issue about the relationship between artist and archaeologist. Whilst I am primarily concerned with the response of the fine artist to archaeological evidence, it must be acknowledged that the humble draughtsmen and topographers who have been such a service to archaeologists have injected something of their own vision into the process of rediscovery. This is perhaps particularly the case in the early nineteenth century, when there was a vigorous school of topographical draughtsmanship flourishing in Britain, and where the camera had not yet emerged to provide a parallel kind of objective record.

It is ironic from this point of view that the very book that had apparently encumbered Martin with tedious fact in his rendering of Pompeii – Gell's Pompeiana – contained a number of imagined reconstructions by one of the best known topographical fantasists of the day, J. P. Gandy. Like Scharf, Gandy was a draughtsman living in London who was hired by an archaeologist to 'improve' sketches – in this case the *camera obscura* sketches of Sir William Gell himself.

Looking at the soulful rendering of the ruined gateway to Pompeii (fig.15), one cannot help feeling that Gandy has done quite a lot more to the scene than flesh out

Fig. 15. W. Gell and J. P. Gandy, View of the Entrance to Pompeii from the North East, engraving, 1817. (Pompeiana, Pl. XV)

Gell's outlines. It is an exercise in Romantic topography. Gandy was adept at glamorising buildings. He was used habitually by the architect John Soane to present his work with appropriate drama; on more than one occasion showing these modern buildings as ruins.

If Gandy could knock down new buildings with such ease, he could also put old ones up. This is what he does on a number of occasions in the illustrations to Gell's book. In Plate XIX he reconstructed the gateway to Pompeii that he showed us earlier on in Romantic ruin. (fig.16) In the text to the plate, Gandy presents his reconstruction in humble fashion. He admits that he has little to go on for most of it. The statue on the pedestal on the left, for example, was deduced simply from a fragment of bronze drapery found at its foot. The quadriga above the gateway is pure invention. Indeed, as Gandy himself put it, only those parts of the image below the horizon line could be guaranteed.

Perhaps what is most disconcerting about Gandy's reconstruction is its sheer plausibility. Despite his proven skills as an architectural fantasist, he is behaving here in a thoroughly sober manner. There are none of the histrionics of Martin in this picture; no violent storms or vertiginous perspectives. Indeed, if one did not know, one would have no reason to believe that this reconstruction was not based throughout on meticulous research.

Fig. 16. W. Gell and J. P. Gandy, An Attempt to give some idea of the principal entrance to Pompeii as it once existed, engraving, 1817. (Pompeiana, Pl. XIX)

I am drawing attention to this point because I want to stress something that will, I imagine, be familiar to all archaeologists. This is that in making any reconstruction, one is almost bound to become involved in guesswork and invention, and however plausible and perceptive one's guesses are, they should never be given the same status as verifiable fact. On the other hand, how is it possible to get any kind of comprehensive image of a site, without some kind of imaginative projection?

VICTORIAN HISTORICIST PAINTINGS

I will not pursue this issue further here. What I want to look at instead is the effect that reconstructions such as those by Gandy had on artists creating historical paintings. In a word, one can say that it encouraged the replacement of one kind of fantasy with another. In the place of Martinesque exaggeration came a more sober type of reconstruction; but one that was still, in essence, a matter of guesswork.

This process was enhanced by the work produced by a growing number of topographers who swarmed to archaeological sites from the 1830s onwards.

One such figure was David Roberts. In the 1820s Roberts had been a scene painter. Like so many others of his generation he was impressed by Martin's dramatic landscape style and showed a debt to it in his own historical work, such as the picture of the

Fig. 17. David Roberts, The Israelites leaving Egypt, 1829. (Birmingham Museum and Art Gallery)

Israelites Leaving Egypt (fig.17), exhibited at the Society of British Artists in 1829.[7] But in the 1830s he began to travel in the East himself, making direct studies of actual sites.

Such representations – alongside the continued publication of images in archaeological books like Layard's – provided, as I have already said, a very different image of antiquity on which historical artists could build. When the history painter Edward Poynter came to produce his *Israel in Egypt* in 1867 he used such studies to give a very different impression of Ancient Egypt from the one seen in Roberts's earlier fantasy. What we have here is something far more like an archaeological reconstruction, with the buildings viewed flat on and the inclusion of meticulous detail. Perhaps one should note too a change in attitude to climate. Roberts's Egypt is filled with the gloomy shadows of Martin. Poynter's has the strong sunlight of Egypt as it was experienced by travellers who had been there in his own time.

Finally, one should note perhaps another effect: the shift from a specific and

---

[7] *The Israelites leaving Egypt*, 1829, is now in the Birmingham City Museum (reproduced Guiterman and Llewellyn, *Roberts*, pl. 62).

famous historical event (the departure of the Israelites under the guidance of Moses) to an everyday activity. For in the picture we are shown the Israelites performing one of the habitual tasks of their servitude. The picture could almost serve as an illustration of how the Egyptians constructed their buildings. No doubt the details are erroneous. But Poynter certainly took care to consult the most up-to-date sources when planning his picture.

This concentration on what one might call the 'domestic' side of history was one that was already associated with archaeology. A few years earlier the architect William Burges had written in the *Gentleman's Magazine*

> Of all the dreams of Archaeologists there is none more frequent than that of endeavouring to transport oneself into the domestic life of any given period.[8]

It had been a possibility already opened up in the eighteenth century, greatly stimulated by the rich information about daily life in the Ancient Roman world that emerged through the excavations at Pompeii. Before this domestic view of antiquity had affected the practice of history painting, it had already had a dramatic effect on the historical novel. Walter Scott's detailed reconstructions of past periods in the Waverley novels had been pioneers. In the Victorian period the practice had been kept alive by such writers as Ainsworth and Bulwer Lytton. The latter, indeed, had done more than anyone else to bring the genre to classical antiquity with his novel *The Last Days of Pompeii*.

The treatment of detailed reconstructions of the past in novels was of immense importance for the new generation of history painters. Perhaps above all, they demonstrated the excitement that could be gained from apparently 'realistic' reconstructions of the past. Furthermore, they also demonstrated that historical accuracy of material detail in no way hampered invention in other directions. Indeed, in a way the emphasis on domestic settings provided a whole new field for fantasy. For the one thing that archaeologists could not provide was any kind of detailed information about the events in the lives of the ordinary people whose domestic arrangements they were describing. Or, if such details were available, they were usually sufficiently slight to allow all manner of supposition.

Poynter's celebrated picture *Faithful unto Death* (fig.18) can bear this out. Painted in 1865, it was based on stories that had grown up around a skeleton, of which the hand was still clutching a spear, that had been uncovered in a recess outside the gates of Pompeii. Already in Gell's account, there is a story attached to this find.

> Conjecture has imagined this the remains of a sentinel, who preferred dying at his post to quitting it for the more ignominious death which, in conformity with the severe discipline of his country, would have awaited him.[9]

---

[8] William Burges reviewing the Japanese court in the International Exhibition of 1863 *(Gentleman's Magazine* (September 1862), 254).

[9] Gell, *op. cit.*, 94.

This story became the basis
for more dramatic treat-
ments – notably by Bulwer
Lytton in the *Last Days of
Pompeii*. And, as is the case
with these things, as the
story was retold its emphasis
changed. When discussing
Poynter's picture, the *Art
Annual* described the subject
as follows:

> It was suggested by the dis-
> covery in the excavations of
> Pompeii of the body of a
> Roman Soldier in full ar-
> mour who is supposed to
> have sacrificed his life to his
> duty by remaining at his
> post.

Not only has this account
softened the image of the
discovery – changing it from
a skeleton, of which the
hand was still clutching a
spear, to a body in full armour – but there has also
been a shift of motive. Gell's
account emphasises the
harsh law of Rome which
would have punished the
sentinel if he had left his
post. Poynter suggests a

*Fig. 18. Sir Edward Poynter, Faithful unto Death, 1865,
oil (Walker Art Gallery, Liverpool)*

nobler motive. His Roman sentry is inspired by a sense of duty, of sticking to one's
task no matter what the consequences.

It need hardly be pointed out how much the image of duty that Poynter conjured
up fitted in with those evocations of heroic contemporary soldiers that one finds in
the period. This was, after all, the age of empire, and it seemed highly appropriate that
the ancient Roman should provide a model for those modern Britons who were
bringing the benefits of law and order to the rest of the world. Poynter's picture can
remind us that the new emphasis on historical accuracy of detail and on the lives of

ordinary people did not prevent the most blatant projections of Victorian values into the reconstructed views of the past. Indeed, as Richard Jenkyns reminded us in *The Victorians and Ancient Greece*, this process was positively encouraged. For the Victorians wanted nothing more than to be reassured that fundamental human values had remained the same throughout the centuries, that they were brothers under the skin with the peoples of those ancient civilisations that they most admired.

The artist who exploited this sentiment most whole-heartedly was Poynter's friend and fellow academician, Sir Lawrence Alma-Tadema. Alma-Tadema was a Dutchman who came to settle in Britain in 1870. Trained as a history painter, he had begun with scenes of the Merovingian period, particularly those relating to Dutch history. But in 1863 he made a trip to Pompeii, and this converted him to the classical world. It was a conversion, one might note, that was timely, for it gave his work a broader, more international appeal. But it was none the less genuine for that. Alma-Tadema was a tireless collector of historical detail and was a pioneer in using photographs of ancient sites to enhance the authenticity of his work.

His picture of the completing of the Parthenon Frieze (fig.19) was exhibited shortly before he made the decision to come and settle in Britain. The fact that it focused on

Fig. 19. Sir Lawrence Alma-Tadema, Phidias and the Frieze of the Parthenon, 1868, oil, 72.4 × 109.2 cm. (Birmingham Museums and Art Gallery).

a part of the Parthenon Frieze then as now in the British Museum, may have had something to do with this. The subject shows an imagined visit by Pericles (who is accompanied by his beloved Asphasia) to inspect the frieze of the Parthenon soon after its completion by Phidias, who is depicted in true Greek profile standing proudly before it. There is, of course, no evidence for such a visit. It is an extrapolation from the comment in Plutarch's *Lives of Famous Generals* that Pericles had entrusted Phidias with the construction of the Parthenon and its sculptures. What Alma-Tadema is doing, of course, is imagining that the viewing of works of art in Ancient Greece was much the same as it was in his own time. What we have here, as one perceptive commentator has observed, is the translation of a Victorian private view into fifth-century Athens.

It should be noted, too, that Alma-Tadema has been as up-to-date as possible in his reconstruction – even to the point of controversy. For one of the most notable features of the Parthenon frieze as it is shown here is that it is coloured. The discovery of traces of colour on Greek sculptures and buildings in the nineteenth century had led to one of the most radical reassessments of the nature of their appearance. For centuries the uncoloured nature of Greek buildings and sculptures had been taken as a sign of their ideality and purity. The Greeks were supposed to have been the masters of pure form, platonically looking beyond the tones and accidents of the everyday to the eternal verities beyond. Now, it would seem, this ideality was to be sacrificed to images of gaudy, almost barbaric, splendour. Already in the 1840s the French architect Hittorf had created a scandal by his coloured reconstructions of Greek buildings and the English sculptor Gibson had shocked the art world with a coloured statue, his so-called 'tinted Venus'. In the 1850s the designer Owen Jones had applied this principle to the Parthenon frieze by erecting a coloured reconstruction of it in the Greek court of the Crystal Palace at Sydenham. It was almost certainly the sight of this that gave Alma-Tadema the idea. Indeed, this sight may have given him the theme for the whole picture. For the frieze is seen here at very much the angle that it could be viewed at Sydenham – or indeed in the British Museum. Originally, as we know, the frieze was placed so high on the Parthenon that it would have been all but unreadable when seen from the ground. By imagining his 'private viewing' , Alma-Tadema has managed to find a way of presenting the frieze as it could be viewed in his own day, but set in antiquity.

By presenting the Parthenon frieze coloured, Alma-Tadema is also in a sense bringing the classical tradition down to size. He is suggesting that perhaps taste in those days was perhaps not so austere and elevated as the aesthetes proposed – that maybe the Athenians were as fond of a bit of vulgar colour as his own contemporaries were.

Working on the principle of the fundamental similarity of humans in all times and places, he also had no qualms about casting Victorians into the costumes of antiquity. In another picture, called the *Picture Gallery*, Alma-Tadema shows his dealer, the celebrated Gambart, masquerading as an imagined Ancient Roman forerunner. [10] Alma-Tadema also took the 'Roman Principle' into his private life. His own house was done up as a Pompeiian villa, and he was in the habit of referring to his study as the 'atrium' and his dining room as the 'triclinium'. At heart the ancients were just like us, Alma-Tadema is saying; except, perhaps, they had a little more fun.

We may smile at these foibles, at these early engagements between the fictional and factual reconstructors of the visual past. We can see all too easily now how much of themselves these observers projected. But we should not smile too broadly. It is easier usually to see the faults of others than our own. We still have to play the game of speculative reconstruction when we try to picture the past, either physically or in our imaginations. And just as we can find fault in the fancies of earlier generations, so future generations will doubtless find fault with ours. We may not be able to see ours, but at least a glimpse at earlier practices can remind us that they must be there.

---

[10] Now in the Art Gallery and Museum, Burley. See Maas, *Gambart*, 242–3, reproduced at p. 224.

'Groping in the Dark':
George Aitchison and the Burden of History

J. Mordaunt Crook

In a characteristic essay G. M. Young once set out to find 'the greatest Victorian': not *Victorianum maximus* ('greatest of the Victorians') but *Victorianum maxime* ('most Victorian of the Victorians'). After some deliberation he chose Walter Bagehot.[1] Using the same criterion – not genius but representativeness – we might look for the most Victorian architect, and choose not Butterfield or Burges or even Gilbert Scott, but George Aitchison. Not for his buildings, which are few, though full of interest; but more for his attitudes, his anxieties, his preoccupations, his priorities. Especially if we choose as our point of perspective, Queen Victoria's Jubilee of 1897. For in 1898 George Aitchison became, uniquely, President of the RIBA, Royal Gold Medallist, and Professor of Architecture at the Royal Academy – simultaneously.

As an architect and designer, Aitchison was seldom short of work. His list of commissions runs to at least fifty items. And two of his buildings – Leighton House, Kensington (1864–6; 1877–89) and a warehouse in Mark Lane, London (1864) – feature in most textbooks of Victorian architecture. The first for its polychromy; the second for its cast iron. But he had another career as well. As a lecturer and public speaker he was hugely prolific. The texts of some 120 performances – and his lectures were performances – have survived. That means more than half a million words; and probably scores of diagrams and models, hundreds of photographs and thousands of lantern slides, now lost. Polychromy, cast iron, marble and mosaic; stained glass, staircases, mouldings; doorways, windows, and balustrades; architectural education; architectural sculpture; Greek architecture, Roman architecture, Byzantine architecture, Islamic architecture, Romanesque architecture, Renaissance architecture; above all Progressive architecture – these were the themes of his lectures and speeches, in

---

[1] Young, 'Greatest Victorian'.

particular at the RIBA and at the Royal Academy. For Aitchison performed most publicly as President of the RIBA from 1896 to 1899 and as Lecturer and Professor of Architecture at the Royal Academy from 1881 onwards and from 1887 to 1905.[2] His style was literary, discursive, occasionally repetitious, sometimes eloquent, always erudite and genial. He had travelled Europe extensively; he was expert in constructional technique; he had a marvellous eye for colour; and he could draw beautifully. His portrait by Alma-Tadema suggests a scholarly, gregarious, rather garrulous bachelor.[3] And yet, throughout these lectures, over a period of half a century, from the 1850s to the 1900s, there is a manifest sense of doubt, of uncertainty, even of despair.

Why? Because, like Victorian architects of all kinds – from T. L. Donaldson to William Burges, from Sydney Smirke to T. G. Jackson, from J. T. Emmett and Robert Kerr to Gilbert Scott and James Fergusson – Aitchison suffered from a burden both intoxicating and asphyxiating, the inexorable burden of history. For an architect that meant the burden of archaeology, with all the attendant dilemmas of eclecticism.[4] In a world of ideas dominated by two conceptual constants – the evolutionary sense and the historicist sensibility – how could architects produce a visual language appropriate to their own age, an age which looked backwards and forwards at the same time? How could they square art and science, past and present, utility and beauty? How could they combine static notions of aesthetic excellence with the progressive imperatives of technology? How, in short, could they serve two masters: History and Progress?

Aitchison's half-century of lectures are a tantalising commentary on this tangled story. Their subject, nominally, is History; but their substance, their thematic pulse, is Progress.

How can we 'become good architects'? Aitchison's reply is traditional: 'by studying architecture historically'.[5] No artist – and here he takes his cue from Joshua Reynolds – can ever 'exclude all imitation of others… He who resolves never to ransack any mind but his own, will soon … be obliged to imitate himself'. Better go back for inspiration to the Ancients. After all, 'poets practise this kind of borrowing without reserve'.[6] To this well-worn linguistic analogy, Aitchison then adds an evolutionary gloss. 'All the progressive arts – and Pascal says architecture is one of them – progress by the improvement of what has gone before… Art, literature, science, and architecture itself, are like… coral islands: each tiny insect adds its mite to the [mass of the mightier] work.'[7]

---

[2] *Builder*, 25 June 1898, 609, and 29 January 1898, 103.

[3] Gotch, *RIBA*, ill.

[4] I have developed this 'revisionist' thesis at some length in the following publications: Mordaunt Crook, Emmett, *Essays*; Kerr, *House*; 'Smirke'; *Burges*; 'Beresford Hope'; 'Architecture and History'; 'Jackson'; and *Dilemma*.

[5] *Builder*, LIV (1888), 61. Not just names and dates: 'it is interesting enough to know who built the Parthenon, or the Pantheon, or King's Cross, but it is no more architecture than playing the fiddle or dancing the polka' (*Builder*, LXXIII (1897), 368). 'Deceased architecture is the architect's lesson-book, as history is the statesman's and poetry the poet's' (*Builder*, LXXI (1896), 382).

[6] *Builder*, LIV (1888), 61, quoting Reynolds, *Discourses*.

[7] Ibid.

Now Aitchison's notion of architectural progress was certainly not original. It owes something to the man he calls that 'great architectural ethnographer', James Fergusson.[8] It owes more to a group of contemporary French theorists, Joseph Louis Duc, Paul Sedille, César Daly and – most of all – Auguste Choisy.[9] But its lineage stretches back – via the Darwinian hypothesis – to the comparative taxonomy of Cuvier and Linnaeus.[10] 'The study of comparative architecture', Aitchison explains, 'is as useful to the architect…as the study of comparative anatomy is to the physiologist'.[11] For therein lie the secrets of architectural evolution. One day it will be possible to reconstruct the culture of an epoch from the fragments of its architectural monuments, just as 'Cuvier could construct the effigies of extinct animals from one of their bones or talons'.[12] 'We cannot have the icthyosaurus nor the pleisiosaurus [today]; if one were to be created it would [surely] die…, for the conditions of its living do not exist. We can have an artificial [specimen] at a pantomime with a man behind the scenes to pull a string and make the wings flap. It is the same with architecture…pantomime Greek, or Gothic, or Renaissance [is no more viable today, that is in 1894, than]…an icthyosaurus, a mastodon or a sabre-toothed tiger.' [13]

So Aitchison's lectures had one overriding aim: to get 'our future architecture…out of the slough of antiquarianism in which it is sunk'.[14] Just as Machiavelli 'extracted the art of government' from fragments of Roman history, so we have to distill the art of architecture – that is the art of making buildings 'joyous…stately, terrible or sublime' – from the archaeology of the past. 'Antiquarianism pure and simple is the death warrant of architecture.' We have to use 'the current architectural language of the day'. Just what that language should be Aitchison never discovered. What he did know was that the function of architects as mere 'costumiers' was 'not a dignified position'.[15]

The lessons of history seemed to Aitchison quite clear. Byzantine architecture had progressed, from a novel method of arcuated and domical construction through

---

[8] *Builder*, LIV (1888), 63, and ibid., L (1886), 404.

[9] See *Builder*, LXVI (1894), 169–72, 193.

[10] Mordaunt Crook, 'Architecture and History'.

[11] *Builder*, LVI (1889), 142.

[12] *Builder*, LXXI (1896), 382.

[13] *Builder*, LXVI (1894), 193. Architecture will evolve, 'by gradual addition to or suppression from an original type, just as widely-differing wings of the albatross and the apteryx have been derived from a common type' (*Builder*, LII (1887), 346–7).

[14] *Builder*, LXX (1896), 109. We want 'a new vitality [in] architecture, so that it may go on improving till it drives out the antiquarian interloper… We want every moulding to tell of its real date by its shape… [Let us therefore] set our grand art [back] on its feet again' (*Builder*, LXX (1896)). As things stand at present, 'we have not even a moulding we can call our own'. Somehow we must 'put the breath of life [back] into architecture, so that it may again become a progressive art' (*Builder*, LXX (1896), 132).

[15] *Builder*, LXX (1896), 109. Similarly *Builder*, LXVI (1894), 87: the 'art of expression is mainly learned from the past, but the artist must be animated by the spirit of the present'; 'Saracen architecture should be studied not to imitate Saracen architecture, but to help us learn the aesthetic part of architecture itself' (*Builder*, LXVI (1894), 153); 'architectural monuments should express the taste, feeling and skill of the nation at the time of their building' (*Builder*, LXVI (1894), 87); they should embody 'the flavour of the age' (*Builder*, LXVIII (1895), 79).

consequential systems of indicative moulding and ornamental form, to a new and distinct architectural style.[16] Similarly Romanesque. Those Romanesque builders, he tells us, were 'the inventors of modern architecture'.[17] How so? Because they got the method right. From pulverised fragments of the Antique they had forged a new structural system of 'titanic grandeur'.[18] Architecture, he repeats, 'involves the creating of organisms'; it is not 'merely the altering of outward forms to please the whim of the day'.[19] Alas, 'the genius of the nineteenth century is mainly devoted to forgery'.[20] Multiplied choice has merely produced multiple plagiarism.[21] 'Modern Gothic', for example, 'is generally as much like the real thing as the Book of Mammon is like the Bible; but even supposing the forgery were so excellent that it would deceive an architect from the Elysian Fields, what then?'[22] It belongs to another age, another people, another Faith. 'We do not want to build in that style now.'[23]

The root of the trouble lay in the changing nature of technology. 'This century', Aitchison announced in 1888, 'differs more from the age preceeding it, than that [era] differed from the stone age'. In travel, transport, and communication, 'we have almost annihilated time and space'. We have invented explosives which rival the 'power...of the earthquake'. Goods can now be produced with a speed once imaginable only in 'fairy stories'. Population and wealth have increased 'in a marvellous degree'. But not without cost. All this machinery has blunted our aesthetic sense with 'every form of exquisite ugliness'.[24] 'Thousands of our fellow-countrymen' have been reduced to 'a livelong misery' so awful that 'negro slavery appears by comparison to be a paradise'; although in global terms 'nothing analogous to this vast accession of wealth has occurred since the Roman Republic'. It is time 'to pause in the race, to survey [these] heaps of gold, to [examine] the disorganisation of society, and to ask...how [it] can be reorganised'.[25]

---

[16] 'The [apparently] eccentric shapes [of its] vaults and domes are purely the result of the unimpeachable logic of construction' (*Builder*, LX (1891), 190). For Byzantine architecture Aitchison chiefly relied on: de Vogüé, *Syrie Centrale*; Dieulafoy, *Perse*; Texier and Pullan, *Byzantine Architecture*; Butler, *Coptic Churches*; de Verneilh, *Byzantin*; Bayet, *Byzantin*; Jackson, *Dalmatia*; Isabelle, *Edifies*; Labarte, *Constantinople*. Of particular importance was the work of Auguste Choisy, Engineer in Chief of Roads and Bridges, Paris, whom Aitchison considered 'a genius' (*Builder*, LX (1891), 187, 190), notably *Histoire*.

[17] *Builder*, LXX (1896), 159. Aitchison's authorities for Romanesque were: Texier, Choisy, Gailhabaud, Du Caumont (to whom, rather than the Rev. W. Gunn, he attributed the stylistic term), Ruprich-Robert, Cataneo, F. De Dartoin (on Lombard architecture), and, of course, Viollet-le-Duc, in particular 'Voute': 'he is always as interesting as a good novel, and a great deal more interesting than most novels' (*Builder*, LXX (1896), 133, 206).

[18] *Builder*, LXX (1896), 227.

[19] *Builder*, LXX (1896), 159.

[20] *Builder*, LVI (1889), 428.

[21] *Builder*, LXX (1896), 133.

[22] *Builder*, LXVIII (1895), 139. Even Burges, 'the most original and vigorous of the band of Neo-Goths', could not make Gothic the style of his own day (*Builder*, LV (1888), 3).

[23] *Builder*, LXXVIII (1900), 129. 'The Gothic revival has done excellent service, but it was doomed from the first to be ephemeral' (*Builder*, XLVIII (1885), 582).

[24] *Builder*, LV (1888), 431. Similarly *RIBA Journal*, 3rd ser. (1901–2), 383.

[25] *Builder*, LV (1888), 431. Unlike Morris, however, Aitchison saw no prospect of a new style emerging out of social revolution (*Builder*, LV (1888), 2).

Meanwhile, architecture alone of the sciences – for it is science as well as art – has compromised its integrity. If the fatal principle of copyism had been employed in other technical fields, 'we should [still] have [catapults] instead of cannon; triremes instead of steam-driven ironclads, ... wick lamps or torches...instead of gas or electricity... Would Argand ever have made his lamp if he had believed the Romans were unsurpassable? Should we have the steam-engine? Should we know the earth went round the sun? Would the law of gravitation have been found out? It should be as contemptible to copy an old building as [to copy] an old book'.[26] 'I cannot believe that the nation that has given us the steam-engine, the railway, the telegraph, the steamboat, and all the triumphs of iron; that has given us Darwin, Tyndall, Huxley and Herbert Spencer; Parkes, Simpson and Lister; Turner, Leighton and Millais; Wordsworth, Browning, Tennyson, and Swinburne, can have sunk so much below the standard of our semi-barbarous forefathers of the thirteenth century as to be incapable of developing [its own] architecture... No,...we have got into a wrong groove, and we must get out of it before architecture ever again becomes a progressive art.'[27]

That 'wrong groove' was the principle of revival, what art historians have come to call the historicist process.[28] Within this carapace of history, Aitchison believed, lurked a real architecture, struggling to get out. But how? 'We...want an architecture of our own time, a new architecture; that is a good wish', he tells his students in 1897. 'But we must know how a new architecture is found. Let us see how it was found in the Middle Ages.'[29] It grew, he implies, by means of a reciprocal evolution: stuctural expression emerging as symbolic representation. Why not in the nineteenth century? It was all a question of cultural norms. 'The embodying...in building...of any great idea came as naturally to the people of the Middle Ages as sending a letter to the papers comes now.'[30] In other words, theirs was an age of imagery, ours is an age of language. Today we have poetry in plenty, but no poetry of form. 'Does society desire to have its aspirations embodied in buildings? No, it wants its highest aspirations embodied in an Act of Parliament.'[31]

******

Aitchison's very first public lecture, at the RIBA in 1857, set out to draw lessons from the polychromy of ancient and medieval buildings, 'so that we may hand down to

---

[26] *Builder*, L (1886), 404. Similarly *Builder*,LXVI (1894), 88.

[27] *Builder*, LXXIV (1898), 610: on receiving the Royal Gold Medal. See also *Builder*, LXXVI (1899), 409: on opening the International Building Trades Exhibition.

[28] 'Historicism' in this sense seems first to have been popularised by Pevsner (*Architectural Review*, LXXXVI (1939), 55 and subsequently *passim*). Its philosophical use – teleological and determinist – is more correctly defined in Popper, *Historicism* (1957; first expounded in *Economica* 1944–5). See Watkin, `Pevsner', 169–71.

[29] *Builder*, LXXII (1897), 267–71.

[30] 'We see the art of building first absorbing all useful and constructional inventions, then gradually converting them into aesthetic features, and producing in special buildings...grand emotional results. The question we naturally ask ourselves is, why we cannot do the same' (*Builder*, LXIV (1893), 166–9). Similarly *Builder*, LXX (1896), 205–6.

[31] *Builder*, LXVIII (1895), 180.

posterity not a lifeless copy…, but a new system of coloured decoration' in keeping with a world of technological change. Even at this early stage, he declined to engage in any battle of styles. In all past styles, he believed, there were lessons for the present. But 'I am waiting', he reminds his audience, 'like the rest of the world for the new style that is to come'.[32] Seven years later it had yet to appear. But he could still berate his contemporaries – living in an age of iron – for failing to use the new material. 'What is the cause of this?', he asks; 'how can we account for this strange supineness?' The answer lies in 'our education and our want of education'. We are very good at handing down traditional techniques 'from one generation to another'. But with iron we are all 'in the dark'. 'Sooner or later…it will come…into general use'; better to use it ourselves than leave it to the engineers. [33]

Now Aitchison came from a background which was as much concerned with engineering as with architecture. T. L. Donaldson, C. R. Cockerell, Sir Charles Barry and T. H. Wyatt were all family friends.[34] But his degree course at University College, London, included some structural science as well as the arts of design. And like his early travelling companion William Burges, he grew up under the shadow of a father much involved with civil engineering. In fact George Aitchison Senior was reputed to have designed London's 'first incombustible building of iron and brick' – Irongate Wharf, on the Thames (c.1845).[35] As a partner in his father's firm in 1859–61, young Aitchison 'saw a great deal of work of an engineering character on the Chester and Holyhead Railway'.[36] In practice in his own right, from 1861, he was responsible for a number of wharves, warehouses, and offices along the Thames, notably Messrs Hubbock's depository and the tobacco warehouse for Victoria Dock. But whereas Burges sublimated his engineering instincts in a riot of medieval forms, Aitchison continued all his life to wrestle with the aesthetic consequences of iron. He saw that the Victorians had equalled the best in literature; they were supreme in science and technology; but their awareness of deficiencies in art and architecture increased as the

---

[32] *RIBA Trans.*, VIII (1857–8), 47: 14 Dec. 1857. In years to come he maintained his enthusiasm for external polychromy, praising the use of mosaics, *sgraffito*, encaustic tiles, glazed bricks and terra-cotta (*Builder*, LXIV (1893), 274).

[33] *RIBA Trans.*, XIV (1863–4), 97, 103: 29 Feb. 1864. He pressed for the foundation of a Professorship of Construction at the Royal Academy, to stifle criticism that the Academy Schools produced only 'draughtsmen and scene painters' (*Builder*, LXVIII (1885), 396). 'Practical geometry, stereotomy and stone-cutting are shamefully neglected amongst English architects' (*Builder*, LII (1887), 636). The Architectural Association is 'a mutual improvement society rather than a school' (*Builder*, LII (1887), 699). The contrast with Paris was striking: in Paris there were even prizes for theoretical exploration, e.g. the Bordin prize ('To seek if there be a common aesthetic law, applicable to the monuments of the great epochs of art') and the J. L. Duc prize ('To determine by special studies the style of modern architecture'). See *Builder*, LVIII (1890), 75.

[34] As a member of F.A.B.S., Aitchison was very much part of the inner circle of the RIBA. See Mordaunt Crook, *Burges*, 73–4.

[35] *RIBA Trans.*, XIV (1863–4), 107. For George Aitchison Snr (1792–1861) of 6, Muscovy Court, Trinity Square, Tower Hill, see *Minutes of Proceedings of the Institution of Civil Engineers*, XXI (1862), 569–71. He left £800. George Aitchison Jnr of 150 Harley Street, left £13,284.10s.1d. (Probate Records, Somerset House).

[36] *Builder*, LXXIV (1898), 609.

century wore on. Looking round him, he saw 'everything…beautiful and picturesque…gradually…being extinguished' by the spread of industrialisation. [37]

So was there any hope? In 1864 he saw a glimmer of opportunity in the very plainness and economy of this new age of utility. 'I think', he told his doubting audience, that 'a purity of outline and elegance of proportion, with an almost total absence of ornament might gradually be made to pervade everything, from our buildings to our teaspoons'. Meanwhile there is no future in 'paraphrases' of the past; in fact they are 'sublimely ridiculous'. Copyism 'cuts at the very root of architecture'; 'it has crippled the natural powers of the architect…it has disgusted the bulk of the people, who take the same interest in it that they do in heraldry'. What then can be done? We cannot just 'put ugly construction into an ornamental box'; we have somehow to 'make the thing itself graceful [and] elegant'.[38] Then comes his peroration, to an RIBA audience clearly becoming a little restive:

> Has…the human mind deteriorated, and are we incapable of making our new constructions beautiful or picturesque? Is the saying of Victor Hugo true, that printing has killed architecture? I trust not…I fervently hope that…it is only through a sort of infatuated perversity that we are now so wanting in artistic invention. The conservatism of mankind is so great that it is only at certain periods of intellectual convulsion that men will dare to doubt and think… The happy invention of Palladio has given us a dispensation from thinking… From that time architecture has been blighted by a servile desire of imitation; we have tried Egyptian, Greek, Roman, Byzantine, Romanesque, Gothic of all periods, Italian and French Renaissance…Arabic, Chinese… Let us now throw [them all] aside…let us hold [them] in abomination.[39]

That was 1864. During the 1870s he has less to say publicly – a wise course for any practicing architect. But he was already turning from architecture to interior decoration. And by the 1880s he had clearly become disenchanted with the whole business of architectural practice. 'Architecture', he announces in 1883, 'has fallen upon evil times'. In part the cause of the decline has been social: architects have thought of themselves as gentlemen rather than bricklayers. 'Architects must free themselves from this nonsense, and strive to be great constructors, doing what they can to impart character

---

[37] 'The labours of the field are performed by hideous engines; the commonest household services are being done by machinery. The moors, heaths, commons and forests make way for fields of cabbages, mangel wurzel and potatoes – trees and hedges will shortly be extirpated. All splendour in dress is laid aside, and we may expect to see the materials of clothing so improved and cheapened, that the labourer in his best clothes, and the king on his throne, shall be almost indistinguishable. Processions and Civic pomp are doomed, warfare itself is becoming as unpicturesque as civil life… Sculpture and painting have ceased to have any marked influence on mankind, and…must be clothed in the forms of past ages, or other countries, to make [them] palatable…ornament is looked on either as an advertisement, or as a humouring of the prejudices of the vulgar' (*RIBA Trans.*, XIV, (1863–4), 105). 'Nearly everyone is dressed alike, to give an appearance of equality, equality being one of the favourite fictions of the day' (*Builder*, LXIV (1893), 209–12).

[38] *RIBA Trans.*, XIV (1863–4), 105.

[39] Ibid.

to…buildings.' 'Architects are before everything constructors, and paper architects are a mere burlesque.' But there was also a deeper cause. Architecture is two things: science and art. 'The scientific mind with no art, and the artful mind with no science are…like two horses pulling in opposite directions.' For example, 'there is a wonderful scope for ingenuity in trying to make a girder sightly.'[40] 'I believe we could make a steam-engine beautiful, or one of the hideous abortions of the engineer, if mankind wanted it.'[41] But there is one obstacle: the utilitarian heresy. 'From the savage upwards', Aitchison explains in 1886, until the middle of the eighteenth century, 'no one ever made anything without an attempt, however rude, to give it some beauty of form… [Alas] this desire ceased amongst civilised nations' with the advent of science, machinery, and the market economy. 'From a toasting fork to a steam-engine, things began to be made for…use, and use only'. As a result, 'we…have building, but not architecture'. [42]

Aitchison's conundrum — how to turn utility into beauty — went of course to the very root of the matter. Given the historicist mindset of his time, that meant: how to make buildings 'beautiful without copying'. Aitchison's answer was hardly original: recapture not the style but the 'mental attitude' of the Middle Ages. [43]

What did that mean? In Aitchison's eyes, architectural design should aim not at an image of the tectonic process — as in the Renaissance — but at an expression of the structural system, as in medieval times. According to this view Romanesque, Byzantine, and above all Gothic represented authentic architecture, that is evolving structural expression. By the same token, Classicism was not an image but a sham. His reasoning ran as follows. Architecture is above all a constructive art. Painting or sculpture imitate the appearance of nature; but architecture imitates its very process: 'it is an attempt to emulate the higher natural organisms, in the making of a shell for man's [own] use.'[44] In effect, form evolves from function. But — and this is the nub of the problem — 'the proper expression of a mere material need does not make architecture'.[45] 'Architecture appeals to emotions which no mechanical methods can produce.'[46] And it is the business of an architect to play upon those emotions as a musician plays upon an

---

[40] *Builder*, LXIV (1893), 207. Similarly *Builder*, LXVI (1894), 153.

[41] *Builder*, L (1886), 404.

[42] Ibid. 'We live in a world of words; the foremost men are engaged in unravelling the secrets of nature or the past, or in making machines to apply the forces of nature to common use. The things wanting are a comprehension of the supreme importance of the visual arts and a sense of the beauty of form; this last is one of nature's gifts to man…it is withering away from want of use' (*Builder*, LXVIII (1895), 180). 'If there is absolutely no desire for anything but bare shelter…a plain dog-kennel or rabbit hutch…then architecture as a fine art must cease' (*Builder*, LXIV (1893), 209–12).

[43] *Builder*, LII (1887), 636.

[44] *Builder*, LXVI (1894), 107. Architects 'create organisms in emulation of Nature' (*Builder*, LXI (1891), 139). Buildings on the Renaissance principle which separate interior and exterior aesthetics, deny their basis in nature: a building which treats a facade independently of its structure 'does not emulate one of Nature's organisms' (*Builder*, LXVI (1894), 108).

[45] *Builder*, LXI (1891), 139.

[46] *Builder*, LXXII (1897), 221.

instrument. For architecture is to building as music is to sound; and its art is as 'inseparably bound up with' its science 'as the soul with the body'.[47] For effective imagery, for his means of communication, any architect has to draw upon the culture in which he lives. A Victorian architect, therefore, must express by his designs the mental 'turmoil' of his day.[48] Alas, Aitchison admits, 'we have abandoned the symbolic, the emblematic and the allegorical'[49]; in fact we live 'in an anti-symbolic age'.[50]

Thanks to the 'pernicious legacy'[51] of the 'abominable Renaissance'[52], architects had been 'groping in the dark'[53] for half a millennium.[54] Somehow Victorian architects had to absorb the semiotic lessons of the Renaissance without copying its tectonic vices. 'If we use', he tells his students in 1894, 'as we eventually must use, iron and steel for those parts which are to bear great weights, great strains, or to bridge wide spans, and [if we] make the ironwork visible, we will not only find that those new materials will take new shapes…[they will] give rise to new advances'.[55] In other words, new needs, new materials, new forms, new aesthetic – in that order.

******

'No man', Aitchison tells his students in 1883, 'can walk down the vast nave of the Crystal Palace and see its filmy construction and its flood of light without thankfulness and admiration'.[56] Here surely was a worthy symbol of 'the Second Iron Age'.[57] 'The difficulty in using iron aesthetically', however, 'is that from its very strength it tends to effacement, setting aside all the difficulties arising from its expansion and contraction, its condensation of damp vapour into water, its rusting, and the difficulty of making

---

[47] *Builder*, LXVIII (1895), 79.

[48] *Builder*, LXVIII (1895), 81.

[49] *Builder*, LVI (1889), 142.

[50] *Builder*, LXVI (1894), 194. Similarly ibid, 107.

[51] *Builder*, LXXIII (1897), 367. 'Architecture became a scholastic exercise in a dead language' (*Builder*, LXVI (1894), 171).

[52] *Builder*, LXVI (1894), 153, 169. Renaissance architects 'were not architects at all, [they] had no idea what architecture meant' (*Builder*, LXXII (1897), 420). 'They not only left a bitter drop in the cup, but that bitterness was rank poison…producing stupor from which we are only now beginning to awaken' (*Builder*, LXXIV (1898), 147–9).

[53] *Builder*, LXI (1891), 138.

[54] Real architecture in England, he believed, had ended with the sixteenth-century staircase at Christ Church, Oxford (ibid.).

[55] *Builder*, LXVI (1894), 88. 'We shall, I think, find out these shapes partly by theory, and partly by experiment' (*Builder*, LXIV (1893), 83–7). 'I suspect that we will have to go back again to the rectilinear form, for that is the form that iron most conveniently…takes' (*Builder*, LXIV (1893), 209–12).

[56] *Builder*, XLIV (1883), 207.

[57] Ibid. 'Though heavy…outside, [it] is wonderful inside and produces strong emotions from the brilliancy of its light, its vastness, slightness and height; and this happens mainly through mere effort to cover a large space economically' (*Builder*, LXIV (1893), 108–10). 'The constructors' of 'the Crystal Palace and…large modern railway station roofs are the really modern Medieval architects', the true cathedral builders of the Victorian age (*Builder*, XXIX (1871), 417).

water-tight joints with…glass… [And of course] it involves four or five times as much time [in design] as similar work in the older materials'.[58] Not that the use of iron was in any way new: there were wrought iron girders in the Baths of Caracalla 1,600 years ago.[59] What was new was the attempt to give metallic forms appropriate aesthetic expression. Architects had traditionally 'joined the art of construction to the art of expression'. With the separation of the architectural and engineering professions, however, engineeers 'simply solved the constructive problems, so that their structures bear the same resemblance to architecture that a woman's skeleton has to the Venus de Milo'.[60] For engineers 'appeal only to the intellectual and not to the emotional side of man'.[61] Somehow the new technology must be brought within the pale of aesthetics.[62] Conversely, architects will no longer be allowed to indulge in pictorial composition. All this involves risks; but 'eccentric ugliness is better than second-hand beauty, if it be the right step forward'.[63]

The most promising steps forward seemed to be visible not in London but in Paris. There Aitchison saw iron used for the first time convincingly, in architectural form, by Baltard, by Hittorf, by Labrouste, by Sedille.[64] Two passages by Emile Zola struck him as prophetic. First the contrast between the sixteenth- to eighteenth-century church of St Eustache and the nineteenth-century Central Market, Les Halles:

> This is a curious conjunction…this end of a chancel framed in an avenue of cast iron… One will kill the other; the iron will kill the stone; and the time is nigh… Don't you see, here is a whole manifesto; it is modern art, realism, naturalism, whatever you like to call it…grown big in the face of ancient art… In any case the church is of bastard architecture; the Middle Ages was dying there, and the Renaissance was only lisping… Have you noticed what churches they build for us now? They are like anything you please, like libraries, like observatories, like pigeon-houses, like barracks; but certainly no one believes the Almighty dwells therein. The masons of the Almighty are dead… Since the beginning of the century one single original monument has been built, a monument which has been copied from nothing, which has sprung up naturally from the soil of the epoch; and that is the Central Market… A swaggering work, and it is only a timid revelation of the twentieth century to come.[65]

The second passage concerns the vision given by Zola to his hero Claude Lantier, of

---

[58] *Builder*, LXVIII (1895), 100. Similarly *Builder*, LX (1891), 82.

[59] *Builder*, LX (1891), 95.

[60] *Builder*, LXX (1896), 109. Similarly *Builder*, LXVIII (1895), 139. For the fragmentation of the building professions, see Mordaunt Crook, 'Pre-Victorian'.

[61] *Builder*, LV (1888), 431. 'The engineers have eliminated beauty from their structures' (*Builder*, LII (1887), 636).

[62] *Builder*, LXVIII (1895), 121.

[63] *Builder*, LII (1887), 700.

[64] For Aitchison's criticism of Baltard's Halles Centrale, see *Builder*, XLIV (1883), 208. He preferred Hittorf's Gard du Nord (using columns cast in Glasgow in 1862); Labrouste's Bibliothèque Nationale ('as agreeable a room as you could wish to see'); Duban and Coquart's Ecole des Beaux-Arts; and 'Les Magasins du Printemps', near St Lazare, by Paul Sedille (ibid.).

[65] Zola, *Belly*.

the birth of modern architecture:

> If ever there was a century in which architecture should have a style of its own, it is the century shortly to begin, the new century…the breeding ground of a new people. Down with the Greek temples; there is no use or place for them in modern society! Down with the Gothic cathedrals; belief in legends is dead! Down, too, with the delicate colonnades…of the Renaissance…[they can] never house modern democracy! What is wanted…[is] an architectural formula to fit that democracy… something big and strong and simple, the sort of thing that [is] already asserting itself in railway stations and market halls,, the solid elegance of metal girders, developed and refined…raised to the status of…beauty.[66]

But how? Where was this new vocabulary of form? There was no easy guide even in the Paris of Emile Zola. For there can be no rule-of-thumb canons of architectural beauty. 'To some extent', as Aitchison explained in 1897, 'our compasses must be in our eye'.[67] 'Aesthetic advance is possible, if we go the right way about it.' Following the American theorist Leopold Eidlitz, he suggests the following formula: first seek out statical solutions to constructional problems, then translate them into symbolic form.[68] 'That is easy to talk about', he admits in 1891, 'but not easy to do; at present [it]…is mainly done by association'.[69] For a start, we lack some of the basic techniques: 'the art of moulding is as much neglected now as the science of statics'.[70] More important, society has become physically so materialistic, and intellectually so 'absorbed in physical science', that it no longer seeks to 'embody [its] aspirations in architecture'.[71] At present our souls are full of deadness…to the highest forms of art'; and a rich man would prefer to give a banquet than build a house.[72]

******

---

[66] Zola, *Masterpiece.* Zola, however, signed the Artists' Protest of 1887 against the ugliness of the Eiffel Tower.

[67] *Builder*, LXXIII (1897), 368 and LXVI (1894), 151.

[68] *Builder*, LXXII (1897), 219 and LXXVIII (1900), 129.

[69] *Builder*, LXI (1891), 138.

[70] *Builder*, LXXIII (1897), 767. Even our mouldings are in 'the antiquarian chrysalid state' (*Builder*, LXVIII (1895), 181). 'A knowledge of statics gives us a true ratio between every part of a structure, and it gives the real shape each part must take; if we were as clever as Nature, it would in all probability give us a beautiful shape. Unfortunately, we are far from being as clever, and…we have to learn by other means how a beautiful shape can be made out of the necessary shape. For this purpose we must study deceased architecture and Nature. Every piece of deceased architecture that we admire can be made to show us the aesthetic laws that govern it and produce its excellence, and these laws are as capable of being employed now as then'. For example, 'a Greek Doric column showed the statical knowledge of its day, but it certainly does not now' (*Builder*, LXXIV (1898), 102). Hence the challenge.

[71] *Builder*, LIV (1888), 62. 'The present generation lives wholly in the present, owing to the discoveries in science and to mechanical invention. This age is cut off by a gulf from the past…our oldest heroes are Smeaton and Brindley, Trevithick, Watt and George Stephenson, the Brunels, Hodgkinson and Fairbairn, Davy, Dalton, Faraday and Wheatstone' (*RIBA Trans.*, N.S. IV, 1887–8, 178). 'In each art nations get the embodiment of what they are' (*Builder*, LV (1888), 432). 'For architecture is a social expression' (*Builder*, LV (1888), 432).

[72] *Builder*, LXVIII (1895), 121. Similarly *Builder*, LV (1888), 433. Not until 'new and noble aspirations again lift men from their present [obsessions] with filling their bellies and their pockets, [will] a new iron architecture…soar above' (*Builder*, LIV (1888), 62). We have painters, sculptors, and architects whose skill matches any in the past "but there is no high ideal in society to be expressed by them' (*Builder*, LV (1888), 432 and LXVIII (1895), 80). Our present ideal would seem to be 'the land of Cocagne, where the little pigs run about ready roasted asking

This sense of gloom pervades Aitchison's lectures. 'We have no national architecture', he notes glumly in 1886; 'whether anything ... stable and progressive is to come out of the present chaos I cannot prophesy'. The current relativistic approach – a different style for each building type – is fundamentally wrong: 'an abominable heresy' produced by 'the present jumble of styles'.[73] 'We have no national architecture at present', he repeats in 1887, 'many of us get our living by tinkering up old buildings ... but it is archaeology not architecture'.[74] We have 'mastered…the bygone styles', he notes again in 1891, and adapted them 'to the wants and uses of the present day… [But] we have [yet] to take [that key] step forward' – translating 'our sense of beauty and aesthetic fitness' into 'the foundation of a new style'. In particular we have still to take our new materials, especially iron, and give them 'the vigorous stamp of architectural beauty'.[75]

'Must we abandon ourselves to despair', he wonders in 1892. Well, not quite: 'a new style is not to be enacted in a day nor in a lifetime'.[76] But by 1894 he is getting restive: 'there is [still] no architecture in Christendom that…can be called good, true and distinctive of the present century'.[77] 'Surely we have something else to say in architecture than they had in the sixteenth century, not to speak of the thirteenth?'[78] By 1895 his patience is wearing thin: 'there is not much time left' for the nineteenth century; let us pray that 'the twentieth century' at least will 'have an architecture of its own', not just 'a chaos of paraphrases'.[79] By 1897–8 he is 'almost in despair'[80]; architecture is in a state of 'suspended animation'.[81] 'I am doing my best to dispel ... dead styles ... from… students' minds'[82]; for 'if architecture cannot progress, it must be swept into the limbo where heraldry, necromancy, astrology and perpetual motion now moulder in peace'.[83]

---

people to eat them' (*Builder*, LXVIII (1895), 121). 'Our…age is marked by its creed of gain, and its love of banquetting, but it is redeemed by a taste for literature, some love for humanity, and a passion for scientific research' (*Builder*, LV (1888), 432). 'Turtle, whitebait, venison, and stuffed truffles, washed down with punch, champagne, old claret and port, are excellent things occasionally, but if all our happiness is centred on them, what can be expected of us?' (*Builder*, LV (1888), 432).

[73] *Builder*, L (1886), 334, 404. Similarly *Builder*, LXXXIX (1905), 595 and LXXIV (1898), 180–2.

[74] *Builder*, LII (1887), 635.

[75] *Builder*, LX (1891), 85. There is some consolation: 'living architecture' does progress, though 'its progress is not always in a direct line' (ibid., 83).

[76] *Builder*, LXII (1892), 179–83. 'Those who reproach architects with not inventing a new style forget that hundreds of years are required to evolve one' (ibid., 75–8).

[77] *Builder*, LXVI (1894), 88.

[78] *Builder*, LXIV (1893), 63–6.

[79] *Builder*, LXVIII (1895), 180, 182.

[80] *Builder*, LXXII (1897), 117.

[81] *Builder*, LXVIII (1895), 81, 99. 'Almost every country has produced a style of its own, [but] this country has yet to take that step' (*Builder*, LXVII (1894), 372: the editor demurred – 'What about English Gothic, the Early English and Tudor Gothic especially?'. 'There are explorers in every direction, [but] the real road has not yet been found' (*Builder*, LXXI (1896), 383).

[82] *Builder*, LXXII (1897), 117–19.

[83] *Builder*, LXXIV (1898), 252. 'The thing we all want is the advancement of architecture. But who is to show us the way?' (*Builder*, LXXV (1898), 425). Are mankind's 'powers of invention' doomed to become 'atrophied [like] the wings of the apteryx?' (*ibid.*, 426).

By the turn of the new century Aitchison is becoming desperate. 'I feel ashamed', he mourned in 1900; 'it is humiliating... It is too melancholy'; architects today are merely keepers of 'a fancy dress shop'.[84] Architects should be 'poets in structure'[85]; and until architecture gets back to its structural roots, 'we are only groping around in the dark', stumbling among the debris of history.[86] 'I am not a prophet', he admits in 1902, but as yet 'I see no signs' of 'something new'.[87]

By this time the editor of the *Builder*, which had patiently published hundreds of thousands of Aitchison's melancholy words, was also getting restive. Repeated eulogies of the Crystal Palace, Statham complained, were really beside the point: after more than a hundred lectures, 'the problem' of iron, the mystery of its aesthetic properties, had yet 'to be solved'.[88] Professors of Architecture, he implied, are not much use if they merely teach us how to doubt.[89] Aitchison was unrepentant: 'when a man is lost in a wood', the best thing you can do is to 'direct him to the road out of it... Architecture has been [lost] in a wood since the fifteenth century'.[90] Even so, he was getting weary. The Jeremiah of the Royal Academy resigned his chair in 1905. He died in 1910.

******

For fifty years George Aitchison had wrestled with the burden of history. To what effect? His lectures cannot be dismissed as eccentric, irrelevant, or peripheral. Generations of students listened; thousands of people read them at second-hand. His anxieties represented the central concerns of the generality of thinking architects. There was immense confusion and deep concern. As Aitchison put it in 1885, 'the leaders of architectural criticism' are 'like the political leaders in [Ireland]; they do not know what they want, but they are determined to get it'.[91] Or as Viollet-le-Duc famously remarked, Victorian architects calling for a new style were like a chorus of opera singers all shouting 'Here we go' — and never moving an inch.[92] But in the end,

---

[84] *Builder*, LXXVIII (1900), 130.

[85] *Builder*, LXXIII (1897), 117–19.

[86] *Builder*, LXXVIII (1900), 130.

[87] *RIBA Journal*, 3rd ser. (1901–2), 199.

[88] *Builder*, LXXXIV (1903), 186, 214. He cites the iron spire of Rouen Cathedral as an instance of how not to use iron; and a house front in George Street, Westminster, by Halsey Ricardo, as an example worth following. When Aitchison announced in 1905 that he would again lecture on Vitruvius, Statham commented: 'We confess that we should have thought enough had been said of late years about Vitruvius, and that lectures...illuminating the art of architecture from a modern standpoint...would have been of more value to the Academy students' (*Builder*, LXXXVIII, 1905, 5). Aitchison had, in fact, already dismissed Vitruvius as treating the 'aesthetic part [of architecture] like a recipe from a cookery book' (*Builder*, LXIV, 1893, 209–12).

[89] *Builder*, LXIV (1893), 209–12.

[90] *Builder*, LXXIII (1897), 368.

[91] *Builder*, XLVIII (1885), 582.

[92] *Builder*, LXVIII (1895), 121.

after half a century of cogitation, Aitchison was no nearer an answer than he had been at the start.

And in a sense there could be no answer. All architects are born to search, and search in vain, for that magical, alchemical formula which turns 'the prose of building into the poetry of architecture'.[93] Aitchison's problem was the eternal architect's dilemma. 'Architecture', he explained in 1898, 'is above all things a constructive art; but…this construction must be clothed in the forms that will give the proper character to the building for the purpose it has to fulfil'.[94] In other words, the Puginian conundrum: propriety or truth? Aitchison never resolved that riddle. Nor did he supply an answer to Donaldson's challenge: 'Are we to have an architecture of our period, a distinct, individual, palpable style of the nineteenth century?'[95] He merely repeated the question *ad nauseam*. As for social comment, Aitchison really adds nothing but repetition to Ruskin's diagnosis of the disintegrative aesthetic. In his favourite field, cast iron, he merely reiterates the dreams of Ambrose Poynter and William Vose Pickett which he absorbed in the 1840s.[96] In his own practice, he never approaches the prophetic achievements of his Parisian contemporaries. By the end of his life he had retreated to the less contentious field of interior decoration. As his interminable lecture series rolls on – through its half a million printed words – he finds little to add to Kerr's antitheses of archaeology and art, and even less to Fergusson's polarities of utility and beauty. Instead he falls back on Choisy's physiological analogy: architecture as organism, architecture as a microcosm of the evolutionary process. Armed with Choisy's conceptual microscope, he examined the architecture of his own day and found it methodologically defective. Then, re-armed with Eidlitz's teleological telescope, he conjured up an architecture of the future: statical equations couched in symbolic imagery.[97] Nothing came of it, at least in his own lifetime. In that sense, Aitchison was a failure, and he shared that sense of failure with a whole generation of reluctant historicists.[98]

But the Victorians judged themselves too harshly. Had Aitchison been able to look back at his own age from the vantage point of the late twentieth century, he would have discovered that his demand for a characteristically Victorian style had in fact

[93] *Builder*, LXVI (1894), 193.

[94] *Builder*, LXXIV (1898), 251–2.

[95] *Builder*, V (1847), 492.

[96] A. Poynter, *On the effects which should result to architectural taste with regard to arranagement and design from the general introduction of iron in the construction of buildings* (RIBA medal essay, 1842); W. Vose Pickett, (1845 edn.). See *Builder*, LXVI (1894), 132.

[97] 'Statics [should] give us…important lessons in aesthetics, for it gives us the proper proportion of each part of a building when we know the height, the weight to be carried, and the strength of material to be used. When these particulars are known and provided for, we may roughly say that we have only to accentuate the important parts by mouldings, or have them advanced by the sculptor, to make it into architecture' (*Builder*, LXXIII (1897), 367).

[98] 'Have we got an architecture that does fulfil all the wants, satisfies the taste, and expresses all the emotions of the day?… If we cannot affirm this, we must admit we have failed' (*Builder*, LXIV (1893), 63–6).

been answered – though hardly in the way he hoped.[99] For eclecticism was indeed the nineteenth century style.[100] If there was a Victorian vernacular – and perhaps that is a contradiction in terms – it was an eclectic vernacular evolving in a complex, pluralistic culture. Gazing at the Victorian age through contemporary, Victorian eyes, Aitchison could see only architectural chaos. Looking at that chaos with late twentieth century – dare we say it – Post-modernist eyes, he would still have seen chaos, but characteristic chaos: the rich, pluralistic chaos of an age of historicism.

Appendix

PRINCIPAL LECTURES, ARTICLES, SPEECHES ETC. BY GEORGE AITCHISON, RA, PRIBA

'On Colour as applied to Architecture', *RIBA Trans.*, VIII (1857–8), 47–54: 14 December 1857 [RIBA]

'On Iron as a Building Material', *RIBA Trans.*, XIV (1863–4), 97–103: 29 February 1864 [RIBA]

'Progressive Use of Iron in Building', *RIBA Trans.*, XXI (1871), 81–2; *Builder*, XXIX (1871), 417 [RIBA conference]

'Iron' and 'Colour', *Builder*, XLIV (1883), 207–8, 273–4 [RA]

'The Late William Burges, A.R.A.', *RIBA Trans.*, (1883–4), 204–9 [obituary]

'On Marble and Marble Mosaic', *Builder*, XLVI (1884), 281–2 [RA]

'On Coloured Glass', *Builder*, XLVI (1884), 382–3 [RA]

'On Staircases', *Builder*, XLVIII (1885), 395–6, 396–7 [RA]

'Architecture in the 19th century', *Builder*, XLVIII (1885), 581–2, 637 [Society for the Encouragement of Fine Arts]

'Architectural Education', *Builder*, L (1886), 331–5 [RA]

'Mouldings', *Builder*, L (1886), 365–6, 402–4 [RA]

'Paul Sédille', *RIBA Journal*, (1886–7), 89–91 [RIBA]

'On Doorways; Windows; Balustrades', *Builder*, LII (1887), 346–7, 380–2 [RA]

'Stray Thoughts on Education', *Builder*, LII (1887), 635–6, 654 [Architectural Association]

'On Architectural Education', *Builder*, LII (1887), 690–700 [General Conference, RIBA]

'Sculpture and its relation to architecture', *RIBA Trans.*, (1887–8), 176–80 [RIBA]

'The History of Architecture', *Builder*, LIV (1888), 61–3 [RA]

'Greek Architecture', *Builder*, LIV (1888), 118 [RA]

'Utilitarian Ugliness in Towns', *Builder*, LV (1888), 430–3 [National Art Congress, Liverpool]

'The Revival of Architecture', *Builder*, LV (1888), 2–3 [reply to William Morris]

'The Roman Thermae', *RIBA Trans.*, ns V (1888–9), 105–22 [RIBA]

'The Origin of Roman Imperial Architecture', *RIBA Trans.*, ns V (1888–9), 158–61 [reply to G. Baldwin Brown, RIBA]

'The Late Mr Pullan', *RIBA Trans.*, ns VI (1888–9), 249–54 [obituary]

'Charles Robert Cockerell', *RIBA Trans.*, ns VI (1888–9), 255–61 [memoir]

---

[99] 'Every modern building...has a 19th century air about it...but I cannot admit that this flavour amounts to a style', for that would involve 'new forms by reason of new wants or new materials... Eclecticism itself would constitute a new style [only] if all pillaged the same things' (*Builder*, LVIII (1890), 75).

[100] During a discussion in 1887, Aitchison was told this by J. A. Gotch, but failed to respond. Gotch explained: 'people [today] do not go on from step to step in one style...as the medievals did'; because Victorian eclecticism was the product of a pluralistic culture (*Builder*, LII (1887), 654).

'Roman Architecture', *Builder*, LVI (1889), 85–8, 103–6, 121–4, 142–5, 162–5, 181–3, 198–201, 204, 224 [RA]

'Roman Architecture', *Builder*, LVIII (1890), 75–8, 94–7, 113–6, 130–3, 135, 137, 152–5, 169–72 [RA]

The Nature and Function of Art by L. Eidlitz, *RIBA Journal*, ns II (1890–1), 389–90 [review]

'Byzantine Architecture', *Builder*, LX (1891), 82–6, 103–7, 123–6, 144–7, 164–7, 187–90 [RA]

'The Advancement of Architecture', *Builder*, LXI (1891), 138–9 [Architectural Association]

'Byzantine Architecture', *RIBA Trans.*, VIII (1892), pp. 221–46 [RIBA]

'Saracenic Architecture', *Builder*, LXII (1892), 75–8, 95–9, 116–9, 136–40, 156–9, 179–83 [RA]

'What is Architecture, and how can it be advanced?', *Builder*, LXIV (1893), 63–6, 83–7, 108–10, 146–50, 166–9, 209–12 [RA]

'The Advancement of Architecture', *Builder*, LXVI (1894), 86–9, 107–11, 131–4, 151–3, 169–72, 192–4 and *RIBA Journal*, 3rd ser., I (1893–4), 243–4, 279–80, 320–3, 363 [RA]

'The Use and Abuse of Marble for Decorative Purposes', *RIBA Journal*, 3rd ser., II (1894–5), 401–7 [RIBA 22 April 1895]

'The Advancement of Architecture', *Builder*, LXVIII (1895), 79–81, 99–101, 119–22, 137–40, 159–62, 179–82 [RA]

'Lord Leighton: some reminiscences', *RIBA Journal*, 3rd ser., III (1896), 264–5

'Romanesque Architecture', *Builder*, LXX (1896), 109–11, 132–4, 158–60, 180–2, 204–6, 227–9 [RA]

'Presidential Address', *Builder*, LXXI (1896), 381–3 [RIBA]

'President's Address', *Builder*, LXXIII (1897), 366–9 and *RIBA Journal*, 3rd ser., V (1897–8), 1–8 [RIBA 1 November 1897]

'The Advancement of Architecture', *Builder*, LXXII (1897), 117–9, 141–3, 165–6, 191–4, 217–9, 296–71, 316 [RA]

'Speeches at the Festival Dinner', *RIBA Journal*, 3rd ser., V (1897–8), 1002–3, 105 [Whitehall Rooms]

'Speech at the Architectural Association Jubilee Banquet', *Builder*, LXXII (1897), 420 [Trocadero Restaurant, Piccadilly]

'Address to the Central Association of Master Builders', *Builder*, LXXIV (1898), 104–5 [Trocadero Restaurant, Piccadilly]

'Address on receiving the Royal Gold Medal', *Builder*, LXXIV (1898), 610 and *RIBA Journal*, 3rd ser., V (1897–8), 412–3 [RIBA]

'Address to Students', *Builder*, LXXIV (1898), 102–3 and *RIBA Journal*, 3rd ser., VI (1898–9), 1–8 [RIBA]

'The Renaissance', *Builder*, LXXIV (1898), 124–6, 147–9, 180–2, 201–1 , 226–7, 251–2 [RA]

'President's Address', *Builder*, LXXV (1898), 424–6 and *RIBA Journal*, 3rd ser., VI (1898–9), 1–8 [RIBA 7 November 1898]

'Address to Students', *Builder*, LXXVI (1899), 83–4 and *RIBA Journal*, 3rd ser., VI (1898–9) 137–41 [RIBA 23 January 1899]

'Address at the International Building Trades Exhibition', *Builder*, LXXVI (1899), 409–10 [Agricultural Hall, Islington]

'Greek Architecture', *Builder*, LXXVI (1899), 109–11, 136–9, 163–6, 187–90, 216–9, 241–4 [RA]

'Progress in Architecture', *Builder*, LXXVIII (1900), 128–30 [RA]

'St Peter's, Rome', *Builder*, LXXX (1901), 105–8, 130–2 and *RIBA Journal*, 3rd ser., VIII (1900–1), 245–55, 453–63; IX (1901–2), 49–61, 77–89 [RA]

'The Learning of Architecture', *RIBA Journal*, 3rd ser., (1901–2), 193–200, 321–6, 381–91, 401–13, 449–58 [RA]

'Coloured Buildings'; 'Coloured Terra-Cotta'; 'Marble', *RIBA Journal*, 3rd ser., X (1902–3), 493–503, 513–22, 529–38

'Metallic Architecture', *Builder*, LXXXIV (1903), 186, 214, 246, 272; *RIBA Journal*, 3rd ser., X (1902–3), 433–40, 469–77 [RA]

'Coloured Glass', *RIBA Journal*, 3rd ser., XI (1903–4), 53–65

'Vitruvius'; 'Excellence in Architecture', *RIBA Journal*, 3rd ser., XIII (1905–6), 21–8, 61–7, 341–6, 451–6.

Robert Willis:
The Religious Revival and its Impact on Architecture

Thomas Cocke

It is right to focus on Robert Willis in connection with the joint celebration of the British Archaeological Association and the Royal Archaeological Institute; not only did he in general terms bring together Church, Architecture, and Science in a way characteristic of the best of his generation, but he was deeply involved with these societies from the start. He was a founder-member of the original British Archaeological Association, being appointed President of the Architectural section, and at the secession he transferred to the Institute of which he remained a devoted supporter, lecturing regularly at its annual meetings for over twenty years (fig.20).

Willis's career can be briefly summarised. Born in 1799 (rather than 1800 as cited in the Dictionary of National Biography),[1] he was a scholar, then Fellow of Caius College, Cambridge: in 1837 he was elected to the Jacksonian Professorship of Natural Experimental Philosophy in the same university which he held to his death. He published over fifty papers not only on 'the principles of mechanism' but on the great medieval buildings of this country and even on the Holy Sepulchre in Jerusalem. His crowning art-historical achievement was posthumous, the publication in 1886, through the collaborative efforts of his nephew, John Willis Clark, of the *Architectural History of the University of Cambridge* in three redoubtable volumes. His vigour extended into his private life. By his wife Mary Anne, daughter of Charles Humfrey, the Cambridge speculative builder and architect, he had produced by 1841 six children under six.

He rarely ventured into the role of designer but in the 1840s he did build a Middle Pointed cemetery chapel at Wisbech, as well as refashioning the west window of St Botolph's, Cambridge and reconstructing the vaults of Great Gate, Trinity and of

---

[1] This information was kindly confirmed by Miss Faith Lyons, descendant of Robert Willis. I am also grateful for the comments of Miss Alexandrina Buchanan who has just completed major research on Robert Willis.

Prior Crauden's chapel at Ely. When preparing designs for buildings to house the new scientific disciplines in the Old Botanic Garden site behind Corpus Christi College (now usually called the Cavendish), his taste was strictly utilitarian.

The key events of the contemporary religious and architectural worlds can be equally swiftly rehearsed. In 1834 Keble delivered his Assize Sermon heralding the Oxford Movement, in 1839 the Cambridge Camden Society (later the Ecclesiological Society) was founded. In 1836 Pugin published his *Contrasts*; Ruskin his *Seven Lamps of Architecture* in 1849; and ten years later Darwin his *Origin of Species*.

Robert Willis was thus one of those intellectual giants of the nineteenth century, whose energy and range intimidate us. While we honour him as the Father of church archaeology, scientists also admire his contributions to physics, physiology, and engineering. His professorship at Cambridge was concerned not with Art or Architecture but with Applied Mechanics. He was involved in experiments on the manufacture of tools and in setting up the Great Exhibition, he advised on the specification for the Great Organ in the rebuilt Crystal Palace at Sydenham; he invented and patented a scale for weighing letters as well as preparing his famous studies on cathedrals.[2] He was no armchair intellectual but someone fully involved in the life of his time.

But there is one other of his qualifications which is rarely discussed. Ordained deacon and priest in 1827, he was the Reverend Robert Willis, as well as Jacksonian Professor and Fellow of the Royal Society. Of course his taking holy orders can be

Fig. 20. Robert Willis MA, FRS (1799–1875). (By kind permission of Dr Faith Lyons)

---

[2] Willis first 'civilly declined' but afterwards accepted the invitation from the Crystal Palace Company (CUL Add MS 5133, item 9). Add MS 5134 f66 is a flyer of 1840 for a 'patent letter balance' invented by Willis and manufactured by Joseph and Edmund Ratcliff of Birmingham.

explained by academic and family tradition. Ordination was generally a prerequisite for a Cambridge fellowship until almost the end of Willis's life. In any case his family was intimately connected with the Church. His paternal grandfather was a priest although his fame was as the humane doctor who treated George III in his madness. One uncle went into the Church, his sister married into it. Yet a man of Willis's intelligence and integrity can hardly have regarded his priestly orders as a formality. It would have been impossible not to be aware of the changing religious attitudes of the 1830s and 1840s both within the Church and without, especially as church buildings and their furnishings moved from being matters of antiquarianism and taste to tests of orthodoxy.

WILLIS, PUGIN, AND RUSKIN

Robert Willis had come early to his interest in ancient buildings. A delicate and precocious child, he had been educated by private tutors, spending some time in Norfolk where he studied the ancient churches. In his early twenties he was able to turn out competent antiquarian watercolours and even analytical studies of a building, such as his series of drawings of the Red Mount Chapel in King's Lynn, numbered as if for engraving, presumably on the model of contemporary articles in *Archaeologia*.[3] By the time of his honeymoon Grand Tour, which he characteristically used to study medieval architecture in Italy, he had adopted a less painterly style, economically jotting down structural and decorative details in pencil outline. At a less academic level, he attended the celebrated Beckford sale at Fonthill Abbey.

During this same period of the 1820s and 1830s Robert Willis was also involved in a host of studies of a technical nature. But his enthusiasm for medieval architecture, so far from being squeezed out, grew until by the 1840s he had become a recognised authority. His first public appearance in this role was in the report he prepared in 1841 for the Dean and Chapter of Hereford concerning the structural stability of the 'dilapidated portions' of the Cathedral, especially the central tower.[4] It set the tone of his subsequent reports, scrupulously polite to the architect involved, cool and factual in the analysis of the problems of the fabric. The mathematical diagram with arcs dotted in and points lettered 'A' or 'B' was the type of illustration he preferred, not the artist's impression. Tours of the cathedrals visited during the annual meetings of the Archaeological Institute gave him an ideal platform to deploy the technique verbally. His delivery was presumably livelier than his prose style, as everyone agreed on the

---

[3] See Willis drawings, Vol.2, ff. 220/1. The four volumes were presented to the Society of Antiquaries by Willis's nephew, John Willis Clark, in 1900. Willis himself had given the Society books he had published, (e.g. *Canterbury* in 1845) although he himself was never a member.

[4] CUL, Cambridge Collection, Cam c832.1, Item 1, Report on the present state of the Cathedral of Hereford and on the causes which have led to it, Hereford, 1842.

clarity and power of his exposition. 'His lucid explanations' were such as to induce 'even the ladies' to visit the 'dark, and close and damp' crypt at Gloucester.[5]

Robert Willis was usually a man of his time in his attitudes to church restoration. He accepted that classical features were wrong in a medieval building. He denounced the 'injudicious half-measures of patching repairs employed [at Worcester Cathedral] in the last two centuries'[6] and applauded the public spirit and judgement of the Ely Dean and Chapter in the vigorous works of 'reparation and restoration' they commissioned from the 1840s.[7]

Yet there sometimes appear signs of a less respectful point of view, more typical of the Hanoverian than the Victorian era. In his 1847 lecture on Ely for the Archaeological Institute he commented that while he could spend hours describing every boss under the Octagon, 'there would be no end of it' and so he moved on.[8] During the same tour he exclaimed at the multitude of saints introduced into the decoration of Bishop West's chapel and alleged that the same saints must have been reproduced several times over to fill all the spaces.[9]

He also could on occasion treat later attitudes and interventions with some objectivity. He recognised the connection between the octagonal plan of the Ely crossing and that of Christopher Wren's St Paul's.[10] He was also willing to record seventeenth-century work, either architectural, as in the colleges at Oxford or Cambridge, or in furnishings. There is a sensitive measured drawing by him analysing the construction of a Jacobean Holy Table at Stoke D'Abernon.[11] Although his history can err – he allegedly attributed the disappearance of the monuments at the east end of Ely to Cromwell stabling his horses there, rather than to the well-documented removal of the choir only seventy years before [12] – he accepted the development of a building in all its stages, never advocating the removal of one style in favour of a 'better'. He knew all the post-medieval writers on architecture. He could for instance contrast without prejudice the varying vocabulary used to describe the elements of a medieval window (e.g. mullions, transom, tracery types) by Wren, Bentham, Milner, Walpole, and Warton.[13] In his paper 'On the Construction of Vaults in the Middle Ages' Willis showed his appreciation of Philibert de l'Orme's lucid analysis of vaulting techniques.[14]

---

[5] CUL, Cambridge Collection, Cam c832.1 Item 12, Report on the Congress of the Archaeological Institute at Gloucester, 1860, 24.

[6] CUL, Cambridge Collection, Cam a 500.7, Item 12, The Crypt and Chapter House of Worcester Cathedral, read at the Ordinary General Meeting of the RIBA, 20 April 1863, 214.

[7] CUL, Cambridge Collection, Cam d 847.11, 4.

[8] Ibid., 5.

[9] Ibid., 6.

[10] Ibid., 4.

[11] Willis Drawings, Vol. 3, ff. 657/8.

[12] CUL, Cambridge Collection, Cam d 847.11, 5.

[13] CUL, Cambridge Collection, Cam a 500.7, Item 9, Architectural Nomenclature of the Middle Ages, 1844, 47–8.

[14] Ibid., Item 5, 212–3.

Robert Willis belonged to a period when many gifted people were taking an interest in medieval architecture but his position was quite distinct. For instance his attitudes to the Middle Ages could not be further removed from those of A. W. N. Pugin. There is no evidence that the two men ever met although it would have been possible during Pugin's restoration of Jesus College Chapel in 1846–7, of which, however, Robert Willis disapproved. His drawing of the north transept arcade he later annotated 'now filled up with Pugin's clumsy work'[15] and in the *Architectural History of the University of Cambridge* he quoted the unfavourable contrast drawn by *The Ecclesiologist* between Pugin's treatment of the central tower at Jesus with that of Cottingham at Hereford and Armagh.[16] Indeed for Willis the significant Pugin would have been the elder Pugin whose *Specimens of Gothic* provided much useful comparative evidence. Willis showed little interest in the liturgical arrangements within the buildings he studied and little enthusiasm for the panoply of Gothic decoration. While his admiration for the majesty of a medieval building was no less than that of Pugin, Willis wanted to know how it worked, not how it looked.

Willis and Ruskin were just as far apart. In *The Seven Lamps of Architecture* Ruskin explicitly referred to Willis's *Architecture of the Middle Ages* and acknowledged its authority.[17] In a note to the 1880 edition of the *Seven Lamps*, Ruskin admitted that 'Willis taught me all my grammar of central Gothic'.[18] The two did meet in 1851 as guests of William Whewell in the Master's Lodge in Trinity and went together on a trip two days later to Ely but again Willis's attitude to buildings was quite different.[19] For instance, though both men had received the conventional gentleman's education in picturesque watercolour, Willis abandoned the use of wash and shading, which Ruskin advocated, in favour of innumerable small pencil sketches to illustrate particular details. In his own notes Willis wanted scientific records not aesthetic impressions and, as we have seen, in his published papers Willis preferred illustration by plan or section.

WILLIS AND THE CAMBRIDGE CONTEXT

The circle with which Willis could share his medieval interests was just as distinguished as the London world of Pugin and Ruskin, even though it is now less famous. Chief among them was William Whewell, Fellow then Master of Trinity, who had published in 1830 a significant book on German medieval architecture, *Architectural Notes on German Churches*, in the midst of his multitude of scientific and administrative duties. He did, however, retain his enthusiasm for Gothic and he and Willis devised an

---

[5] CUL, Add MS. 5036, f. 309 verso.
[16] Willis, *Cambridge*, II, 148.
[17] *Ruskin*, Works, VIII, 87–8, 95 note.
[18] Ibid., xl. See also Pevsner, 'Willis', 27.
[19] Pevsner, 'Whewell', passim.

appropriate lierne vault for the interior of the early sixteenth-century Great Gate at Trinity in 1849. Other Trinity colleagues were Adam Sedgwick, the great geologist, and George Peacock, who became Dean of Ely and obviously relied much on Willis in formulating his restoration programme.[20]

This Cambridge group, while titanic in intellect and energy, tended towards conservatism in social and religious questions. It is not surprising that their initial welcome to the Camden Society turned to hostility, once medieval ecclesiology and archaeology were seen to promote radical changes. Willis rarely invoked the Deity or speculated on contemporary religious matters. One exception is his comment, after the fall of the spire at Chichester: 'Under the Divine Blessing, we may... hope to see the tower and spire rising and pointing to the skies as before'.[21]

However he felt bound to make a specific and public protest against the way in which the Camden Society had treated Church matters in the article on Ambrose Poynter's new church of St Paul's in Cambridge published in the first issue of *The Ecclesiologist*. Although a Vice-President, he not only deprecated 'the flippant tone [which] appears to us singularly offensive' but attacked the way in which some desired 'to convert the society into an engine of polemical theology, instead of an instrument for promoting the study and the practice of Ecclesiastical Architecture'. He stressed that:

> the objects of the Camden Society are co-extensive with the whole Church of England, and as its members are not confined to any particular party in the Church, it is, therefore, in the highest degree improper that any school of religious belief which is by the Church permitted to exist within her body should, in our publications, be spoken of with disrespect.[22]

Although the influence of Willis and of his eleven co-signatories, most of them senior dons at Trinity, was great enough to secure a reissue of the offending number with a toned-down version of the article, the incident marked a parting of the ways between Willis and the Society; that was hardly surprising, considering the irreconcilable difference between the pragmatic and measured Willis, testing each statement according to the best evidence, and the high fliers of the Camden Society like Alexander Beresford Hope and John Mason Neale, who delighted in bold prejudice and exaggeration. While Willis agreed with them in his enthusiasm for church restoration, he deplored the provocative spirit in which they went about it. When the Sextry Barn at Ely was

---

[20] The recent catalogue of the documentary sources for the post-medieval restoration of Ely Cathedral; prepared by Dr Mark Collins, confirms Willis's prominent role in the restoration of the south-west transept of Ely Cathedral in the 1840s. (Information kindly supplied by Gavin Simpson.)

[21] CUL, Cambridge Collection, Cam a 500.8, Item 2, The Architectural History of Chichester Cathedral, with an Introductory Essay on the Fall of the Tower and Spire (Chichester 1861), xxiv.

[22] Report of the 23rd meeting of the Cambridge Camden Society held on 6 December 1841 at which Willis took the chair. (*Ecclesiologist*, I (1842), 25).

demolished in 1842, the Camden Society protested noisily and condemned the Dean and Chapter in print. Willis responded by a meticulous drawn and written record (fig.21). In the course of his article he did for once allow himself a few sharp asides at the extremism of the Society. Willis, correctly dating the Barn to *c*.1250, considered its

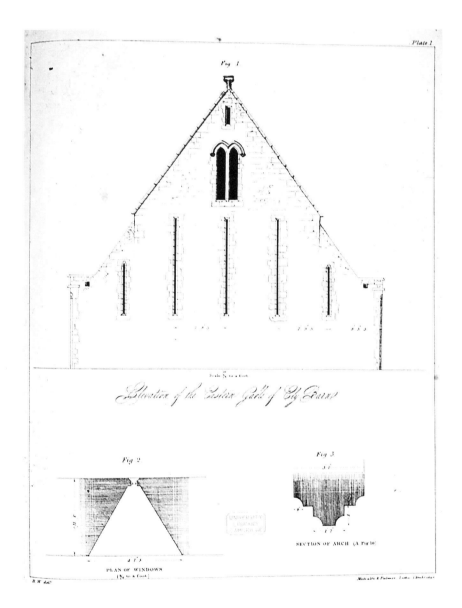

Fig. 21. Sextry barn, Ely
(Reproduced from their photograph by permission of the Syndics of Cambridge University Library).

plain vernacular details to be of more interest to architects than antiquarians but remarked how

> the anonymous writers of the Camden Society have insisted very strongly upon the symbolical nature of the arrangement of a church into nave and side-aisles, as involving the sacred number three, and have not only endeavoured to persuade their readers that this was an original motive for this division, but that it ought to be adhered to still for the same reason.[23]

Willis believed 'the original motive to have been purely derived' not from ecclesiology but 'from reasons of construction, and indeed the history of architecture shows it to have been so'. With scarcely concealed sarcasm he ended his article citing the 'violation [at the Sextry Barn] of another symbolical maxim of the Ecclesiologists which...they seem to have been at length reluctantly compelled to give... up', the presence of a triplet of lancets at both west and east ends. Such a triplet 'so symbolically sacred, according to Ecclesiologists, that it ought never to be employed even at the west end of a church, was here to be found at both ends of a medieval barn'.[24] The shaft went home. In a convoluted sentence the magazine referred to the 'compliment paid to us' by Willis in connecting the Society 'with one of the main sources of the interest which attached to the barn, by furnishing an argument against some theories which he seems to attribute to us'.[25]

Apart from this episode there is little evidence of Willis's attitude to Church questions. It is perhaps surprising that he never received any Church preferment – the great Adam Sedgwick was a canon of Norwich – but neither did he apparently look for secular honours beyond his Professorship and his Fellowship of the Royal Society. He had no need for extra income as he evidently enjoyed considerable private means. In 1870 he renounced his orders under the Clerical Disabilities Act of that year, which for the first time provided clergy with that facility.[26] This may have been due to Darwinian doubts or to reluctance to have an official status which he did not choose to practise. His eldest son was a curate at this time and went on to become the incumbent of a Somerset parish.

In Robert Willis's aversion to controversy he is perhaps more representative of his contemporaries than conspicuous people such as Pugin or Ruskin. It was not only the backward-looking or less gifted who deprecated attack on the Established Church. Willis's guiding principles seem to have been to respect the existing arrangements and to support those in authority. In his published papers he would always pay tribute to the proprietor of the building whether the Dean and Chapter of a cathedral or a private individual as at Glastonbury Abbey. He was scrupulous in his consideration

---

[23] CUL, Cambridge Coll., 8.
[24] Ibid.
[25] *Ecclesiologist*, II (1843), 169.
[26] I owe this information to my colleague Dr Brenda Hough of the Church of England Records Centre.

for the architects actually on the job, such as Cottingham at Hereford and in one incident, when consulted over the construction of some movable screens at Norwich Cathedral, he would only offer a sketch to show how his idea worked 'as I have no desire to interfere in any way with the proper functions of our clever friend, Blore'.[27]

I suggest that the main lesson to be learned from the scanty evidence for Willis's concern in religious matters is that one must not be beguiled by Pugin's *Contrasts* into drawing too sharp a divide, setting forward-looking churchmen whose right thinking in ecclesiology was matched by a knowledge of church archaeology against purblind conservatives. Robert Willis was sensitive to the ideas and enthusiasms of his time but he was too careful a scholar and too conscientious a scientist to allow his views to override the evidence. It is a fine tribute to him and to the Cambridge world in which he moved that through these qualities his work is still studied for its content, not for its period charm.

---

[27] CUL, Add MS 8170 f. 90, letter of 9 March 1846. Although the letter, addressed to 'Mr Dean', has been annotated by the cataloguer of the papers as 'of Ely', the cathedral in question must be Norwich, from its date and its reference to alterations in the choir.

Real Antiquity and the Ancient Object:
The Science of Gothic Architecture and the
Restoration of Medieval Buildings

Chris Miele

The before and after view was a favourite device of Victorian architects (figs 22 & 23). The transformations recorded in these images are shocking to late twentieth-century sensibilities, but to a nineteenth century eye restorations and reconstructions, far from destroying the authenticity of a medieval building, actually enhanced it. The Victorian architectural public simply did not place as high a premium on genuine ancient remains as we do today. Provided that copies were accurate and reconstructions based on reasoning from sound evidence, few people thought to question their validity. Underlying these different views are correspondingly different philosophies of history. The overwhelming majority of architects, critics, and historians writing before 1860 believed that architectural history and archaeology were inductive sciences with as much claim to objectivity and predictive accuracy as palaeontology, geology, or botany. Architectural forms were shaped by historical laws which, once described, could be mastered to direct future developments. Of course nowadays history, including the history practised by hard-headed empiricists, is far from being a simple objective enterprise. It is a matter of fact tempered by ideology and the discursive practices of history itself. Even historians who work with quantifiable evidence are loathe to predict large-scale historical developments. In line with these beliefs, no art historian working in a western tradition would ever argue that reconstructions have the same value as originals. Originals have, to paraphrase Walter Benjamin, a real presence in space and time, an absolute identity that cannot be replicated at will.[1]

Consequently, what W. R. Lethaby wrote earlier in this century about his Victorian forebears and their notions of history still rings true.

---

[1] Benjamin, 'Reproduction'.

Fig. 22. St Nicholas, Great Yarmouth. Woodcut illustration showing the church prior to its restoration by John Pollard Seddon. (Ecclesiologist, 1864, 34. Reproduced by permission of the author)

*Fig. 23. St Nicholas, Great Yarmouth. Woodcut illustration of the church following the proposed
restoration. (*Ecclesiologist, *1864, 35. Reproduced by permission of the author)*

It is impossible to give any notions of the violences and stupidities which were done in the name of 'restoration'. The crude idea seems to have been born of the root absurdity that art was shape and not substance; [that] our ancient buildings were appearances of what we call 'style'. When the architect had learned what his textbooks taught of the styles he could then provide thirteenth- or fourteenth-century features at pleasure, and even correct authentic old ones.[2]

Lethaby was right. Victorian restoration *was* informed by the idea that the value of architectural remains lay solely in their shape, that Gothic forms were sharply focused snapshots of a true antiquity that lay elsewhere, captured in 'textbook' notions of historical style. But what Lethaby failed to see, so caught up was he in rejecting Victorian values, were the ways in which his own highly spiritualised view of ancient art bore the negative imprint of Victorian historicism. The value of a genuine artefact always increases in direct proportion to its rarity. So while Victorian restoration did unquestionably compromise the authenticity of medieval buildings, it also provided the right conditions for the cult of the original to flourish. The 'textbook' approach and that of the connoisseur depend upon one another. For a time one may gain the upper hand but ultimately the two cannot exist separately. This was as true in Lethaby's day as it had been half a century before, in the middle decades of the nineteenth century, when, if you scratched the hard, shiny, and unsentimental surface of Victorian Gothic architecture, you were likely to get a glimpse of another sort of Gothic. From time to time an errant architect or critic would argue that only genuine ancient things deserved to be called 'ancient' and that such things were always of greater value than facsimiles, restorations, and reconstructions. This is exactly what happened in the early 1840s in response to George Gilbert Scott's plans to restore the ancient church of St Mary at Stafford.

SCOTT, PETIT, AND THE RESTORATION OF ST MARY STAFFORD

In 1840 George Gilbert Scott was asked to draw up plans for the restoration of St Mary Stafford. Like the near contemporary design of St Giles Camberwell, Stafford gave the young architect a chance to convince his critics in the Camden Society that he had learned the science of 'Ecclesiology'.[3] During 1840–1, when he was busy with his plans for Stafford, Scott consciously remade his Gothic manner, exchanging the spindly lancet style of his early churches (such as, for example, Holy Trinity in Shaftesbury of 1841) for a style that was sculptural, rugged, loaded with authentic medieval details, and, most important of all, pleasing to the influential Cambridge Camden Society. In later years Scott would describe this sudden shift in words which suggested a religious

---

[2]   Lethaby, *Webb*, 145.
[3]   Scott to E. J. Boyce of the Camden Society, 31 November 1841, 8, Box 4, G. G. Scott Papers. See also G. G. Scott *Recollections*, 103–6.

conversion, wishing to give a respectable gloss to what was in part professional opportunism. The approval of the Camden Society spelled a way out of the demoralising world of competitions and frantic appeals to the Poor Law Guardians.[4] Churchwork was genteel and virtually immune from the cycle of building booms and busts that racked the early Victorian building economy.[5]

The Stafford designs were ready by the summer of 1841 and set up in the west end of the church for the parishioners to inspect. In the accompanying report Scott assured his clients that the restoration was based on sound reasoning from incontrovertible evidence (figs 24 & 25). He promised that historical knowledge would give back to the church its 'hoary aspect of antiquity', implying that in its present unrestored state St Mary's was neither old nor venerable, a claim that appears to contradict the plain facts since the plans called for the complete rebuilding of roughly one third of the church to new designs.[6]

Fig. 24. St Mary, Stafford, as recorded in an engraving of c. *1800. (Reproduced by permission of the author)*

[4] G. G. Scott, *Recollections*, 88.
[5] See Miele, 'Victorian'.
[6] Masfen, *Views*, 7.

Fig. 25. St Mary, Stafford, as restored by George Gilbert Scott, 1841 and following.
(RCHME Crown Copyright)

Scott had his supporters and detractors in the vestry. The core of the opposition
disliked the collision of styles along the south, and most prominent elevation, where
the restored early Gothic transept came up hard against the original late Gothic nave
with hardly any concession to compositional principles. Surely, he was asked, it would
be better to make the entire church over into a perfect specimen of the Perpendicular
style? Scott and his defenders argued that by refusing to create a harmonious whole
the architect was actually demonstrating his commitment to historical truth. Instead
of improving the church by applying the outmoded ideals of the picturesque, he was
faithfully interpreting archaeological evidence, following the 'course dictated by the
building itself', as Scott put it.[7]

Stylistic heterogeneity and archaeological truth eventually won the day, silencing all
Scott's opponents except for one, the Reverend John Louis Petit (1801–68). Petit is

---

[7] Petit, *Restorations*, 2.

one of those Victorian amateurs who were widely regarded in their day but are now known mostly to experts: an original thinker, a widely admired draughtsman, a pioneer in the appreciation of vernacular architecture, an amateur architect, an apologist for the Romanesque revival on the Continent, and an important influence on Ruskin.[8] In short, he was a formidable opponent, all the more so because his objection amounted to a flat denial that any architect could give back the 'hoary aspect of antiquity' to an ancient fabric. The bone of contention was the south transept, which Petit criticised on archaeological and on philosophical grounds. The implications of this two-pronged attack are so far-reaching that each in its turn deserves consideration.[9]

Fig. 26. Scott's reconstruction of the south transept of St Mary, Stafford. (Published in Masfen, Views. Reproduced by permission of the author)

First, as to archaeology: Scott dated the unrestored south transept to the years following the collapse of the crossing spire in 1593. Had it not been restored into oblivion, the late sixteenth-century transept would now be admired as an interesting specimen of Gothic survival. However, in Scott's day all Gothic architecture executed after the Reformation was thought to be lacking in the essentially Christian spirit of real medieval work. The case for rebuilding the transept was compelling. Working from documents and fragments Scott concluded that the original east end and transept had been in an early thirteenth-century style, transitional between the Early English and the Decorated (fig.26). The Reverend Petit had no trouble with Scott's overall conclusions and even approved of the restored chancel where the traces of the original design were said to have been very clear. In the matter of the chancel, however, the eyewitness accounts of an Anglican clergyman are

8   Pevsner, *Writers*, 100. See also Watkin, *Rise*, 72–3.
9   For Scott's version of the dispute, Masfen, *Views*, 21–31, and G. G. Scott, *Recollections*, 97–100. Petit, *Restorations*, reproduces their correspondence.

suspect since Petit was probably not so much accepting the proof of archaeological evidence as he was yielding to the High Church taste for aggressively rebuilt and decorated chancels. This preference had been developing at least since the 1820s and in the wake of the Oxford Movement came to reflect a militant form of Anglicanism. Chancels had to radiate power and purity as blazing icons of faith, and it was just short of heresy to suggest that one go unrestored even at the expense of letting other parts of a church come to near ruin. In all likelihood Petit restricted his critique to the more secular and 'public' side of the church, the south elevation, rather than run the risk of confusing archaeology and theology.

The fragments on which Scott based the restored transept consisted of sections of the plinth and the weathermoulding of the former transept roof as well as several carved jamb shafts and three window keystones. Petit agreed that the end wall of the transept had probably been lit by three slender lancets and that it had terminated in a steeply pitched gable, but he saw no evidence to suggest that the window jambs were as elaborately moulded as Scott made them out to be, nor did he think that diminutive offset buttresses had run up through the plinth to frame the central lancet. Petit was certain that the mouldings around the lancets had been fewer and simpler and that the trio of lights had been set under a recessed comprising arch. His transept, in short, was of a decidedly Early Gothic character, while Scott's transept was suspended in the process of style change, with features taken from the Early English and Decorated styles but with the balance tipped to the latter by the transept's overall effect. Scott's reconstruction supported the widely-held view that a wall pierced by traceried lights (a developing characteristic of the Decorated style) came about by experiment with a fixed repertory of English forms.

The south transept was debated from October 1841 to January 1842, when, with no sign of either party giving in, it was agreed to submit the matter to arbitration by a joint committee of the Cambridge Camden and Oxford Architectural Societies. In May 1842 the Oxbridge committee found in favour of Scott with a few words of warning. Scott's might not be the only correct interpretation of the fragments but it was at least consistent with the evidence. What his transept lacked in specificity was more than made up for by the quality of the design, which was based on a sound understanding of medieval principles; it was accurate in a general sense because the architect had used his knowledge of historical style to fill in factual gaps.[10] The decision was a great compliment to Scott's skill as an archaeologist and as a modern Goth, a seal of approval that he would recall with pride in later years.[11]

Petit's second objection was based on purely philosophical grounds, and was not even addressed by the joint committee perhaps because it called into question the very notion of certainty and authenticity that underpinned its decision. Petit stated explicitly

[10] 10 and 28 May 1842, Oxford Arch. Soc., Corr.
[11] Masfen, *Views*, 28–31.

that restorations that relied on the interpretation of fragmentary evidence and large-scale reconstructions could never be accurate because archaeology and architectural history were not objective and perfectible systems of knowledge, no matter how soundly they might be based on inductive analysis from objective evidence. The proof he offered for his scepticism was both concrete and elegantly simple. The people of Stafford who had known St Mary's before the restoration would know with absolute certainty that the restored church was not the one their forefathers had looked on, and this knowledge broke the continuous chain of perception that was the only guarantee of authenticity and of age.[12] This concern for the townspeople was a little insincere. Petit was merely using the nameless inhabitants rhetorically to apply a perennial problem of philosophy to a critique of restoration. In essence, Petit was arguing that our knowledge of objects and causes, in this case our recognition of ancientness, derives from sense perceptions alone, the 'constant conjunction of experience', to quote David Hume. The alternative position is, to run the risk of oversimplifying, that knowledge is generated by relating the evidence of the senses to mental structures that are only partly dependent on experience. Petit was arguing that no amount of archaeological learning could overcome the identity of the unrestored transept as it was established by common sense, the innocent eye of an ordinary viewer. If antiquity is defined strictly in relation to native perception, then only stones that are ancient in and of themselves, those that have been looked on continuously by human beings over centuries, are literally ancient. Such ancient things have something like the quality that Michael Fried called 'objecthood'; they confront the viewer as independent and complete entities, having a life of their own that comes from being unique. This identity cannot be copied or reconstructed under any circumstances.

Scott was not, it must be said, of a philosophical turn of mind, but he could see the implications of Petit's 'literal antiquity' very well, and responded accordingly, admitting that

> Though [the south transept's] appearance will be different from what has been seen by present inhabitants, or by some few generations before them, and though it may appear modern to those who measure antiquity by the extent of their own memories...it will, in fact, have a far more ancient character than it has now.[13]

Scott's brand of antiquity was the product of characteristic marks that were totally divorced from their supporting material.[14] Of course Scott could see the difference between a literally ancient thing and its modern replica or reconstruction, it was just that this difference had no value for him because architectural history told him the true form of the ancient thing. In Scott's mind the unrestored church of St Mary was

---

[12] Ibid., 22–3.
[13] Ibid., 25.
[14] On other contemporary meanings of 'character', Rowe, 'Character', 72.

merely a reflection of its former great self as known through historical precepts. It was as if ancient matter was merely the neutral mould on which the true form of antiquity was impressed, and once the skin of antiquity has been stripped away by copying or reconstruction, the stone itself was a useless carcase fit for the antiquarian collector or for sale as building rubble. In this view material functions as a point of reference or index to a system of historical description. Ancient stones are valuable to the extent that they fulfill their representational function, and I believe that this is the best explanation for Scott's use of the word 'character', which he means in its first sense, as a letter in an alphabet or a word in any written system.

Consciously or not, Scott was defining antiquity in Platonic terms: literally ancient buildings are mere manifestations, illusory and fleeting instances of antiquity that come into being and then decay without altering the true form of antiquity. It is the view of a philosophical Realist, hence it is fitting to call antiquity as known in relation to character 'Real Antiquity', a designation I make mindful of the fact that 'Real' here has a meaning opposite of its everyday use. Real Antiquity is an amalgam of observations that have been collected together, regimented, and analysed by historians in much the same way as artists since the Renaissance had studied ancient sculpture and human anatomy to derive an ideal image of the human form.[15]

TAXONOMY, THE PARADIGM, AND THE DISCOVERY OF TRUE ANTIQUITY

By the time Scott had mounted his defence, the search for the form of Real Antiquity had been underway for close to a century. The great transformation in medieval research began around 1750. Before then the study of medieval remains tended to concentrate on written records not the physical evidence of ancient fabrics.[16] The periodic interest that early topographical writers and antiquarians showed in medieval buildings did not lead to a system of classification based on morphology or sequence.[17] After 1750 medieval research developed as a result of conscious methodological refinements calculated to make architectural history into a science of classification that worked by inductive analysis, like botany or geology.[18] From constant matching and grouping there emerged a taxonometric system able to locate any artefact precisely in a chronological sequence of morphological differences.[19]

What is most important for the present context is not the derivation of this architectural taxonomy but the effect that it has on the status of the literally ancient thing, since taxonomy made it possible for Scott to believe that he had given antiquity

---

[15] For an analogous and near contemporary debate on the status of the original in relation to the copy, see Holmes's 1859 essay on photography, 'Stereoscope' and chapter two in Ewen, *Politics of Style*.

[16] Momigliano, 'History' and Piggott, 'Antiquarian'.

[17] With the exception of John Aubrey's precocious manuscript. Colvin, 'Aubrey'.

[18] Frew, 'Aspect'.

[19] Rodden, 'Development' and Hull, 'Taxonomy'.

back to Stafford church by rebuilding almost half of it. The function of taxonomy is to convert particular objects into cues that refer to an abstract system of knowledge. The process of referencing subordinates the existence of individual artefacts to general concepts in order to make an identification, and nowhere is this absorption of the specific within the universal more apparent than in the selection of one particular monument as a paradigm, the first stage in the evolution of any science of classification. A paradigm is not a law itself but an object in the world that reflects a principle as nearly as tangible substance can and in this way serves as a fixed standard of measurement for similar structures. There is always a gap in resemblance between this ideal specimen and the principles it illustrates, a difference that can never disappear, because the true form of any law must be conceptual and finds its most perfect expression in language.

Once an object has been selected to be a paradigm its substance undergoes a dramatic transformation. Take a monument that has been a paradigm of early thirteenth-century style since at least the 1770s, Salisbury Cathedral.[20] As a style paradigm it assumes a leading position among buildings with similar forms, possessing the highest value within the style-class of Early English architecture. In order for the idea of the Early English to remain vivid, Salisbury must be constantly replicated to preserve the integrity of our idea of the style, and as a result picturesque decay cannot be tolerated, at least in the days before photographic recording. Images of Salisbury, fragments of its style-identity, are parcelled out among other monuments to make style identifications, and any comparable features assume something of the eternal value of the paradigm. These style-typical features must also be replicated in order for any building's historical identity to be preserved. A building having features comparable to Salisbury, such as, for example, the splendid church at West Walton in Norfolk, loses something of its uniqueness by becoming a specimen of the Early English through its resemblance to Salisbury, and the points of style correspondence must be kept fresh lest West Walton lose its position in the narrative which we know as the history of medieval architecture. But isolated from the casual architectural tourist, it can at least tolerate more picturesque incident than a paradigmatic monument. West Walton has, in other words, a lower order of Real Antiquity than Salisbury and as a result a little more individuality.[21]

In the 1770s the way forward to an architectural taxonomy was shown by James Essex (1722–84), the Cambridge architect and antiquarian who called for a programme of collaborative research to define a system for dating medieval architecture by visual analysis and comparison with style paradigms whose dates were known by reference to documents.[22] Correspondence through learned societies and journals was necessary to collect data and test hypotheses, and the truth would be reached in the crucible of

---

[20] Bentham, 'Remarks' and Pevsner, *Wiltshire*, 392.

[21] E. A. Freeman (*Preservation*) propounded the idea that the status of different monuments in the history of medieval architecture had to be taken into account when considering proposals for their restoration.

[22] Essex, 'Lincoln', 150 (read 16 March 1775).

discussion and debate.[23] Essex is a good example of the first generation of architectural taxonomers not simply because he understood that architectural history had to begin with an objective analysis of forms, but also because, like any budding natural historian, he believed that historical knowledge had to have a practical application, in his case the restoration of ancient buildings and the design of new ones in a convincing medieval manner. For Essex taxonomy seems to have held within it the promise of a truthful restoration, a causal linkage revealed in papers on Lincoln Cathedral and the Round Church at Cambridge he read to the Society of Antiquaries in 1775 and 1781. In them documentary research is matched with visual observations in order to produce drawn reconstructions of obscured Romanesque fabrics. The analysis and restoration of the Round Church is particularly interesting for showing the give-and-take that exists even in this early phase of architectural taxonomy between universal concepts and individual instances. Conjecturally restored to its pure form and convincingly dated, Essex used the Round Church as a point of reference, an ideal schema for other churches with western rounds that are then, in turn, given a specific historical identity.[24]

For all his methodological sophistication, Essex's analyses were hampered by lack of precise terms, a shortcoming younger contemporaries were keen to redress. The appointment of Richard Gough (born 1735) in 1771 as Director of the Society of Antiquaries encouraged the emergence of a mature architectural taxonomy and a programme of research similar to the one Essex outlined.[25] Gough wanted to use the Society as a forum for collaborative historical research founded on the testing of evidence in debate.[26] The title of the journal founded in 1770 during his ascendancy, *Archaeologia*, was selected for its scientific connotations. The basis of the new science was to be neutral, topographical description and record collecting of the kind pioneered by William Camden in his *Britannia*. Gough brought out a new edition of this great work in 1789 because he believed Camden's neutral format provided an excellent armature on which scholars could build a complete documentary history.[27] Gough extolled the virtues of the early, heroic days of antiquarianism, the late sixteenth and early seventeenth centuries, when scholars made the search for an objective, scientific record of history their chief goal.[28] Implicit in this call for a return to basics was a criticism of the antiquarian writers who had served as pamphleteers during the troubled period of the Civil War and Commonwealth, distorting historical evidence for political expedience. Unlike these unprincipled scholars, Camden and his immediate followers had, as Gough put it, 'first restored Antiquity to Britain, and Britain to Antiquity', a formula that suggests that scholarship manufactures antiquity by apprehending its

---

[23] Cocke, 'Attitudes' especially 78–84 and Watkin, *Rise*, 53–4.
[24] Essex, 'Lincoln' and `Round Churches' (read 24 May 1781) See also Cocke, `Essex'.
[25] Evans, *Antiquaries*, 135–6, 143–6, 160, 191–2.
[26] Gough, *Topography*, xii.
[27] Camden, *Britannia*, vii.
[28] Piggott, 'Camden', 209–10.

true form and that outside the confines of precise historical knowledge antiquity simply does not exist.[29] As a strong-minded revisionist, Gough had very definite views about what was wrong with his immediate predecessors. From the heights scaled by Camden, antiquarians had become

> men of uncultivated minds, fit only to pore over musty records, and grovel among ruined walls; shut up in closets from the commerce of life and secluded from information even in their own way...Whoever sits down to compile the history and antiquities of a county [he concluded] should confirm the evidence he collects from books and manuscripts...or by correspondence with other students.[30]

Gough's own work is fascinating for the attention it pays to what is today known as methodology. Perhaps his best known publication, *Sepulchral Monuments in Great Britain*, part one of which appeared in 1786, begins with a lengthy defence of the decision to present artefacts in eight classes, from those with triangular lids, to brasses, wall tombs, and so on, and then within each class to establish regularities, such as the placement of symbols, so that all the objects considered are carefully plotted on a two-dimensional grid of historical meaning. Gough believed that monuments were primarily important as records, reflecting as a neutral medium the forces that shaped medieval society, a preoccupation reflected in the book's full title, *Sepulchral Monuments in Great Britain, Applied to Illustrate the History of Families, Manners, Habits and Arts, at the Different Periods from the Norman Conquest to the Seventeenth Century*. The reputation of this book as a document in the Romantic movement is totally at odds with its author's intention to discern the true shape of history beneath decaying, chiselled surfaces of monuments.[31]

A most important figure in the reforming circle of Gough at the Antiquaries was the Catholic priest, Vicar Apostolic of the Western District of England, the Reverend Dr John Milner (1752–1826). In the 1790s Milner pressed the need for a single system of description on his colleagues and readers. Without this system, notions of style would remain imperfect exposing medieval buildings to the risk of ill-judged or misinformed restorations.[32] An adequate system of description would teach the correct rules of medieval architecture, making it as impossible to mix the medieval styles as it would be to mingle the details of one classical order with another.[33] Even though Milner resorted to this common analogy, he understood that the styles of medieval architecture were utterly unlike the classical orders. Doric, Ionic, and Corinthian were synchronous systems that could be used together in the same monument, and although there was some idea, derived from Vitruvius, that the Doric predated the Ionic, and

---

[29] Camden, *Britannia*, ix.
[30] Gough, *Topography*, I, xxii.
[31] Gough, *Sepulchral*, lxxxiii-viii, cxii, cxvii.
[32] Milner, 'Ecclesiastical', preface, xi.
[33] Milner, *Treatise*, 123–4. The text was written in 1798 but only first published in 1813.

the Ionic the Corinthian, these historical associations had become so remote as to be meaningless. Milner realized that a new and accurate system ought not to describe medieval styles as simple static essences but be able to portray the evolution of one style into another. There is a persistent tension in all historical taxonomies between an image of stasis and the obvious fact that forms change over time. By the turn of the century he had solved the problem by using the terms, 'First Pointed', 'Second Pointed', and 'Third Pointed'. Although to our way of thinking these categories are obvious, they were far more amenable to taxonomy than most then in use because they referred not only to sequence but also to the distinctive physical feature of the Gothic, the pointed arch itself.[34]

Another late eighteenth-century innovator was John Carter (1748–1817), a draughtsman for the Society of Antiquaries, who also abandoned the classical analogy for a system of classification derived from an analysis of medieval buildings themselves. Although Carter used the word 'order' in the title of his two volume work on the history of ancient and modern British architecture, he identified medieval buildings as having 'Class One', 'Two', or 'Three' characteristics.[35] Carter's prose style was a model of clarity, far in advance of Milner's, even if his dates were flawed. And where Milner's work relied on medieval documents, Carter, who could not read Latin, had to focus almost exclusively on visual evidence. He was perhaps more willing to interpret buildings on the evidence of their forms alone than any of his contemporaries, and when the vagaries of a fabric tested his analytic skill he did not shrink from the challenge. Take his description of the west front of Dunstable Priory, a wild and ungainly jumble of features by anyone's standards:

> ...as all conjecture seems to have been exhausted to account for the mixture of styles seen in this front...it is not the less fortunate in presenting to us those many characters which are found in our Saxon edifices down to the sixteenth century; but will also be a further confirmation of the progress of the pointed architectural system as we have delineated it...[36]

There is no need to explain its freakish appearance by reference to a document, nor is there any sense that the lack of architectural coherence harms its monumental quality. The random and savage appearance actually intensifies the Priory's historic value, making it a veritable textbook of medieval style history.

THOMAS RICKMAN (1776–1841) AND THE *ATTEMPT*

Although the need for a shared system of description and classification was widely recognised in the first quarter of the nineteenth century, no single model emerged to

---

[34] Ibid., xii-xviii, 90–1, 103–7, 112–4, 118, and *Dissertation*, 26–7.

[35] Carter, *Orders*.

[36] Ibid., I, 35, pl. XL.

coordinate the efforts of a growing number of scholars until Thomas Rickman's *Attempt to Discriminate the Styles of English Architecture from the Conquest to the Reformation* of 1817.[37] Rickman's *Attempt* is known today largely because it formalised the now familiar sequence of styles: Norman, Early English, Decorated, and Perpendicular. (Rickman's only contribution was in fact 'Perpendicular'; 'Norman' was widely used before him, Milner had coined 'Early English', and Britton 'Decorated'.)[38] But his real and lasting achievement consisted in taking the work of earlier taxonomers to its logical conclusion by devising a complete primer to medieval architectural styles with barely any reference to actual monuments in the body of the text. The *Attempt* presents the styles as coherent systems, each described by the same terms in exactly the same sequence: Early English doors, windows, arches, piers, buttresses, etc., then Decorated doors, windows, arches, piers, buttresses, and so on, until all the kit components of every style have been noted. In this modest handbook there is no suggestion that some aspects of medieval building remain to be explained; the *Attempt* assumes that the totality of medieval style can be comprehended by its terms. Planning is mentioned only in passing and methods of construction or composition hardly touched on. Reading Rickman cold gives the impression that the entire historic value of a structure lay locked in its characteristic features, each of which finds a place in a specific chapter and subheading of the *Attempt*. The first and most basic level of historical analysis is complete when the forms of the structure have been transposed into categories, 'Rickmanese', as Summerson unkindly called it.

The *Attempt*'s great achievement was to separate style from instances of style. Milner and Carter had described medieval style in terms of medieval monuments. Rickman reversed the equation describing medieval monuments in terms of medieval style. Rickman refers only rarely to actual buildings in early editions of the *Attempt*, removing them to an appendix gazetteer in which the buildings are grouped under style rubrics. Rickman deliberately made the book pocket-sized so that it could double as a travel guide, and in subsequent editions he expanded the gazetteer, throwing the net of taxonomy ever wider without significantly changing his descriptive formula. The taxonomy was truthful, later editors noted, though perhaps in need of a little adjustment.[39] So while the actual specimens varied, Rickman's antiquity was left untouched, riding high above ancient matter.[40] In this process of subordination, literally ancient objects lost their real presence since all objects in the same class were made to resemble one another to a certain extent. There is no room in this sort of antiquity for the authentic original; instead all literally ancient things share in a common antiquity that exists separate from the stuff of which they are made.

---

[37] Watkin, *Rise*, 56–9.
[38] Baily, 'Rickman', 313.
[39] As J. H. Parker noted after buying the copyright to Rickman's *Attempt* (*Oxford Arch. Soc., Rules*, 1844, 15, note C).
[40] Aldrich, 'Gothic', LXV (1985), 427–33, 428–9 and T. M. Rickman, *Rickman*, 38.

The dissolving of unique buildings in the cauldron of medieval style is most strikingly illustrated by the simple engravings published in the *Attempt*. Although dismissed by some contemporaries as mere imaginary illustrations, they were in fact benchmarks in the history of the Gothic Revival precisely because of their hypothetical nature.[41] Rickman did not reproduce actual monuments as paradigms, but designed each to be a picture of style itself, an image that reflects the slippage between original and reproduction that is the necessary result of any taxonometric system and an essential precondition of Victorian restoration. The plate labelled 'Norman' shows a sequence of bay elevations with the details in each varied to demonstrate that the style remains entire despite the substitution of one form for another. This is precisely the level of authenticity that Scott was aiming to achieve at Stafford, not an authenticity of individual details but an authenticity of possibilities and likelihoods.

It has to be said that the now vast literature on British architectural historiography pays scant attention to the effects of taxonomy on the course of the Revival, as if the relationship between words and things was incidental. Illustrated *compendia* are judged more important than phrases, a state of play that has harmed Rickman's reputation. Indeed, Charles Eastlake was not sure how to present Rickman in his 1872 *History of the Gothic Revival*. Eastlake grudgingly acknowledged the enormous popularity of the *Attempt* but concluded that Rickman had lacked talent and inspiration. At one point he suggested that the fault lay with Rickman's Quakerism, which had prevented him from exploring the higher sacramental and artistic truths manifested by medieval churches, but nothing could have been further from the truth.[42] Rickman's thinking was in fact heavily influenced by the programme of the Liverpool Philosophical Society at whose meetings he delivered his first papers on architecture. The Society was dedicated to the advancement of the inductive natural sciences and did not allow any ethical or religious doctrines to enter into its official proceedings.[43] Although Rickman's training as an apothecary had prepared him for this approach. Like Carter he had little choice in the matter since he too could not read Latin.[44]

Rickman's brand of architectural history deliberately focused on the shapes of things, just as Georges Cuvier, the great French comparative anatomist and palae-ontologist, had to rely on the mute, physical evidence of fossils. Real Antiquity makes carved stones into things that are very like fossil remains. Fossils are not literally ancient things but impressions left by absent things, valuable as records once they have been sorted and then used as evidence to reconstruct the past. Carved stones were reflections too, images of the real form of ancientness which resided elsewhere. The methods of classification used by Cuvier and Rickman worked from the same

---

[42] Eastlake, *Revival*, 125–6, 130.

[43] Baily, 'Rickman', 135.

[44] Ibid., 148–9.

[41] Britton, *Antiquities*, V, 97, as noted in Aldrich, 'Rickman', 427–33.

premise, namely, that the chief physical characteristics of an entity, in Rickman's case the treatment of openings in the wall or in Cuvier's case the method for taking nourishment, determine the nature of the entire style or species. And like Cuvier, Rickman wanted the results of his system to lead other scholars to synthesise a general theory of the past. In the spirit of collaboration he invented a blank questionnaire to speed the recording and sorting of medieval churches according to the taxonomy of style.[45]

Although there is no direct evidence to suggest that Rickman read Cuvier's *Lectures on Comparative Anatomy* (an English translation was published in 1802), later Revivalists compared the two explicitly. Addressing the Leicester Architectural Society in 1865, Matthew Holbeche Bloxam (1805–88), the Rugby architectural historian who was a friend and admirer of Rickman, wrote that

> Mr. Rickman...was the father of modern architecture in the scientific sense...he first discovered that one age built in a particular manner, and another age in another style...and men of ability...could tell them from the slightest fragment, almost within a year, when the first part of a church was built and when the second was erected, by canons as certain as those which enabled Cuvier, from a single bone to reproduce the whole animal; for they had laws in their own minds as closely connected with the minds of the builders of former ages, as laws upon which the Creator had constructed each wonderful fabric. Those laws were not founded on caprice but reason...[46]

Rickman's *Attempt* gained in popularity over the 1820s, with a handful of scholars adopting its terms and new editions appearing in 1825 and 1835.[47] In the 1830s several writers praised the *Attempt* and recommended its nomenclature as the most precise: there was Bloxam's own primer, which went through a staggering nine editions between 1829 and 1849, Whewell's *Architectural Notes on German Churches* of 1830 (with editions in 1835 and 1841), Willis's *Remarks on the Architecture of the Middle Ages...* of 1835, and Parker's *Glossary* of 1836. This generation of pocket-sized field guides was directed to a new corps of architectural observers, fieldworkers, and specimen collectors drawn from every walk of genteel life, the same people who compiled statistical profiles of local species of butterfly or geological features. The scientific impulse combined with increased leisure time led to the foundation of amateur societies that blended archaeology, architectural history, and natural history in their official proceedings. The first purely architectural societies to be founded after 1839 were organized on the model of earlier scientific societies[48] and promoted the spread of Rickman's taxonomy further.[49]

---

[45] Ibid., Appendix VII.
[46] Bloxam, 'Leicester', lviii.
[47] Simpson, *Fonts*, i-ii and Whewell, *German Churches*, 132.
[48] Rudwick, 'Foundation' and Piggott, 'Arch. Socs.'. on the history of palaeontology, Rudwick, *Fossils*.
[49] *Oxford Arch. Soc., Rules*, 3–4.

ECCLESIOLOGY AND THE CHURCH SCHEME

The claims of the Cambridge Camden Society, founded in May 1839, to promote an exacting science of 'Ecclesiology' must be seen in the light of this earlier development. 'Ecclesiology' was based on taxonomy and a precise classificatory vocabulary. 'Nothing', wrote one of the Society's anonymous reviewers,

> conduces more to the diffusion and popularity of any science than its being provided with a sufficient complement of names for every part and subdivision of the subject to which it belongs. This appears to be the true secret of the almost universal taste for botany, and other minutely classified sciences, which immediately followed upon the publication of the Linnaean system...[50]

The Camdenians wanted to impose near laboratory conditions on the study and description of medieval architecture and to this end they called upon their eager membership to help in the collection of data. Their most widely circulated publication, *A Few Hints on the Practical Study of Ecclesiastical Antiquities*, was intended to 'point out what should be observed, and how to observe it by the rule laid down'. Random observations or the testimony of a picturesque view did not lead to firm conclusions since these could not be compared systematically or sorted statistically. *Few Hints* concludes with a twelve-page questionnaire, what the Society called the 'Church Scheme', to be filled out on a church visit. It had blanks for nearly every imaginable variation in style or arrangement, allowing any monument to be transposed into a series of brief notes. Similar questionnaires had been used since the seventeenth century to collate local history publications and had been instrumental to Rickman's study.[51] The Camden Schemes were printed in far greater numbers than any before, and sold at bulk discounts to members and corresponding societies. There was a plan to pool resources with the Oxford Architectural Society to create a Scheme library recording every single medieval church in England and Wales, as well as foreign examples. This consortium was later joined by the Exeter Diocesan Architectural Society.[52] The affiliated societies called on members to complete Schemes for remote churches to help in the creation of this national monument library[53] and by 1841 over 400 Schemes were available for study in the Camden Society's rooms.[54] A church that had been pushed through the Church-Scheme sieve by the Camdenians became an image of Real Antiquity, a sequence of historical signs. And the Scheme promoted comparative analysis of a large number of monuments by making it easier to record historic structures to a fixed standard. The discovery of correct principles would result

---

[50] Willis, [review].
[51] Piggott, *Stukeley*, 11; Lhwyd, 'Parochalia'; and Gunther, *Lhwyd*.
[52] Oxford Arch. Soc., Corr., Dep. d. 538, 22 November 1841, 22 February 1842, 29 June 1843. EDAS, *Transactions*, II (1847), 15.
[53] Camden Soc., *Few Hints*, 20.
[54] Camden Soc., *Annual Report*, 1841, 57–68. *Camden Soc., RIBA.*

from the analysis of a large study sample. Restoration as advised by the Cambridge Camden Society and the dozens of societies established during the 1840s consisted in the purification and completion of the sequence of shapes analysed in Church-Scheme fashion.

For some Camdenians Church-Scheme compilation became an all-consuming passion. John Mason Neale (1818–66), a founder member of the Society, visited and recorded twenty-six different churches on six days in January and February 1840, fourteen near Cambridge and the rest along the Sussex coast where he was overseeing the restoration of St Nicholas Old Shoreham to designs by J. C. Buckler.[55] In April and May he covered eight counties in five days recording thirty-one churches.[56] In all his notes Neale followed Rickman's method closely; indeed they are remarkable for their brevity and the sheer lack of interest shown in the picturesque qualities of ancient architecture (fig.27). Neale was positively hostile to the tradition of the amateur 'sketcher' whom he thought wasted time on insignificant details in search of a pretty picture (echoing a bias articulated by Gough in the 1780s).[57] He even went so far as to accuse picturesque view-makers of triviality, which he saw reflected in their casual manner of conduct within sacred precincts and in the souvenir and tourist trade that catered to them.[58] When in the course of his pious wanderings Neale met a clergyman, he lost no opportunity to advise on possible courses of restoration. He was often invited to have a look at churches in need of restoration or even to lecture a collection of local clergymen at luncheons held in his honour.[59] Neale is reputed to have kept up this kind of tourism for his whole life. In 1861, aged forty-three, he boasted of having visited and analysed over ninety churches in a three-week tour of Spain, raising his lifetime total of churches visited, he calculated, to 2,746.[60] Such careful reckoning illuminates the Ecclesiological fixation on specimen collecting and objectivity.

What was the undoing of such a seemingly perfect combination of theory and practice? The answer is certainly too complex to set out in a conclusion, but there is room enough to present a few thoughts on the matter. The challenge to what Lethaby termed the 'textbook' approach to architecture with the emergence of the conservation movement came about as a result of scarcity or, more appropriate in these days of ecological awareness, resource depletion. Statistics gathered in 1872–3 showed that most of the 8,000–odd medieval churches in England and Wales had suffered some measure of restoration since 1840, and, furthermore, that the pace of restoration had accelerated since 1855.[61] The news sparked the anti-restoration lobby to life, prompting

[55] *Camden Soc., Lambeth.*
[56] Ibid., Vol. II.
[57] Gough, *Topography*, xxiii-iv.
[58] Neale, *Hierologus*, iv-v; and Paley *Guide*, vii, and *Restorers*.
[59] Miele, *Gothic*, ch. 11.
[60] Lawson, *Neale*, 29–34, 61, 333–4.
[61] 'Church Building', *Parliamentary*.

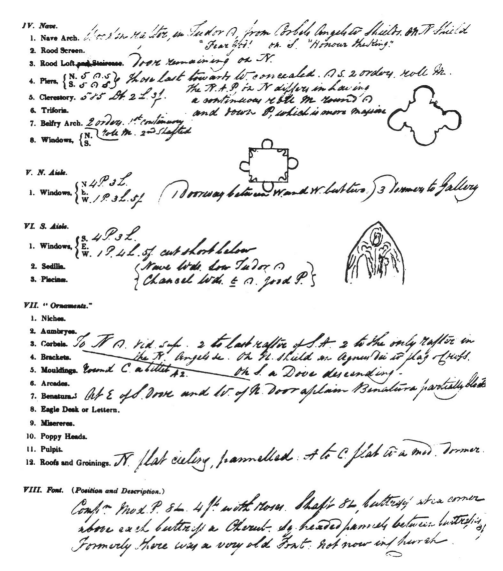

Fig. 27. *Church Scheme compiled by John Mason Neale on 31 December 1839 for St Dunstan, Stepney.*
(Lambeth Palace Library MS 1977, f. 137v. Reproduced by kind permission of the Archbishop of
Canterbury and the Trustees of Lambeth Palace Library)

one of its prophets, John Ruskin, to reject the RIBA Gold Medal in protest on the
grounds that the official body of the architectural profession had stood idly by while
unscrupulous practitioners had by over-restored the nation's patrimony to line their

pockets.[62] The survey confirmed what many architectural tourists would have suspected: in the 1840s unrestored churches were still common; after 1865 they were hard to come by. Ceaseless restoration put more and more images of Real Antiquity into circulation, mass-producing it according to a restricted range of principles and standard types as set out in architectural handbooks like the *Attempt* and in the principles of Ecclesiology. Like any mass-reproductive process, this manufacture of Real Antiquity converted the original, literally ancient things that managed to escape unscathed into valuable items. The idea of the authentic original emerged against a backdrop of cheapened, mass-produced multiples. Walter Benjamin's reflections on the work of art in the age of mechanical reproduction offer what I believe to be the best reason for the rise of the conservation movement:

> Even the most perfect reproduction of a work [of art] is utterly lacking in one element: its presence in time and space, its unique existence at the place where it happens to be...One might subsume the eliminated in the term 'aura' and go on to say: that which withers in the age of mechanical reproduction in the aura of the work of art.[63]

The 'aura' of antiquity is precisely the quality that William Morris and his colleagues in the Society for the Protection of Ancient Buildings wanted to maintain. The duty of the SPAB, Morris told the audience at the first annual meeting, was to 'guard the life and soul of monuments', not their shapes and forms. It is ironic that this highly spiritualised view of architecture, what Riegl termed the 'cult of monuments', should be framed by Morris just as his commitment to a Materialist view of history was deepening.[64]

It is an inconsistency shared by several of his left-wing followers. Lethaby, to take the most conspicuous example of someone who trained at the feet of Morris and Webb at committee meetings of the Society for the Protection of Ancient Buildings, developed a mystical theory of architecture from an interest in building materials and craft. Later one wing of the early Modern Movement would adopt this mixture of matter and spirit for its very own, dubbing it the *Zeitgeist*. Here the ironies multiply. For if the taxonomers are rightly blamed for using the methods of natural science to contradict the evidence of the senses, applying their discoveries ruthlessly to the restoration of ancient buildings, then so too can we find fault with their critics, the promoters of the Arts and Crafts Movement, for striving after the metaphysical seed at the heart of innate matter, both ancient and modern. Rickman and Scott located authenticity in the stratosphere of historical style, in the dessicated conceptual space of architectural histories and handbooks. But Morris, by calling ancient remains sacred,

[62] 'Ruskin and the RIBA Gold Medal' in Ruskin, *Works*, XXXIV, 513–6, and Miele, 'Victorian'.
[63] Benjamin, 'Reproduction', 220.
[64] Riegl, 'Monuments'.

by arguing that ancientness was an inimitable and elusive quality, and by refusing even to attempt to prize antiquity from its lithic shell, fetishised the past. Surely without meaning to, Morris made it possible for less sophisticated followers to develop an unhealthy love of old things, to believe that the past must be approached in hushed tones, with back stooped and eyes averted. Unwittingly he encouraged the most retrograde elements within the heritage industry to thrive.

Antiquity Inventoried: Museums and 'National Antiquities' in the Mid Nineteenth Century

Arthur MacGregor

The founders of the Archaeological Institute and of the British Archaeological Association were possessed of a particular view of antiquity in which the past of our own country was accorded a greater significance than had been acknowledged by the majority of their antiquarian predecessors or was yet recognized by the public at large. Although precocious in their own land, the sentiments that they embraced were entirely in harmony with contemporary developments in continental Europe, where national consciousness had been mobilised in the previous decades as never before. In addition to its political dimensions this movement found expression in the art and literature of the Romantics and in the establishment of museums that served as veritable shrines to the national characters of their respective founding nations. The National Museum in Budapest, for instance, played a key role in the forging of a distinct Magyar identity, rejecting the cultural as well as political imperialism implicit in Austro-Hungarian rule; in Prague a similar part was played in forwarding Czech interests within the Habsburg empire by the founding in 1818 of the National Museum whose importance then is still proclaimed by its dominant position in Wenceslas Square; the founding of the Germanisches Nationalmuseum in 1852 represented only the most striking event in a whole chain of developments that followed the conclusion of the Congress of Vienna in which the disparate German principalities came to acknowledge a common cultural as well as ethnic identity; while in Copenhagen the decision in 1807 to establish a new national museum may be seen not as a product of administrative rationalisation but rather as a proclamation of Denmark's expanding view of its own distinctive identity.

Britain's insular character and comparatively long-established political stability may have diluted to some degree the imperatives of nationalism, but the Romantic movement that was its cultural offspring had its adherents here,[1] with Sir Walter Scott playing perhaps the most influential role. The founding of the twin archaeological societies, although not overtly nationalistic in character, can usefully be seen in the light of this movement: the practice of carrying their annual conference to the provinces had an evangelising dimension that contrasted with the established routine of the Society of Antiquaries of London, as did their broadly-based and accessible membership structure – both characteristics that reflected the popularising character of the Continental movements already mentioned.

SCOTT AND THE SCOTTISH ANTIQUARIES

Sir Walter himself may form a useful starting point for the exposition of a broader suggestion that antiquities began to impinge more directly on the national consciousness at this time. Scott's antiquarian cast of mind had led him to amass at Abbotsford an extensive collection, comprising numbers of historical relics, some of them associated with the characters who peopled his works, others of more general antiquarian interest.[2] When a new edition of the *Waverley Novels* came to be prepared in 1842, ten years after Scott's death, the publishers seized on the idea of enlisting these antiquities, as it were, in the cause of art:

> This is the age of graphically illustrated Books [they declared] and it remained to affix to these Works, so interwoven everywhere with details of historical and antiquarian interest, such Engraved Embellishments as...[the author's]...personal tastes and resources would most probably have induced him to place before students of antiquity and lovers of art.

Where the collection at Abbotsford could not supply appropriate images the publisher's artists were packed off to find alternatives in the museum of the Society of Antiquaries of Scotland.[3]

Confirmation of this newly forged relationship can be found in the first printed catalogue of the collections of the Scottish Antiquaries, which appeared in 1849: here, with a piquant symmetry, the publishers of the illustrated edition of the *Waverley Novels* are acknowledged for allowing *their* illustrations of the Edinburgh antiquities to be reproduced in the catalogue.[4] The complementary relationship between the broad sweep of Romanticism and the particular role of the antiquarian museum could hardly be more neatly encapsulated.

---

[1] For the prelude to my own account of antiquarian developments in the mid-nineteenth century, see Piggott, 'Prehistory'. See also the observations on the links between antiquarianism and nationalism in Levine, *Amateur*, 62, 73–4.

[2] For example, Scott was for a time the owner of that noted piece of La Tène metalwork, the 'Torrs chamfrein', acquired in 1920 by the National Museum of Antiquities in Edinburgh. Towards the end of his life he began to prepare a catalogue of his collection, with the title 'Reliquiae Trottcosinae – or the Gabions of the late Jonathan Oldbuck, Esq.' (i.e. the eponymous collector of Scott's novel, *The Antiquary*): see Maxwell Scott, *Abbotsford*.

[3] See Scott, *Waverley*, especially the publisher's preface to vol. I.

[4] *Antiquaries of Scotland*, xii.

Something of the language of the period surfaces in the historical account of the Antiquaries that prefaces this publication. The Society had been founded in 1780, it explains, in the hope of securing 'a more comprehensive study of the Historic Monuments and the National Antiquities of Scotland than individual zeal could hope to effect; the establishment of an archaeological museum in the Scottish Capital had also been a primary aim'. The latter ambition had been achieved in a modest way,[5] but the burden of this self-appointed task weighed heavily on the Society, which acknowledged that, at best, its ambitions could 'be very imperfectly accomplished by the most zealous private exertions' and that its national importance strongly merited the intervention of government. The Secretary, Daniel Wilson, observed: 'In Paris, Berlin, Copenhagen, Brussels, Petersburg, Munich, Rome, Naples, and Athens, the Archaeological Collections are objects of national care. In London and Dublin they are in like manner maintained from the public money'.[6] The Society hoped for an early acknowledgement from government of the importance of their collections, which duly came with their adoption by the state in 1851.[7]

TOWARDS A MUSEUM OF NATIONAL ANTIQUITIES

In holding up London as an example for the establishment of a museum of national antiquities, the Antiquaries in Edinburgh were being more than a little disingenuous. Four years earlier, in his *Archaeological Album*, Thomas Wright (a moving spirit in the founding of the British Archaeological Association) had complained that 'In the British Museum, our native antiquities appear to be held in very little esteem... It is discreditable to the Government of this country that we have no museum of national antiquities'.[8] At the British Archaeological Association's Winchester meeting in 1845, Thomas Pettigrew, the Association's Vice-President and Treasurer, similarly regretted that the British Museum housed 'only particular specimens, not a series minutely illustrative of the antiquities of various nations and times, and it is especially defective in that which more particularly relates to us, and which should distinctly characterise a national collection'.[9] In the same vein, a correspondent in *The Builder* expressed regret that no provision had been made in the new British Museum building for national antiquities and observed:

> Such a collection would be of higher value, and of less expense, than the blocks of granite brought from Egypt at so much trouble and cost, which, however, singular as curiosities,

---

[5] In 1848, the year prior to publication of the catalogue, the collections were open to the public two days a week and a respectable 6,000 visitors had been admitted.

[6] Ibid., xi–xii.

[7] See Stevenson, 'Museum', 31–85, 142–211, esp. 80–5.

[8] Wright, *Album*, 149.

[9] Pettigrew, 'Antiquarian', 3.

have no claim upon the delineator of national manners, and are all but valueless to the artist. It is for want of a receptacle for national antiquities, that we find so many pieces of pottery, carvings, and stained glass, in the hands of dealers, or in private collections; and there is no doubt, that if a proper building were set apart, many private collections would be presented to the public.[10]

On 27 June of the same year pleas were made in Parliament for the establishment of a Museum of National Antiquities during which similar expressions were made, one advocate going so far as to suggest that 'such an institution would have the best effect on the manners and morals of the people'.[11]

Pettigrew returned to the debate in 1851:

> We are absolutely at this time, in the middle of the nineteenth century, without any collection that can be called truly British. It is true that we have a British Museum, but in vain will you seek, within the walls of that now gigantic building, any collection of British remains...A collection of our national antiquities, so much to be desired, could not but be of the highest benefit to archaeological knowledge...[12]

While the officers of the British Museum included some who shared this view,[13] the all-powerful Trustees were yet to be won over by it. In 1849 a commission of inquiry into the affairs of the Museum, newly rehoused in Smirke's neo-Grecian edifice, received some less-than-encouraging answers to questions put to two of their number. 'Have you ever turned your attention to the question of extending and improving the collection of British antiquities in the British Museum as distinct from all others?', the commissioners asked the eminent antiquary W. R. Hamilton; 'I have not', he replied. 'Have you turned your attention at all to the question of the establishment of a separate Department of British Antiquities in the Museum?', they asked Viscount Mahon (who was also President of the Society of Antiquaries); 'No', he answered.[14] Events were about to unfold, however, that were to expose the complacency of the

---

[10] Hall, 'Preservation', 182

[11] Reported in *The Builder*, III no. 126 (1845), 313–14.

[12] Pettigrew, 'Archaeology', especially 168. Pettigrew evidently regarded the *JBAA*, where this article was published, as a kind of literary alternative to such a museum, serving as 'a storehouse and treasury of materials for future enquirers and for the information of the historian'.

[13] Edward Hawkins, Keeper of the Department of Antiquities, had announced as early as 1828 his intention of reserving a room in the proposed new building for British antiquities. This had still not materialised when, in 1844, Lord Prudhoe (later 4th Duke of Northumberland) proposed that he should donate his collection of bronzes from the Stanwick hoard on condition that '...a room were appointed at the Museum for the reception of national antiquities'; although the offer was accepted, the Trustees failed to honour their part of the bargain, pleading later that the Stanwick hoard formed 'little more than a basis for such a collection': see Kendrick, 'BM' 139, and also note 19 (below).

[14] Quoted by Kendrick, BM, 139. In mitigation for the Trustees' seeming complacency, Kendrick (p. 143) points out that the rehousing of the Museum in its new building, not to mention the arrival of some spectacular monuments from Lycia and from Nimrud, had no doubt preoccupied the Trustees to the extent that an undue preoccupation with the more pedestrian remnants of British material culture would have seemed little short of eccentric.

Trustees in this matter to unprecedented scrutiny and to censure, and that ultimately were to lead to permanent changes in the Museum's collecting policy and in its permanent structure.

At the centre of this tumult lay the material comprising the collection of the Reverend Bryan Faussett (1720–76), deriving largely from Faussett's own excavations in Kent and representing the fruits of the earliest coherent campaign of excavations in cemeteries of the Anglo-Saxon period.[15] Following Faussett's death, custody of the finds, together with five volumes of excavation records, passed successively to his son and to his grandson, and there they remained, effectively unknown and forgotten, until 'rediscovered' by Charles Roach Smith in 1843. A founder-member of the British Archaeological Association and its joint Honorary Secretary, Roach Smith (1807–90) may have been reconnoitering in advance of the Association's visit to Canterbury in 1844 when he called on the Reverend Dr Henry Godfrey Faussett at Heppington. What he discovered there led to the inclusion in the Canterbury programme of an excursion to Heppington in order to view the collection, with the members visiting 'in detachments' the small room in which it was kept, supervised by Roach Smith and watched over by the local constabulary.[16]

Following Godfrey Faussett's death in 1853 it was perhaps natural that his executors, having resolved to sell the collection, should have turned to Roach Smith for advice, and being well aware of its significance, his immediate response was that first refusal should be given to the British Museum.[17] The value of the collection was fixed at £665.

Members of the Archaeological Institute were alerted by Richard Westmacott to the approach made to the British Museum following delivery of a paper on excavations in the Anglo-Saxon cemetery at Linton Heath, Cambridgeshire, by the Hon. Richard Neville; Westmacott professed the opinion that 'the addition of so valuable a mass of evidence bearing on a period hitherto of great obscurity, and of which the National

---

[15] Faussett never recognised his finds as Anglo-Saxon but interpreted them as belonging to communities of 'Romanised Britons'. (Some of them did indeed come from burials of the Roman period, no doubt contributing to his confusion.) Credit for recognition of their true significance goes to the Revd James Douglas, who incorporated some of Faussett's evidence in his pioneering account of his own excavations in Kent (Douglas, *Nenia Britannica*). For a recent account of Faussett and his collection see Chadwick-Hawkes, 'Faussett'.

[16] Smith, *Retrospections*, 10. So enthused was Godfrey Faussett by all this attention that he expressed a wish that the BAA might arrange for publication of the finds, but nothing came of this proposal. Smith was somewhat critical of the BAA's failure to act in this matter. He also noted that the comparatively affluent Society of Antiquaries of London 'did not turn their eyes' in the direction of the Faussett collection, 'but then they had made no pilgrimage and had not committed themselves; they did not profess intense zeal in antiquarian science, nor warm admiration of national antiquities; and therefore have not so much to answer for as those who had gone so far and taken such pains to effect so little' (Smith, *Coll.*, III, 181–2).

[17] See Faussett, *Sepulchrale*, v: 'Although I could not be ignorant of the indifference with which our national antiquities have been and are regarded by the Government', says Roach Smith, 'I thought it possible that what could not be looked for from good taste, or from patriotism, might be conceded to dictation or to interest'. So moderate was the monetary value placed on the collection, he says, that no fewer than three private persons declared themselves willing to purchase it in the event of the BM declining.

Depository at present comprises scarcely any vestige, would prove a most important auxiliary to archaeological enquiries'.[18] J. O. Westwood concurred, expressing his desire and that of 'many English antiquaries' that the collection 'should be purchased to form part of the National Series, the commencement of which had been viewed by them with lively interest'.[19] He further suggested that 'the occasion was one in which the members of the Institute would do well to represent to the Trustees of the British Museum their strong sense of the importance of securing such collections for public information'.[20] These sentiments were duly expressed in a letter dated 7 November 1853, addressed by the Secretary of the Institute, George Vulliamy to the Trustees:

> The Committee of the Institute are deeply impressed with the importance of rendering the series of national antiquities recently commenced in the British Museum as complete as possible...[and express]...their anxious hope that the Faussett Collection...may not be permitted to pass into private hands, or be transferred to some foreign museum, whilst English archaeologists have no sufficient means of studying the remains of the Anglo-Saxon age in any public depository at present existing.
>
> [The committee] have anxiously hoped for the full realisation of the anticipations they had formed, when the liberality of his Grace the Duke of Northumberland, in 1846, devoted his valuable collection of antiquities towards the formation of a national series, and his Grace conferred upon the Institute the high honour of making that society the medium of his presentation of those antiquities to the British Museum. By recent arrangements, the Central Committee of the Institute have been empowered to transfer to any public museum in this country such antiquities as may come into the possession of the society, and which, by their rarity and importance, may more properly claim a place in the depositories most available for public instruction. The Committee have accordingly in contemplation to offer to the Trustees of the British Museum certain objects which may supply valuable accessions to the series now in formation.[21]

J. Y. Akerman, Secretary of the Society of Antiquaries of London, revealed to the same meeting that his Society had made similar representations and that their president, Viscount Mahon, 'had received assurances that in the event of the Faussett collection being secured for the British Museum, Mr [William] Wylie, who had formed a very valuable assemblage of Saxon relics at Fairford...had generously pledged himself to present the whole to the National Collection'.[22]

---

[18] *Archaeol. J.*, XI (1854), 51–2.

[19] The latter reference is no doubt to the 'British Room of Antiquities' established at the Museum in 1850, whose embryonic character is confirmed a year later by its dismissal as being 'as yet too insufficiently arranged to admit of classification and description' (Vaux, *B M*, iv).

[20] *Archaeol. J.*, XI (1854), 52.

[21] The letter is reproduced in BM Trustees, 'Faussett Coll.', 317–18. On the Duke of Northumberland's collection, see note 13 above.

[22] *Archaeol. J.*, XI (1854), 52–3. Wylie's intentions had first been made clear in a letter of 14 November 1853, addressed to Akerman himself: having expressed his incredulity that the Trustees should decline the Faussett collection, he empowers Akerman to make it known that, if they were to recant, '...I shall have much pleasure in

Roach Smith weighed into the debate with gusto, most notably through the medium of his occasional publication, *Collectanea Antiqua*, produced for subscribers from 1848 onwards. 'The public voice had long been raised against the unaccountable absence of National Antiquities in the National Museum', he asserted, and continued:

> Foreigners had long reproached us for the neglect with which we treated the valuable remains of ancient art illustrative of our history...They asked, when they visited the British Museum, for the halls and chambers consecrated to British, to Romano-British, to Saxon, to Norman, and to English Antiquities; and were astounded when told that such apartments existed not.[23]

To the waves of barbed shafts launched by Roach Smith and others, the Trustees remained immune. They declined to sanction the purchase, and having once so resolved they refused to be budged. Their intransigence stirred Roach Smith to new extremes of vehemence: the constitution of the Trustees was 'a monstrous anomaly'; the membership was marked by 'a general incompetency'; it was doubtful whether three out of their total of forty-seven could distinguish between Anglo-Saxon and Chinese works of art; it was symptomatic that refusal of the collection had been urged because its constituent pieces did not constitute 'high art'.[24]

Later he reproduced the text of a defence of the Trustees' actions, conveyed in a parliamentary statement by one of their number, Lord Seymour, and reported in *The Times* of 4 July 1854: every class of antiquities had its own adherents, the statement said, and the Trustees had very limited funds with which to satisfy the public appetite for material from every corner of the world; classical and other antiquities, if not purchased by the British Museum, were likely to be lost to the nation, whereas antiquities found in England, if not purchased by the Trustees, 'would be very likely to find a place in some provincial museum, and would therefore not be lost to the country'. Roach Smith's re-publication of this statement by no means heralded a more temperate attitude to the Trustees: indeed, he was utterly scornful of it, and took the noble lord

---

adding, as a free gift, the relics it was my fortune to collect in the Fairford Graves...There would then be a pretty nucleus of a collection of our own really national, because Teutonic antiquities' (BM Trustees, 'Faussett Coll.', 320, reproduced in 'Copies of all Reports... on the subject of the Faussett collection', 320). With the failure of the Faussett initiative, Wylie donated his collection instead to the Ashmolean Museum: see MacGregor and Bolick, *Ashmolean*, 6. Roger White (in *Mayer*, 122) notes that further Anglo-Saxon items were lost to the BM as a result of this débacle, for J. Y. Akerman, having formerly announced his intention of depositing there finds from his excavations in Gloucestershire and Oxfordshire, later decided to give them to Liverpool.

23 Smith, *Coll.*, III, 182–92. Readers of the *Archaeol. J.* were also informed that 'the contempt with which objects essential to a series of National Antiquities have long been viewed' had been compounded by the Trustees' rejection of the Faussett collection, and were reminded 'how disadvantageous to science is the want of enlightened intelligence' among the administration there (*Archaeol. J.* XI (1854), 90–1, 94).

24 In Faussett, *Sepulchrale* (p. vi), however, he lays ultimate blame at the feet of Government: 'When our Government shall be composed of statesmen instead of placemen; of men who look to the credit, the prosperity, and the glory of the country, more than to the maintenance of themselves in power...then, and then only, may it be expected that our national antiquities will be cared for and protected; and that, at the same time, the ancient national literature will be appreciated and its students encouraged'.

and his fellow board members severely to task:

> The country now knows, from the declaration of the Trustees themselves, that the British Museum is not, in their opinion, intended for British Antiquities. Let the Corporation of the City of Liverpool at once come forward and occupy the place repudiated by the managers of the Anti-British Museum, and establish an Institution strictly devoted to NATIONAL ANTIQUITIES.[25]

Reference to Liverpool serves to introduce the White Knight who was to redeem the Faussett collection. He was Joseph Mayer (1803–86), a goldsmith of that city and an inveterate collector of antiquities.[26] As an active and influential member of the Historic Society of Lancashire and Cheshire, Mayer had played an important part in organising the British Archaeological Association's conference at Chester in 1849, and from that time he formed a strong acquaintance with Roach Smith, whose steadfast patron he was to become. He had even opened to the Liverpool public an Egyptian museum, designed 'to give those of his fellow citizens unable to get to London for themselves some idea of the glories of the past displayed in the British Museum'.[27] Given all these factors, it is a matter for no surprise that Mayer, having been an enthusiastic supporter in the first instance of moves to persuade the British Museum to buy the Faussett collection,[28] and having even considered purchasing the collection and presenting it to the British Museum himself,[29] quickly stepped in when it was rejected and bought the entire collection on his own account. The purchase was celebrated with a lecture on Anglo-Saxon antiquities by Thomas Wright at the Philharmonic Hall (fig.28), with the collection placed on display to the participants, and more permanently, with the publication of Faussett's notebooks in a handsome volume entitled *Inventorium Sepulchrale*, edited by Roach Smith and financed by Mayer.[30]

---

[25] Smith, *Coll.*, III, 266–9.

[26] Mayer was an assiduous collector of finds from the medieval village of Meols on the Wirral estuary: about one third of the *c*.3,000 items treated in Hume, *Meols* are said to have belonged to Mayer, while excavations in the course of building the railway line to Lancaster provided another prolific source; see Margaret Gibson, in *Mayer*, 6. He had travelled widely on the Continent and had already drawn unfavourable comparisons between the status accorded to archaeology in Britain compared with that in France, Germany, and Denmark; he had also been instrumental in the presentation of a petition to the Treasury urging the allocation of funds 'for preserving and collecting objects of National interest' (quoted by Roger White, in *Mayer*, 119).

[27] See Margaret Gibson, in *Mayer*, 8.

[28] 'Hurrah! for the Faussett Collection', he had written to A. W. Franks, and of the antiquities he expressed the following sentiment: 'I hope you will get them ... they should be yours but if you refuse them they shall not be separated if I can help it' (letter from Mayer to Franks, 24 November 1853, in BM, Department of Medieval and Later Antiquities; quoted at greater length by R. H. White, in *Mayer*, 120).

[29] This information is contained in a letter from Roach Smith to Thomas Bateman, to which attention has been drawn by Michael Rhodes (Rhodes, 'Faussett', especially 39). Faussett apparently withdrew the offer after the BM authorities had refused access to the Faussett Papers to Roach Smith while the purchase was under consideration by them.

[30] In the preface to the *Inventorium Sepulchrale* (see Faussett, *Sepulchrale*) Roach Smith attributes two motives to Mayer's munificence in financing this work, the first that 'he wished to shew that it was with no restrictive or selfish

Fig. 28. The Philharmonic Hall at Liverpool on the occasion of Thomas Wright's lecture on the Faussett collection, 27 September 1854. Joseph Mayer is shown being presented with an illuminated address. (Photograph by Roger White: reproduced by his kind permission and by courtesy of Liverpool City Record Office)

The purchase had been a very considerable coup in the face of the failure of the British Museum to buy the collection. In time the Mayer museum changed its name to reflect its new character (further consolidated in 1857 with the purchase of W. H. Rolfe's Kentish antiquities), and curiously it was to be this private institution that in 1867 proudly adopted the title of the Museum of National and Foreign Antiquities.[31]

feeling he had purchased the antiquities', the second out of piety to the memory of Faussett, 'because his Journal shows him to have been a pains-taking and a truth-loving investigator, and a conscientious steward of the treasures he had brought to light'.

[31] Despite its impressive title, the 'Mayer Museum', as it was popularly known, was not highly evolved in organisational terms: it has been described as constituting at this time 'a munificent gift trembling on the verge of chaos' (Margaret Gibson, in *Mayer*, 43).

Its independent existence was to be short-lived, however, for in the same year the entire collection was transferred by Mayer to the care of the municipal authorities of Liverpool.

ROACH SMITH AND THE ANTIQUITIES OF LONDON

Roach Smith's bruising encounters with the British Museum and indeed with almost every branch of archaeological authority can have done him little good when, shortly afterwards, prompted by ill health, financial difficulties, and the expiry of his business lease, he decided to sell his own collection. It had been formed over a period of twenty years during which Smith had practised his profession as a pharmacist in the City of London. Excavations for the extension of the Bank of England in 1834 had provided the opening prelude to two decades of intensive collecting activity that culminated in 1854 with the publication of his *Catalogue of the Museum of London Antiquities*. Here he describes the processes by which the collection had accumulated, the bulk of the items having been bought from workmen involved in building works, in road making, bridge widening, and sewer trenching. While acknowledging that his museum had 'formed itself out of a series of accidents', Smith reveals a clear sense of what he calls his 'self-imposed stewardship', all his endeavours being directed towards the accumulation of 'materials to illustrate the early history of the metropolis'.[32] Elsewhere he makes it clear that the task had been shouldered partly on account of the failure of the City authorities to perform the task that was rightly theirs. 'There is so contemptible an apology for [a public museum]...in the City of London', he wrote, that 'it must be allowed that nowhere in the Kingdom is there to be found a corporation composed of people more unintellectual and uneducated'.[33] Smith himself had on more than one occasion offered items for display in this embryo museum (located in one room in the Guildhall) but to his chagrin they had been pronounced 'not...adapted for the collection contemplated by the Corporation'.[34]

When the time came for Roach Smith to dispose of his collection, his overriding concern was that it should remain entire and that if at all possible it should escape the fate of what he termed 'the grave of science, a *public auction*'.[35] The Corporation of London was given the opportunity of acquiring it, but declined to commit itself: ironically, a major factor in this decision was financial uncertainty due to impending legislation that would make free libraries and museums a charge on the rates.[36] The

---

[32] Roach Smith elsewhere expressed the view that 'The real value of antiquities should be determined by the extent to which they are capable of being applied towards illustrating history' (Faussett, *Sepulchrale*, ix).

[33] Smith, *Coll.*, I, 4.

[34] Guildhall Library committee minutes, 24 January 1848, quoted in a most valuable article by Dafydd Kidd (Kidd, 'Roach Smith', 112).

[35] Ibid., 130. A similar image is conjured up in Faussett, *Sepulchrale*, (p. iv), where public auctions are characterised as 'the common grave of antiquarian gatherings'.

[36] Ibid, 129. The Public Libraries and Museums Act 1855 reached the Statute Book later in the same year.

British Museum, having been offered it for £3,000, made a counter-offer of £2,000.[37] What happened then was recounted later by Roach Smith himself:

> When the time came for me and my Museum of London Antiquities to be separated, Lord Londesborough sent me a cheque for £3,000. This I was compelled to return; he could not keep the Museum in its integrity; and I had ever resolved that it should not be dispersed by auction; so I accepted the £2,000 offered by the Trustees of the British Museum, thus ensuring for the whole collections a safe resting place in the national institution.[38]

The cost that Roach Smith was willing to bear in order that the collection should remain intact is a striking affirmation of the seriousness of purpose that characterised his collecting activities. That he and his many supporters who lobbied intensively for the purchase of the collection by the nation were justified in this elevated opinion of its value is confirmed by the fact that once acquired by the British Museum, the collection effectively formed the foundation of an entirely new department, dedicated to British and Medieval Antiquities and Ethnography.

The City of London, so comprehensively anathematised by Roach Smith, had meanwhile made a shade more progress in its collecting activities than he had been willing to acknowledge. It was true that by 1840 the contents of the museum established at the Guildhall sixteen years earlier[39] could still be enumerated in a brief, four-page appendix to the catalogue of the Library[40] and could yet be contained in a single anteroom. Still, there had been improvements. It had been anticipated, for example, that redevelopment of the Royal Exchange site was likely to produce important archaeological discoveries and accordingly arrangements were made at the outset of this work that:

> any articles of interest then disinterred should be secured for the Gresham Committee. In the Specification for the Works, issued in 1840, the Contractor and Excavator were required, in taking out the soil, to deliver up 'any plate, coins, antiquities, or curiosities, whether in metal or otherwise, or any carved stones or carvings in marble, pottery, terra-cotta, or tessure, which may be found in the course of the excavations: it being understood that all such matters or things are to be taken up with all requisite care and are to remain the property of the...Committee.

---

[37] The lower sum was based on a valuation drawn up by A. W. Franks, who, despite his modest opinion of the collection's monetary worth, was a strong advocate of its acquisition. In 1855 he reported to Edward Hawkins as follows: 'The collection would be a great and valuable addition to the British Room and the acquisition of it would go far to remove from us the reproach under which we are labouring of neglecting the antiquities of our own Country, while we accumulate those of other lands' (BM, Officers' Reports LIV, 10 February 1855; quoted in Wilson, *Franks*, 24).

[38] Smith, *Retrospections*, I, 167.

[39] The Library Committee had been instructed by the Court of Common Council on that occasion 'To consider the propriety of providing a suitable place for the reception of such antiquities relating to the City of London and suburbs, as may be procured or presented to this Corporation, and to report thereon to this court' (*Guildhall Museum*, vii).

[40] *City Corporation Library*, 369–72.

Copies of an order to this effect were to be prominently displayed for the benefit of the workmen on the site and all antiquities found in the excavations were to be 'brought to the clerk of the works, who would remunerate the parties according to the value of the articles found'; each was to be labelled with the time and place of discovery, with the name of the finder, and with the amount of cash paid to him.[41] These conditions were recorded in a catalogue of the finds prepared for publication by William (later Sir William) Tite in 1848, by which time the excavations had been completed and the material was stored in the museum at the Guildhall.

There was yet general agreement that this institution was far from adequate. In an essay entitled *Why Not? A plea for a free public library and museum in the City of London*, published in 1855, Charles Reed made passing reference to the Guildhall collection, but doubted that it merited the title of museum. The British Museum was judged equally inadequate to the needs of the City, partly on account of its comparative remoteness but also because it was so full '...that the difficulty is to get the Trustees, not to purchase, but literally to accept, contributions'. The institution he envisaged,

> embracing objects of interest in art and nature, ancient and modern, would, under proper regulations, be a place of great resort; and it would be the natural depository of all those remarkable specimens of early Roman and British work, which enrich every part of the City, and are turned up every day by the spade of the excavator...In the course of years [he predicted] we should have in *our* Museum a worthy companion to that which the nation now boasts her property.[42]

Despite all this criticism (or perhaps because of it) the 'worthy companion' that was to emerge in the long run was the Guildhall Museum itself, rehoused in more appropriate premises and reopened to the public in 1876.

EPILOGUE

A number of other positive gains emerged from the often bad-tempered but invariably engrossing museological discourse of the mid-nineteenth century. At the British Museum, the founding of the Department of British and Medieval Antiquities and Ethnography in 1866 effectively put an end to charges that national antiquities were inadequately valued at national level and, under the keepership of A. W. Franks, the Department quickly established itself as of international class.

In Edinburgh, meanwhile, the conveyance of the Society of Antiquaries of Scotland's museum to government control brought more than merely relief to the Society from the burden of its administration: the title National Museum of Antiquities, which emerged into regular use within a few years of its establishment, conveyed more

---

[41] Tite, *Excavations*, xxxvii-xxxviii.
[42] Reed, *Why Not?*, 10, 21–2.

adequately the role that the Museum was to fulfil in Scotland's wider antiquarian consciousness.

In the preface to the English edition of his influential *Primeval Antiquities of Denmark*, published in 1849, J. J. A. Worsaae commented that in Britain such antiquities 'have never hitherto been brought into a scientific arrangement...[and in consequence]...have neither furnished those results to history, nor excited that interest with the public in general, which they otherwise would have done'; he continued with the hope that '...the day is not far distant when the British people will have formed a national museum of antiquities commensurate with the importance of their remains'.[43] As we have seen, considerable advances were made within a few years of Worsaae's pronouncement, with far-reaching implications for the understanding of antiquities of all periods. No single National Museum embracing the whole of the kingdom ever did emerge, but the lessons of the debate centred on the few institutions I have mentioned were taken to heart in smaller museums up and down the country, contributing to the truly national regard for the materials and lessons of antiquity of which we are the inheritors.

---

[43] Worsaae, *Denmark*, iii, vii.

British Archaeologists in the Aegean

B. F. Cook

British archaeology is not synonymous with archaeology in Britain, and this was especially true in the Victorian period, when a classical education was every gentleman's birthright, when speeches in the House of Commons could be embellished with quotations from Horace or Virgil, and when even a Prime Minister might write a book on Homer.[1] In such an intellectual climate it is hardly surprising that appeals for financial support for archaeological expeditions in classical lands could not only be made direct to Parliament but could receive there a sympathetic hearing and a generous response.

Archaeology was still at the stage of 'digging up things', but the things that were dug up were beginning to find their way directly into public collections rather than into private hands, and among the public collections in this country the pre-eminent place had already been claimed by the British Museum. The early years of Queen Victoria's reign saw an important new development in the acquisition of classical material, Greek and Roman antiquities, for the British Museum. The Museum had included some classical antiquities in its collection from the very beginning, thanks to the omnivorous taste of Sir Hans Sloane,[2] but in its early years it was almost entirely dependent for new acquisitions on the generosity of private individuals. Even when Parliamentary grants were sought for particular purchases, the occasion was invariably the opportunity to acquire an existing collection like those of Sir William Hamilton, Charles Townley, and Lord Elgin.[3]

The 1840s saw the beginning of a new era, in which public money would be made

---

[1] Gladstone, *Homer*.
[2] Edwards, *British Museum*, 269–303; Miller, *Cabinet*, 36–41; Jenkins, *Classical Antiquities*.
[3] Fothergill, *Hamilton*; Cook, *Townley*; St Clair, *Elgin*.

available for expeditions to acquire Greek and Roman antiquities on a large scale from sites in the Aegean. Even so, these expeditions did not just happen: each expedition depended on the initiative of a particular individual.

The Expedition to Xanthos

For the first of these expeditions we must go back almost to the very beginning of Queen Victoria's reign. It was in the spring of 1838 that Charles Fellows (fig.29), on his first journey in Turkey, discovered the ancient sites in Lycia,[4] and it was Fellows, more than anyone else, who was responsible for the British Museum's collection of sculptures from Xanthos. The following autumn he went to Lycia again. It was proposed that Fox Talbot, the pioneer of photography, should accompany him,[5] but nothing came of the idea and in the end Fellows took with him the artist George Scharf the younger. Although travelling as an individual and at his own expense, Fellows volunteered to point out objects suitable for acquisition by the British Museum, but he was assured by Lord

Ponsonby, then British Ambassador at Constantinople, that it was unlikely that a *firman* (permit) for their removal would be granted. After his return to England in March 1840, Fellows published the first of his travel books.[6]

In October of the following year a message came to the Museum's Trustees to the effect that a *firman* was ready and that prompt action was required to take advantage of it. Fellows was asked to provide descriptions of the objects to be collected, with appropriate maps and plans, but preferred to supervise the project personally: 'I felt certain that the removal of one stone would bring to light others, probably better preserved and more valuable, and that the *visible* formed but a fraction of what might be obtained, but could not be enumerated in written orders, which might probably be only

Fig. 29. Sir Charles Fellows (1799–1860). (BM)

---

[4] Michaelis, *Century*, 93.
[5] BM Orig. Papers, XXIX (Aug. 1843 - Jan. 1844). I owe this reference to Marjorie Caygill.
[6] Fellows, *Journal*.

literally obeyed'.[7] This sceptical view was later to be more than adequately confirmed. Fellows accordingly wrote to the Secretary of the Museum offering his services to the expedition: he did not expect remuneration and would pay his own expenses, but expected 'a free passage out and home' on a naval vessel 'and rations with the officers'. His offer was accepted promptly, and within two days he was on a steamer bound for Malta. From there he joined HMS *Beacon*, a surveying ship commanded by Captain Graves.

It was after Fellows met Graves that his troubles began, for the Captain's orders were simply to collect the *firman* from Smyrna, to sail to Xanthos, and there to embark the objects pointed out by Fellows and take them to Malta. No funds had been allotted, but Fellows offered to advance what was necessary on the assumption that the British Museum's Trustees would reimburse him. On arrival at Smyrna on 15 November 1841, it turned out that the so-called *firman* was only a letter asking for details of what was wanted, so that the local authorities could report on the practicability of the project. What was worse was that Ponsonby had also requested a series of reliefs built into the fortifications of the Castle at Bodrum.

Fellows had already been proved correct in his supposition that supervision on the spot would be more effective than written instructions from England. His next initiative was to prove equally important: he sensibly decided to ignore the sculptures in Bodrum, and persuaded Captain Graves to accompany him by steamer to Constantinople, there to seek a *firman* for Xanthos only. This *firman* was speedily granted in the form of a letter from the Grand Vizir to the Governor of Rhodes, instructing him 'in consequence of the sincere friendship existing between the two Governments [i.e. Turkish and British]' to allow Captain Graves to embark the antiquities if they were 'lying down here and there, and…of no use'.[8]

The expedition's equipment, including spades, pickaxes, and crowbars, was purchased in Smyrna and *Beacon* sailed to Rhodes, taking sixteen days for a voyage that could be done by steamer in thirty hours. Permission having been granted by the Governor, Fellows and his party were landed at the mouth of the Xanthos river on 26 December. Since the river was swift it took four days to get their stores upstream. (The return journey could be accomplished in three-quarters of an hour.) The aim was to collect the Harpy Tomb, the tomb of Payava (known to Fellows as 'the horse tomb'), and some reliefs incorporated in the fortifications. Fellows, however, expected to find more, and in this he was justified, for a search of the hillside below some surviving foundations disclosed the remains of the Nereid Monument.

Captain Graves now proved a less than enthusiastic collaborator. He left orders that neither of the two large tombs was to be dismantled, since the necessary machinery was not available, and that no boats were to be constructed to take the stones

---

[7] Fellows, *Xanthian Marbles*, 3–4.
[8] Ibid., 10–11.

down river, as Fellows requested, without further specific orders from Malta, for
which he declined to send. All hands were to leave on 1 March.

Faced with the literal interpretation of orders that he had foreseen, Fellows had
again to decide how best to accomplish the aims of the expedition. What he decided
was to ask the carpenters to spend their time making crates, and to concentrate
himself on pointing out the sculptures of the Nereid Monument for collection. The
sailors joined in the task with more enthusiasm than archaeological skill:

> The pleasure and excitement of these
> discoveries were entered into even
> by the sailors, who often forgot the
> dinner-hour or worked after dusk to
> finish the getting out of a statue: in-
> deed great care was needed to pre-
> vent their being in too much haste
> to raise up the figures, for while the
> marble was saturated with the mois-
> ture of the earth the slightest blow
> chipped off the light folds of the dra-
> pery; these hardened as they dried
> in the air.[9]

A more conventional exercise of the
sailors' skills was to lower the reliefs extracted from the fortifications some 200 feet on hawsers.
Meanwhile Fellows discovered that,
despite the orders of Captain
Graves, the Harpy tomb and the
'horse tomb' were to be dismantled: he tactfully left the sailors to
it. In the absence of suitable machinery, they simply threw ropes
over the Tomb of Payava and hauled
it down (fig.30).

In the end there were eighty-two
crates, which Fellows had to leave
behind in Xanthos. When he arrived

*Fig. 30. Xanthos: sailors dismantling the Tomb of Payava,
1842. Drawn by Charles Fellows. (BM)*

in Rhodes aboard HMS *Beacon* on 5 March he found a letter from the British Museum
acknowledging his actions to obtain the *firman* and confirming that his expenses would
be refunded. The following month Fellows returned to England whilst the steamer

---

[9] Ibid., 27–8.

Medea went to Xanthos to collect the crates. The Payava tomb was left for the next season, but in December 1842 the rest of the material arrived in England aboard HMS *Cambridge*. Fellows himself was warmly thanked by the Trustees and he was later knighted.

THE MAUSOLEUM AT HALICARNASSUS

Fellows had wisely abandoned Ponsonby's request for the sculptures in the Castle at Bodrum, which the Turkish authorities were not then prepared to relinquish. A subsequent British Ambassador, Sir Stratford Canning (later Lord Stratford de Redcliffe), did receive permission to remove them, and again it fell to the Royal Navy to accomplish the task.

It was assigned to HM Sloop *Siren*, commanded by H. Edgell, who left a lively account of the voyage.[10] The frieze blocks were extracted from the walls of the Castle by his crew, for whom it seems to have been an enjoyable exercise of their skills with ropes and tackle. This was not of course an archaeological expedition, even though it did bring to the British Museum all the surviving fragments that had then been recognised of the Mausoleum, one of the Seven Wonders of the World.

The arrival of the slabs in London aroused much interest, rekindling speculation on the precise location of the Mausoleum. Among those involved in these speculations was Charles Newton, then an Assistant in the British Museum's Department of Antiquities. In 1852 Newton left the Museum for the diplomatic service, and on being posted as HM Vice-Consul at Mytilene he was instructed 'to use such opportunities as presented themselves for the acquisition of antiquities for the British Museum'.[11] Newton was an Oxford-trained classicist, and considered himself an historian rather than an archaeologist.[12] For historical purposes he was especially eager to acquire inscriptions: an important group of inscriptions and other antiquities excavated by Newton on Kalymnos, was presented to the British Museum by Lord Stratford de Redcliffe.[13] Visits to Bodrum in 1855 and 1856, however, fired Newton with the ambition of organising an expedition there, in particular to collect some sculptured lions in the Castle walls that had been attributed to the Mausoleum by Ludwig Ross.[14]

To this end, after consultation with A. Panizzi, the British Museum's Principal Librarian, Newton asked the Foreign Secretary to obtain for him the services of a naval vessel for six months, the assistance of a small party of Royal Engineers (including a photographer), and £2,000.[15] Given the intellectual climate of the time these

---

[10] Edgell, *Journal*: a manuscript belonging to Edgell's granddaughters, who have kindly lent it to the British Museum

[11] Newton, Travels, I, 2.

[12] Reprint of Newton's memorial address in Jebb, 'Newton,' lii.

[13] See Newton, 'Calymnos' (I owe this reference to Dr D. M. Bailey); Newton, *Travels* I, 304–15; *BM Ancient Greek Inscriptions* II, 53–102, nos 231–344.

[14] Ross, *Reisen*.

[15] Newton, *Discoveries*, II, part 1, 85; *Travels*, II, 67.

Fig. 31. Excavation at Halicarnassus, c. 1856, with photographic tent in the background.
Photograph, Cpl. B. Spackman, RE. (BM)

requests seemed not unreasonable and were promptly granted. The naval vessel was HM Steam-Corvette *Gorgon*, with a crew of 150 under Captain Towsey. The contingent of four Sapper NCOs, including Corporal B. Spackman as photographer, was commanded by Lieutenant R. M. Smith, RE. The Navy provided more than logistical support: members of *Gorgon's* crew assisted with the digging, and some of the officers were persuaded by Newton to help by hand-colouring photographs of the mosaics uncovered in a Roman villa and photographed in sections by Corporal Spackman using a movable platform.[16] The mobile darkroom in which he processed his plates is visible in another of Spackman's photographs (fig.31).

Newton made regular reports on his progress to the Foreign Office,[17] and from one of these we learn of his plans to excavate the alternative sites proposed for the Mausoleum by Spratt and Ross, in an attempt to determine which was correct.[18] In the event both were proved wrong and the Mausoleum was eventually found on a differ-

---

[16] Newton, *Discoveries*, I, pl. XXXVIII; *Travels*, II, 16.
[17] *Budrum Papers*, passim.
[18] Ibid., 3.

ent site that had first been pointed out by Lieutenant Smith. (Newton never admitted this, and most subsequent writers have credited him with the discovery.)[19] Excavation yielded more slabs of the frieze and a large quantity of free-standing sculptures, including several parts of lions, one of which joined a piece that had been extracted from the Castle.[20]

All of this material, together with sculptures excavated at Cnidus and along the Sacred Way at Branchidae near Miletus, was removed to England by naval vessels in a fairly routine transport operation.[21] The sailors' skills were tested rather more by the recovery of a huge marble lion that had originally surmounted a tomb on a promontory near Cnidus. The lion was crated and lowered down a 200–foot cliff using huge spars and an enormous amount of tackle, the kind of machinery that had been lacking at Xanthos (fig.32).

Fig. 32. C. T. Newton and the lion of Cnidus.
After a photograph by Cpl. B. Spackman, RE. (Newton, Discoveries, *pl. LXI)*

---

[19] Dickson, *Murdoch Smith*, 33; Jenkins, *Archaeologists*, 176–83; Cook, *Relief Sculptures*, Introduction, III.
[20] Waywell, *Free-Standing*, 182, no. 405.
[21] *Budrum Papers*, 24–7 and 35–8.

Richard Pullan, an architect and surveyor, arrived late in 1857 to make accurate drawings of the finds, but the plans of all the sites excavated were drawn by Lieutenant Smith. (Smith was a capable and enthusiastic young officer who later excavated at Cyrene with Commander E. A. Porcher, RN, and after a distinguished military career he was appointed Director of the Royal Scottish Museum, Edinburgh.)[22] Newton acted as what would today be called Field Director. Although he was a pioneer in the use of photography to record the excavation, his archaeological technique was, even by the standards of his day, rather primitive. Admittedly he was greatly hampered in his attempt to uncover the site of the Mausoleum by the houses and gardens that covered it. Negotiations for the purchase of the separate plots took time, and meanwhile Newton had the Sappers excavate by mining underneath. Elsewhere in Bodrum, to save time, some of the spoil was back-filled into old trenches. At the Mausoleum it was piled up in a mound (on which Lieutenant Smith erected a flagpole!).[23] No detailed record was kept of daily progress and Newton even commented that it was not practical to mark on the site-plan the locations of any but a few particularly important finds.[24] Nonetheless the discoveries made by the expedition, in terms both of acquisitions for the British Museum and of additions to knowledge of this extraordinary monument (including traces of colour on both sculptures and architectural details), made it one of the most successful of its period.

TEMPLE OF ARTEMIS AT EPHESUS

Newton had begun the search for one of the Seven Wonders of the World, the Mausoleum, with a substantial Government grant and a good deal of naval and military support; John Turtle Wood (fig.33) began the search for another, the Temple of Artemis at Ephesus, with five redundant railwaymen employed at his own expense. His only official support was in obtaining a *firman* to excavate for twelve months with permission to export the finds, on condition that duplicates should be left for the Turkish Government, and subject to agreement with the owners of the land.[25]

Wood was an architect, then resident in Smyrna, from where he travelled daily by train to Ayasolouk, the nearest station to the site of Ephesus. The return journey took seven hours and allowed a mere six and a half hours on the site before the only train back. At Ephesus he 'used to wander about the plain seeking for mounds or other indication of the site of the great Temple', while his workmen dug all day under the supervision of a ganger. Later he managed to live near the site in a chalet originally constructed for engineers working on the railway. The whole enterprise was not with-

---

[22] Smith and Porcher, Cyrene. Dickson, *Murdoch Smith.. DNB*, s.v. Smith, Sir Robert Murdoch.
[23] Newton, *Discoveries*, I, pl. XII.
[24] Ibid., II, part 1, 99.
[25] Wood, *Ephesus*, 16.

Fig. 33. John Turtle Wood. (BM)

out discomfort and danger: Wood was often poorly fed, and used to dine with a loaded revolver in full view on the table to deter brigands.

Initially he excavated in the city of Ephesus itself, and even after he received a small grant from the Trustees of the British Museum, he was given only grudging permission to spend part of it on the search for the Temple. Excavation was at first concentrated on the odeum and the theatre since 'it was desirable that for any sums of money expended by the Trustees there should be some substantial return'.[26]

One of Wood's major acquisitions from Ephesus itself was a long inscription in honour of Q. Vibius Salutaris cut on the blocks of the wall at the entrance of the theatre.[27] It was this inscription that provided the essential clue to the discovery of the Temple, since it included a description of a ceremony in honour of the goddess in which a procession left the city for the Temple by way of the Magnesian Gate. Wood found this gate in 1867 and in May 1868 began to trace the road by sinking pits at intervals to an average depth of almost 4 metres. It was not until May 1869 that Wood found proof, in the form of an inscription of Augustan date, that he had reached the Temple precinct. This proof came none too soon, since the Trustees' grant that year had been accompanied by a hint that it would be the last if the Temple were not found. The search had begun six years earlier but Wood calculated that the actual duration of the search was about twenty months and the cost less than £2,000.

Excavation of the Temple (fig.34) continued until 1874, when work was suspended on the express orders of Newton. It had been conducted on a large scale with over a hundred workmen employed at a time for extended periods. By 1872 the Trustees had granted about £4,000 for the work, and in that year a Treasury grant of £6.000 was obtained. The area of the excavation eventually measured some 500 × 300 feet, and

---

[26] Ibid., vi.
[27] Ibid., 79–81; *BM Ancient Greek Inscriptions*, III, 117–42 and IV, 238–50, no. 481.

Fig. 34. Wood's Excavation of the Temple of Artemis. (Wood, Ephesus, *facing p. 192)*

Wood estimated that 132,222 cubic yards of soil had been removed, much of it tipped (by agreement) on the neighbouring fields to a depth of nearly 2 metres. The soil was at first removed in wheelbarrows, the estimate for building a light railway having been too high, but later horses and carts were also used.

This expense, which included the cost of buying the site (fig.35), was further justified by the finds, including some of the sculptured column-drums and piers that had contributed to the Temple's reputation in antiquity. Wood also recovered evidence for the dimensions of the Temple, enabling him to produce a plan and some rather conjectural elevations and sections.[28]

---

[28] Wood, *Ephesus*, 262–8.

The scale of the operation made it impossible to supervise the work closely enough to prevent the workmen from making away with any small finds of value: Wood accepted this as the price of clearing the site rapidly. The foundations of a church that had been constructed in the Temple were simply demolished, the work being 'partly effected by the aid of gunpowder in small quantities'. Wood's working methods were not without criticism even at the time. In 1867 the German archaeologist Kekule complained to Newton that Wood had extracted the blocks with the Salutaris inscrip-

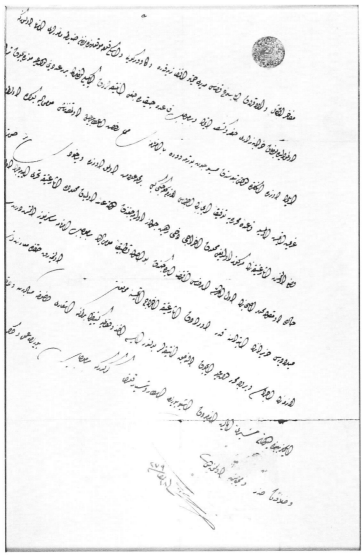

Fig. 35. Title-deed for the site of the Temple of Artmeis at Ephesus. (BM)

tion without noting their relative positions and that the excavations were 'not being conducted in a systematic manner'. Newton sympathised with Wood's situation: he was working under difficult, unhealthy, and even dangerous conditions, without the kind of support that Newton himself had had in Bodrum; but he urged Wood at least to number the blocks and to make a diagram of their relative positions before removing them. Kekule's further complaint, that a consignment of marbles had been lost at sea, was justified; the only defence was that now a request had been made for the aid of a man-of-war. Newton promised to inform Wood by telegraph if the request was granted.[29]

In January 1868 a party of sailors and Marines from HMS *Terrible* spent twenty days packing sculptures and moving them from the site to the railway for transport to the ship at Smyrna. Another party from HMS *Caledonia* spent most of January 1871 crating and moving sculptures from the Temple. The largest column-drum was loaded at Smyrna with a steam-crane lent by the contractors for the new quay. In London it needed twenty dray horses to move it from the docks to the Museum. In March 1873 HMS *Antelope* left Smyrna with twenty-four cases and three loose blocks, and in the following month HMS *Swiftsure* took thirty-one cases and sixteen blocks. This naval assistance was invaluable and Wood had by this time the support of two NCOs from the Royal Engineers, but when the final consignment of marbles was to be removed Admiral Rolph merely provided men, boats, and tackle to load the antiquities on a merchantman, since his own five ships were not bound for England or Malta.

TEMPLE OF ATHENA POLIAS AT PRIENE

In 1868–9, while Wood was halfway through his long campaign at Ephesus, an expedition of a very different nature was undertaken at nearby Priene by Richard Pullan, who had worked with Newton at Bodrum. Pullan was financed by the Society of Dilettanti, as he had been at Teos in 1862 and the Smintheum in 1866, and his primary aim was not to acquire objects for the British Museum but to add to knowledge of Ionic architecture by a detailed study of the temple of Athena Polias. By training he was an architect and surveyor, and he was also a competent watercolourist. Having visited the site in 1861 he proposed to the Dilettanti that he should excavate and provide measured drawings, notes, and photographs within a year at a total cost of £500.

Like other excavators he had some difficulty obtaining a *firman*, and had also to face problems with brigands and malaria, but he succeeded through a mixture of 'endurance, persistance and courage'.[30] He employed fifty workmen, some of them to clear the site, others to move blocks of marble for recording. His cavalier attitude to the blocks, which were simply thrown down into the nearby valley after they were

---

[29] Letter from Newton to Wood, 7 November 1867, in BM Dept of Greek and Roman Antiquities.
[30] Carter, *Priene*, 10.

Fig. 37. Temple of Athena Polias at Priene, c. 1869. After a photograph by R. P. Pullan.
(Antiquities of Ionia, IV, pl. XV)

measured, now seems shocking, but in other respects his archaeological technique was if anything in advance of the standards of his day. Like his mentor Newton he used photography to record progress, (fig.36) but he kept much more detailed notes of the work as it progressed, recording the location of blocks on a grid. He seems to have intended a rather more detailed publication than that eventually produced by the Dilettanti,[31] and the evidence for the use of a grid has only recently been recovered by Joseph Coleman Carter, whose study of the sanctuary and its sculptures includes an important, though long-delayed site-report.[32] Since the details were not published at the time, the technique was not immediately emulated, and Pullan's use of the grid was the first in the Mediterranean area by a large margin.[33]

Although collecting had not been part of the original plan, Pullan began in February 1869 to consider the possibility of removing some of the material by camel. When Newton arrived on the site on 7 April this idea became a practical possibility, especially as he was armed with funds supplied by John Ruskin. In addition to part of the *cella* wall of the temple, which was covered from floor to ceiling with inscriptions, forming a kind of civic archive, the fragmentary relief-sculptures from the coffers and

---

[31] *Antiquities of Ionia*, IV.
[32] Carter, *Priene*.
[33] Ibid., 5–9.

a selection of architectural members were sent by mule and camel to Balatschik, and thence by rail to Smyrna, where they were taken aboard HMS *Antelope*.

ARCHAEOLOGY, POLITICS, AND TECHNOLOGY

An overview of these various expeditions reveals a number of characteristics in common. Perhaps most obvious — certainly most painful — to a modern archaeologist is the primitive nature of the archaeological methods, not all of which can be excused as being acceptable by the standards of the day. Some shortcomings may be accounted for by the use of naval and military personnel, endowed with enthusiasm rather than archaeological training and experience, for example the demolition of the Tomb of Payava at Xanthos and the use of gunpowder at Ephesus. Wood's failure to keep detailed records of finds at Ephesus met with severe criticism in the 1860s, when there was already less excuse than Newton had had at Bodrum a decade earlier. Newton had at least employed both Smith and Pullan to make drawings and must be given credit for realising the potential of photography. Of all the technological advances of the age photography was to prove the one of most lasting benefit, but at the time the one that was most crucially important was the harnessing of steam power.[34] Fellows complained bitterly of the delays he suffered on HMS *Beacon*, a sailing vessel, and the achievement of successive expeditions in shipping large quantities of marbles to England would have been impossible without the availability of steamships. Steam was essential too for the railway, without which Wood could not have made his day trips from Smyrna to Ephesus, and without which the finds from Ephesus and Priene could not have been moved to Smyrna for embarcation. At Smyrna, too, the contractors' steam-crane was enormously useful if not absolutely indispensible for loading the heaviest of the sculptured column-drums.

It need hardly be said that this practice of collecting on a grand scale was wholly dependent on the cooperation of the Royal Navy. It would, however, be misleading to ascribe this to a deliberate policy of cultural imperialism or colonialism on the part of the British Government.[35] This would be to judge nineteenth-century practice from the standpoint of twentieth-century ideology: the actual evidence points in a quite different direction. Although Government funding was forthcoming for Newton at Bodrum and, eventually, for Wood at Ephesus, Pullan's work at Priene was privately financed by the Society of Dilettanti, and the expenditure incurred at Xanthos and Ephesus were, initially at least, met personally by Fellows and Wood and only later refunded by the Trustees of the British Museum. That collecting antiquities was not a matter of deliberate Government policy is demonstrated by the absence of a consistent pattern of financial provision. Indeed, the Government's failure to provide ad-

---

[34] Cf. Michaelis, *Century*.
[35] Dyson, 'Archaeology', 205.

equate financial backing was severely criticised in 1862 by Edward Faulkner, who contrasted it detrimentally to French practice.[36] Even the support of the Royal Navy, which was essential to so many expeditions, especially for transport of the finds to England, was not planned in advance as part of Government policy but was provided only if ships happened to be available, in contrast, for example, with the help provided for the Austrian expedition to Samothrace in 1873.[37] This is evident from the limited help provided by the Navy for Wood's last shipment from Ephesus. It is also evident from Lord Stratford de Redcliffe's need to persuade Rear Admiral Grey that sending HMS *Medusa* with Newton on board to various destinations in the archipelago would serve also to show the flag in areas where piracy was rife and would therefore, he felt, meet with Government approval.[38]

Nor is 'colonialism' the correct term for the relations between England and the Ottoman Empire, which were conducted throughout on a proper basis of diplomacy. The Ottoman Empire is one of the common threads that bind together the expeditions to Xanthos, Bodrum, Cnidus, Ephesus, and Priene with others of the same period to Carthage and Cyrenaica. The Ottoman regime had no strong attachment to pre-Islamic cultures, and was willing to part with their remains for diplomatic purposes and the necessary *firman* was in each case obtained through regular diplomatic channels.

Another common thread is that in every case the initiative for an expedition and the energy to see it through, lie to the credit not of the Government, or even the British Museum, but of dedicated individuals. To the names of Fellows, Newton, Wood, and Pullan it is necessary to add that of Lord Stratford de Redcliffe, who as Sir Stratford Canning had obtained the slabs of the Mausoleum frieze from the Castle at Bodrum for presentation to the British Museum, and who later provided Newton with so much necessary support in the archaeological work he undertook whilst he was Vice-Consul.

Underlying all the efforts of these professional and amateur archaeologists was a genuine interest in the classical past. Their enthusiasm led them to face difficulties, hardships, and even danger in the quest. Archaeology provided a new and exciting source of information to supplement what was already known from the literary record. Newton was the great pioneer of this new discipline in Britain. Through his excavations and publications, through his lectures and his support for the foundation of the Society for the Promotion of Hellenic Studies and of the British School at Athens, Newton more than anyone else was responsible for the establishment of Classical Archaeology as a speciality separate from the study of British antiquities.[39] There is a

---

[36] Falkener, *Ephesus*, ix.
[37] Michaelis, *Century*, 117.
[38] Letter from Lord Stratford de Redcliffe to Rear Admiral The Hon. F. W. Grey, 25 November 1855, London, private collection. I am grateful to Dr Ian Jenkins for bringing this letter to my attention.
[39] Cook, 'Newton'.

certain irony in this, since Newton was much involved in the activities of the newly founded Archaeological Institute before and during his sojourn in Mytilene. He prepared a map of British and Roman Yorkshire under the direction of the Institute's Central Committee for the annual meeting at York in 1846,[40] and he was one of the secretaries at that meeting; he produced 'Notes on the Sculptures at Wilton House', for the Salisbury meeting in 1849;[41] he gave his analytical lecture, 'On the Study of Archaeology', at the Oxford meeting in 1850;[42] and he reported on 'Excavations and Discoveries at Calymnos', to the Shrewsbury Meeting in 1855.[43]

Newton and those who followed him gladly embraced these new techniques of obtaining information, and were always ready to take advantage of the possibilities opened up by new developments in technology. In May 1856 Newton wrote from Rome to his friend Panizzi at the British Museum: 'Since you were last in Rome the Appian Way has been uncovered. I drove out on it the other Sunday and looking up saw the Electric Telegraph running along the side of the road. The 19th century is full of strange *rapprochemens*'[sic].[44]

---

[40] Newton, *Map*.
[41] Newton, 'Wilton'.
[42] Newton, 'Archaeology'.
[43] Newton, 'Calymnos'.
[44] BL Add. Ms. 36717, f. 483.

Bibliography

ABBREVIATIONS AND JOURNALS

Archaeol. J.	*Archaeological Journal*
BL	British Library
BM	British Museum
CUL	Cambridge University Library
DNB	*Dictionary of National Biography*
EDAS	*Exeter Diocesan Architectural Society Transactions*
JBAA	*Journal of the British Archaeological Association*
Mon. Mag.	*Monthly Magazine*
ns	new series
Phil. Mag.	*Philosophical Magazine*
RA	Royal Academy
RIBA	Royal Institute of British Architects
RIBA Trans.	Royal Institute of British Architects, *Transactions*

MANUSCRIPTS AND SPECIAL COLLECTIONS

BL Add. Ms.	British Library Additional Manuscripts
BM Orig. Papers	British Museum Original Papers
Camden Soc., RIBA	British Architectural Library, RIBA, Ecclesiological Society Papers, Church Schemes, 5 vols
Camden Soc., Lambeth	Lambeth Palace Library Archives, Cambridge Camden Society, Church Notes and Collected Church Schemes Compiled by John Mason Neale and Others
CUL, Cambridge Coll.	CUL, Cambridge Collection, Cam a 500.7, Item 8, A Description of the Sextry Barn at Ely, lately demolished (Cambridge Antiquarian Society 1843), 8
Edgell, *Journal*	H. Edgell, *Journal of HM Sloop* Siren *from May 14th 1845*
Oxford Arch. Soc., Corr.	Bodleian Library, Calendar of Correspondence of the Oxford Architectural and Historical Society, 1835–1900

G. G. Scott Papers	British Architectural Library, RIBA, Scott Papers, ScGGS
Willis drawings	Architectural drawings of Robert Willis, Society of Antiquaries, London.

ABBREVIATED REFERENCES

Aldrich, 'Gothic'	M. Aldrich, 'Gothic Architecture Illustrated: The Drawings of Thomas Rickman in New York', *The Antiquaries Journal*, LXV (1985), 427–33
Aldrich, 'Rickman' (thesis)	M. Aldrich, 'Thomas Rickman (1776–1841) and Architectural Illustrations of the Gothic Revival' (M.A. thesis, Toronto 1983)
Allen, *Naturalist*	D. E. Allen, *The Naturalist in Britain* (London 1976)
Anon, 'Salisbury Plain'	Anon, 'Salisbury Plain', *Mon. Mag.*, 19 (1 July 1805), 623
Antiquities of Ionia	*Antiquities of Ionia*, published by the Society of Dilettanti, 5 parts (1769–1915), IV (London 1881)
Antiquaries of Scotland	*Synopsis of the Museum of the Society of Antiquaries of Scotland compiled by D. Wilson* (Edinburgh 1849)
Babbage, *Science*	Charles Babbage, *Reflections on the Decline of Science in England, and on Some of its Causes* (London 1830)
Baily, 'Rickman' (thesis)	J. Baily, 'Thomas Rickman, Architect and Quaker, the Early Years to 1818' (Ph.D. thesis, Leeds 1977)
Banks, 'Guadaloupe'	J. Banks, 'Observations on the Nature and Formation of the Stone incrusting the Skeletons...of Guadaloupe...', *Transactions of the Linnean Society of London*, 12 (1819), 53–61
Bayet, *Byzantin*	C. Bayet, *L'Art Byzantin* (Paris 1883)
Bellers, 'Description'	F. Bellers, 'A description of the several Strata of Earth, Coal, Stone etc found in a coal pit ... at Dudley', *Philosophical Transactions of the Royal Society*, 17 (1712), 541–4
Benjamin, 'Reproduction'	W. Benjamin, 'The Work of Art in the Age of Mechanical Reproduction', *Illuminations*, ed. H. Arendt (New York 1968)
Bentham, 'Saxon Churches'	J. Bentham, 'Historical Remarks on the Saxon Churches', in *Essays*, ed. J. Taylor, 77–8; reprinted from J. Bentham and B. Willis, *The History and Antiquities of the Conventual Church and Cathedral of Ely* (Cambridge 1771)
Bloxam, 'Leicester'	M. H. Bloxam, 'On some of the sepulchral Monuments and Effigies in Leicestershire, a paper' (address to Leicester Architectural Society, 1865), (Northampton 1866), *Associated Architectural Societies: Reports and Papers*, Vols 1–42 (London 1850–1937)
BM Ancient Greek Inscriptions	*The Collection of Ancient Greek Inscriptions in the British Museum*, II (Oxford 1883), III (Oxford 1890), IV (Oxford 1893–1916)
BM Trustees, 'Faussett Coll.'	'Copies of all Reports, Memorials, or other Communications to or from the Trustees of the British Museum, on the subject of the Faussett Collection of Anglo-Saxon Antiquities', *Parliamentary Accounts and Papers, 1854*, xxxix, 315–23
Boylan, 'Buckland'	P. Boylan 'Dean William Buckland (1784–1856): a Pioneer in Cave Science', *Studies in Speleology*, 1 (1967), 237–53
Boylan, 'Buckland' (thesis)	P. Boylan, 'William Buckland 1784–1856: Scientific Institutions, Vertebrate Palaeontology and Quaternary Geology' (Ph.D. thesis, University of Leicester 1984)
Britton, *Antiquities*	J. Britton, *Architectural Antiquities, 5 vols.* (London 1827)
Britton, *Auto-biography*	J. Britton, *The Auto-biography of John Britton*, 3 vols (London 1849, 1850)

Broderip, 'Stonesfield Slate' — W. J. Broderip, 'Observations on the Jaw of a Fossil mammiferous Animal found in the Stonesfield Slate', *Zoological Journal*, 3 (1828), 408–12

Brookes, 'Establishment' — S. A. Brookes, 'L. A. M. A. S.: A Victorian Establishment.', *Transactions of the London and Middlesex Archaeological Society* 36 (1985), 203–22

Browning, *Aurora Leigh* — Elizabeth Barrett Browning, *Aurora Leigh. A Poem in Nine Books* (London 1857)

Buckland, *Reliquiae Diluvianae* — W. Buckland, *Reliquiae Diluvianae*, 1st edn (London 1823), 2nd edn (London 1824)

Buckland, *Vind. Geologiae* — W. Buckland, *Vindiciae Geologiae; or the connexion of Geology with Religion explained* (Oxford 1820)

Buckman, 'Tessellae' — James Buckman, 'On the Substances employed in forming the Tessellae of the Cirencester Pavements and on their chromatic arrangement', *Archaeol. J.*, VII (1850), 347–54

Budrum Papers — *Papers respecting the Excavations at Budrum. Presented to both Houses of Parliament by Command of Her Majesty* (London 1858)

Burchfield, *Kelvin* — J. D. Burchfield, *Lord Kelvin and the Age of the Earth* (London 1975)

Butler, *Coptic Churches* — A. J. Butler, *The Ancient Coptic Churches of Egypt* (Oxford 1884)

Camden, *Britannia* — W. Camden, *Britannia*, 2nd edn, enlarged by R. Gough, 4 vols (London 1806)

Camden Soc., *Annual Report* — Cambridge Camden Society, *Annual Report*, 1841

Camden Soc., *Few Hints* — Cambridge Camden Society, *A Few Hints on the Practical Study of Ecclesiastical Antiquities* (Cambridge 1843)

Cardwell, *Organisation of Science* — D. S. L. Cardwell, *The Organisation of Science in England* (London 1972)

Carlyle, *French Revolution* — Thomas Carlyle, *The French Revolution. A History*, 3 vols (London 1837)

Carlyle, *Past and Present* — Thomas Carlyle, *Past and Present* (London 1843)

Carson, *Numismatic Soc.* — R. A. G. Carson, *A History of the Numismatic Society 1836–1986* (London 1986)

Carter, *Orders* — J. Carter, *The Ancient Architecture of England, (Part I the Orders of Architecture during the British, Roman, Saxon and Norman Aeras)* 2 vols (London 1795–1814)

Carter, *Priene* — Joseph Coleman Carter, *The Sculpture of the Sanctuary of Athena Polias at Priene*, Reports of the Research Committee of the Society of Antiquaries of London, XLII (London 1983)

Chadwick-Hawkes, 'Faussett' — Sonia Chadwick-Hawkes, 'Bryan Faussett and the Faussett Collection: an Assessment', *Anglo-Saxon Cemeteries: a Reappraisal*, ed. Edmund Southworth (Stroud 1990), 1–24

Challinor, 'Webster' — J. Challinor, 'Some Correspondence of Thomas Webster, Geologist (1773–1844) -II', *Annals of Science*, 18 (1962), 147–75

Chandler, *Dream* — Alice Chandler, *A Dream of Order: the Medieval Ideal in Nineteenth-Century English Literature* (London 1971)

Chippindale, 'Bicknell' — C. Chippindale, 'Clarence Bicknell: Archaeology and Science in the 19th Century', *Antiquity*, LVIII (1984), 185–93

Choisy, *Histoire* — Auguste Choisy, *Histoire de l'Architecture*, 2 vols (Paris 1899), lectures at the Ecole Polytechnique 1898–9

'Church Building', *Parliamentary* — 'Survey of Church Building and Church Restoration, 1840–75', *Parliamentary Accounts and Papers*, LVIII (1876)

City Corporation Library — *A Catalogue of the Library of the Corporation of the City of London: instituted in the year 1824* (London 1840)

Clark and Hughes, *Sedgwick* — J. W. Clark and T. M. Hughes, *The Life and Letters of the Reverend Adam Sedgwick*, 2 vols (Cambridge 1890)

Cobbett, 'Reformation'
William Cobbett, *A History of the Protestant 'Reformation' in England and Ireland; showing how that event has impoverished and degraded the main body of the people in those countries* (London 1824); published in parts 1824–6; *Part Second. List of Abbeys, Priories, Nunneries, Hospitals, and other Religious Foundations... Confiscated, Seized on, or Alienated, by the Protestant 'Reformation' Sovereigns and Parliaments* (London 1827)

Cocke, 'Attitudes'
T. H. Cocke, 'Pre-Nineteenth-Century Attitudes to Romanesque Architecture', *JBAA*, 3rd ser., XXXVI (1973), 72–97

Cocke, 'Essex'
T. H. Cocke, 'James Essex, Cathedral Restorer', *Architectural History*, XVIII (1975), 16–21

Coleridge, *Constitution*
S. T. Coleridge, *On the Constitution of Church and State, According to the Idea of Each*, 3rd edn (London 1839)

Colvin, 'Aubrey'
H. M. Colvin, 'Aubrey's *Chronologia Architectonica*', *Concerning Architecture, Essays on Architectural Writers and Writing Presented to N. Pevsner*, ed. J. Summerson (London 1968)

Conybeare, *Letters*
J. Conybeare, *Letters and Exercises of the Elizabethan Schoolmaster John Conybeare, with notes and a fragment of Autobiography by the Very Rev. W.D. Conybeare*, ed. F. C. Conybeare (London 1905)

Cook, 'Newton'
B. F. Cook, 'Sir Charles Newton, KCB' (with a list of Newton's writings as an appendix), *Proceedings of the Eighteenth British Museum Classical Colloquium, London, 7–9 December 1994* (forthcoming)

Cook, *Relief Sculptures*
B. F. Cook, *The Relief Sculptures of the Mausoleum*, forthcoming

Cook, *Townley*
B. F. Cook, *The Townley Marbles* (London 1985)

Cox, 'Smith'
L. R. Cox, 'New Light on William Smith and his Work', *Proceedings of the Yorkshire Geological Society*, 25 (1942), 1–99

Credland, 'Flint Jack'
A. G. Credland, 'Flint Jack – A Memoir', *Geological Curator*, 3 (1983), 435–43

Cumberland, 'Buckland'
G. Cumberland, 'Strictures on Professor Buckland's Inaugural Lecture', *Mon. Mag.*, 52 (1821), 301–5

Cumberland, 'Deluge'
G. Cumberland, 'On the Deluge', *Mon. Mag.*, 40 (1815), 209–10 and 404–5

Cumberland, 'Effects of Deluge'
G. Cumberland, 'On the Effects of the Deluge', *Mon. Mag.*, 40 (1815), 130–3

Cumberland, 'Mosaic System'
G. Cumberland, 'In Defence of the Mosaic System', *Mon. Mag.*, 40 (1815), 18–20

Cunnington, *Antiquary*
R. H. Cunnington, *From Antiquary to Archaeologist* (Aylesbury 1975)

Curwen, *Gideon Mantell*
The Journal of Gideon Mantell – Surgeon and Geologist 1818–1852, ed. E. C. Curwen (Oxford 1940)

Daniel, *Origins*
Glyn Daniel, *The Origins and Growth of Archaeology* (New York 1971)

Dart, 'Hyena'
R. A. Dart, 'The myth of the Bone-accumulating Hyena', *American Anthropologist*, 58 (1956), 40–62

Davies, *Earth in Decay*
G. L. Davies, *The Earth In Decay – a History of British Geomorphology* (London 1969)

Davy, *Consolations*
Sir Humphrey Davy, *Consolations in Travel* (London 1830)

Dawson, *Banks*
W. R. Dawson, *The Banks Letters* (London 1958)

Dean, 'Age of the Earth'
D. R. Dean, 'The Age of the Earth Controversy: Beginnings to Hutton', *Annals of Science*, 38 (1981), 435–56

Dean, *Hutton*
D. R. Dean, *James Hutton and the History of Geology* (Ithaca 1992)

De La Beche, *Theoretical Geology*
H. De La Beche, *Researches in Theoretical Geology* (London 1834)

De Luc, 'Guadaloupe'
J. A. De Luc, 'On the fossil skeleton found in Guadaloupe', *Mon. Mag.*, 37 (1) (1 June 1814), 399–401

de Verneilh, *Byzantin* — F. de Verneilh, *L'Architecture Byzantin de France* (Paris 1851)

de Vogüé, *Syrie Centrale* — de Vogüé, *Syrie Centrale*, 2 vols (Paris 1865–97)

Dickson, *Murdoch Smith* — William Kirk Dickson, *The Life of Major-General Sir Robert Murdoch Smith* (Edinburgh/London 1901)

Dieulafoy, *Perse* — M. Dieulafoy, *L'Art Antique de la Perse* (Paris 1884–9)

Douglas, *Nenia Britannica* — Revd James Douglas, *Nenia Britannica: or a Sepulchral History of Great Britain* (London 1793)

Dyson, 'Archaeology' — Stephen L. Dyson, 'From New to New Age Archaeology', *American Journal of Archaeology*, XCVII (1993), 195–206

Eastlake, 'Revival' — C. L. Eastlake, *History of the Gothic Revival* (London 1872); ed. J. Mordaunt Crook (Leicester 1970), revised 1978

Edmonds, 'Buckland' — J. M. Edmonds, '*Vindiciae Geologiae*, published 1820; the inaugural lecture of William Buckland', *Archives of Natural History*, 18 (1991), 255–68

Edwards, *British Museum* — Edward Edwards, *Lives of the Founders of the British Museum* (London 1870)

Ellenberger and Gohau, 'Stratigraphie' — F. Ellenberger and G. Gohau, 'A l'aurore de la stratigraphie paléontologique: Jean-André De Luc, son influence sur Cuvier', *Revue d'Histoire des Sciences*, 34 (1981), 217–57

Englefield, *Isle of Wight* — H. C. Englefield, *A Description of the principal picturesque Beauties, Antiquities and Geological phænomena of the Isle of Wight with additional observations on the strata of the island, by T. Webster* (London 1816)

Essex, 'Lincoln' — J. Essex, 'Some Observations on Lincoln Cathedral', *Archaeologia*, IV (1777), 149–59

Essex, 'Round Churches' — J. Essex, 'Observations on the Origin and Antiquity of Round Churches; and of the Round Church at Cambridge in Particular', *Archaeologia*, VI (1782), 163–78

Evans, *Antiquaries* — J. Evans, *A History of the Society of Antiquaries* (London 1956)

Evans, 'Prehistory' — J. D. Evans 'On the Prehistory of Archaeology', *Antiquity and Man*, ed. J. D. Evans, B. Cunliffe, and C. Renfrew (London 1981), 15–16

Evans, 'RAI' — J. D. Evans, 'The Royal Archaeological Institute: a Retrospect', *Archaeol. J.*, 106 (1949), 1–11

Ewen, *Politics of Style* — S. Ewen, *The Politics of Style in Contemporary Culture* (1990)

Eyles, 'Smith' — J. M. Eyles, 'William Smith: Some Aspects of his Work', *Towards a History of Geology*, ed. C. J. Schneer (Cambridge, Mass. 1969), 142–58

Falkener, *Ephesus* — Edward Falkener, *Ephesus and the Temple of Diana* (London 1862)

Farey, 'Bakewell' — J. Farey, 'Observations, in Objection to some new Arrangements, and Simplifications of the Strata of England, proposed by Mr Bakewell', *Phil. Mag.*, 42 (1813), 103–26

Farey, 'Cumberland' — J. Farey, 'On Mr Cumberland's Theory', *Mon. Mag.*, 54 (1822), 300–2

Farey, 'Cuvier' — J. Farey, 'Geological Remarks and Queries on Messrs Cuvier and Brogniart's Memoir on the Mineral Geography of the Environs of Paris', *Phil. Mag.*, 35 (1810), 113–40

Farey, 'Deluge' — Anon [J. Farey], 'Reflections on the Noachian Deluge and the attempts lately made at Oxford, for connecting the same with present Geological Appearances', *Phil. Mag.*, 56 (1820), 10–14

Farey, 'List' — J. Farey, ['List of Strata'], *Phil. Mag.*, 36 (1810), 102–6

Farey, 'Notice' — Anon [J. Farey] 'Notice of volumes 1 to 4 of Sowerby's *Mineral Conchology*', *Mon. Mag.*, 55 (1823), 543

Farey, 'Smith' — J. Farey, 'Mr Smith's Geological Claims stated', *Phil. Mag.*, 51 (1818), 173–80

Farey, 'Strange'   J. Farey, 'An Extract of all such Matters concerning Fossil Shells and Plants, as are mentioned in the remarks of John Strange, Esq. read to the Society of Antiquaries in ... 1779...', *Phil. Mag.*, 54 (1819), 139–40

Farey, 'Stratification'   J. Farey, 'On the Stratification of England...' *Phil. Mag.*, 25 (1806), 44–9

Faussett, *Sepulchrale*   *Inventorium Sepulchrale: an Account of some Antiquities dug up...by the Rev. Bryan Faussett*, ed. C. Roach Smith (London 1856)

Fellows, *Journal*   Charles Fellows, *A Journal written during an excursion in Asia Minor* (London 1839)

Fellows, *Xanthian Marbles*   Charles Fellows, *The Xanthian Marbles; their Acquisition and Transmission to England* (London 1843), reprinted in Charles Fellows, *Travels and Researches in Asia Minor* (London 1852), 422–56

Fitton, *Notes*   W.H. Fitton, *Notes on the Progress of Geology in England* (London 1833, published by R. Taylor)

Fitton, 'Strata'   W. H. Fitton, 'On the Strata from whence the Fossil described in the preceding Notice was obtained', *Zoological Journal*, 3 (1828), 412–18

Flinn, 'Essay Review'   D. Flinn, 'Essay Review', *Geological Journal*, 27 (1992), 87–90

Fothergill, *Hamilton*   Brian Fothergill, *Sir William Hamilton: Envoy Extraordinary* (London 1969)

Fox-Strangways, 'St Petersburgh'   W.T. H. Fox-Strangways, 'Strata of the Environs of St Petersburgh, in the Order of Geological Position', *Phil. Mag.*, 55 (1820), 323–8

Freeman, *Preservation*   E. A. Freeman, *The Preservation and Restoration of Ancient Monuments: a paper with notes* (Oxford 1852)

Frew, 'Aspect'   J. Frew, 'An Aspect of the Early Gothic Revival: The Transformation of Medievalist Research, 1770–1800', *Journal of the Warburg and Courtauld Institutes*, XLIII (1980), 174–85

Gell, *Pompeiana*   Sir William Gell and John P. Gandy, *Pompeiana: The Topography, Edifices and Ornaments of Pompeii*, (London 1817–19)

Gifford and Rapp, 'Arch. Geology'   J. A. Gifford and G. Rapp jr, 'The early development of archaeological geology in North America', *Geologists and Ideas: a history of North American Geology*, ed. E. T. Drake and W. M. Jordan (Boulder, Col. 1985), 409–21

Gladstone, *Homer*   W. E. Gladstone, *Homer* (London 1878)

Gotch, *RIBA*   *The Growth and Work of the Royal Insistute of British Architects, 1834–1934*, ed. J. A. Gotch (1934)

Gough, *Sepulchral*   R. Gough, *Sepulchral Monuments in Great Britain, Applied to Illustrate the History of Families, Manners, Habits and Arts, at the Different Periods from the Norman Conquest to the Seventeenth Century* (London 1786, 1796) 2 vols published

Gough, *Topography*   R. Gough, *British Topography, or an Historical Account of What Has Been Done for Illustrating the Topographical Antiquities of Great Britain and Ireland*, 2 vols (London 1780)

Grayson, *Human Antiquity*   D. Grayson, *The Establishment of Human Antiquity* (London 1983)

Guildhall Museum   *Catalogue of the Collection of London Antiquities in the Guildhall Museum* (London 1903)

Guiterman and Llewellyn, *Roberts*   H. Guiterman and D. Llewellyn, *David Roberts*, exh. cat. (Barbican Art Gallery, London 1986)

Gunther, *Lhwyd*   R. T. Gunther, *Early Science in Oxford. Vol. XIV: Life and Letters of Edward Lhwyd* (Oxford 1945)

Hall, 'Depositories'   E. Hall, 'Effects of the Depositories of Rivers on the Sea', *Mon. Mag.*, 43 (1817), 113

Hall, 'Preservation' E[dward] H[all], 'The Preservation of National Antiquities', *The Builder*, III no. 115 (1845), 182

Hallam, *State of Europe* Henry Hallam, *A View of the State of Europe during the Middle Ages*, 2 vols (London 1818), 10th edn, 3 vols including supplementary vol. (London 1853)

Hardman, *Ruskin and Bradford* Malcolm Hardman, *Ruskin and Bradford. An Experiment in Victorian Cultural History* (Manchester 1986)

Hearl, *Barnes* T. W. Hearl, *William Barnes 1801–1886* (Dorchester 1966)

Hilton, *Atonement* B. Hilton, *The Age of Atonement* (Oxford 1988)

Hitchcock, *Early Victorian Architecture* Henry-Russell Hitchcock, *Early Victorian Architecture in Britain*, 2 vols (London 1954)

Hoare, 'Oct. 1807' R. C. Hoare, 'Note for 4 October 1807', *Wiltshire Archaeological and Natural History Magazine*, 22 (1885), 234–8

Hoare, *South Wiltshire* R. C. Hoare, *The Ancient History of Wiltshire* 2 vols (London 1812–21), vol. 1 (*South Wiltshire*)

Holmes, 'Stereoscope' O. W. Holmes, 'The Stereoscope and the Stereograph' (1859), reprinted in *Photography and Print*, ed. V. Goldberg (Albuquerque 1981)

Hull, 'Taxonomy' D. L. Hull, 'The Effect of Essentialism on Taxonomy: Two Thousand Years of Stasis', *The British Journal of the Philosophy of Science*, XV (February 1965), 314–26

Hume, *Societies* A Hume, *The Learned Societies and Printing Clubs of the United Kingdom* (London 1847)

Hume, *Meols* Abraham Hume, *Ancient Meols* (London 1863)

Inkster, 'Mechanics Institutes' I. Inkster, 'The social context of an educational movement. A revisionist approach to the English Mechanics Institutes 1820–1850', *Oxford Review of Education*, 2 (1976), 277–307

Isabelle, *Edifices* C. E. Isabelle, *Les edifices circulaires et les domes* (Paris 1855)

Jackson, *Dalmatia* T. G. Jackson, *The Architecture of Dalmatia* (1887)

Jacobs, 'Cephalopod Shells' D. K. Jacobs, 'The support of Hydrostatic Load in Cephalopod Shells', *Evolutionary Biology*, 26 (1992), 303–6

Jahn, 'Scheuchzer' M. E. Jahn, 'Some notes on Dr Scheuchzer and on *Homo diluvii testis*', *Toward a History of Geology*, ed. C. J. Schneer (Cambridge, Mass. 1969), 192–213

Jardine, *Strickland* W. Jardine, *Memoirs of Hugh Edwin Strickland* (London 1858)

Jebb, 'Newton' R. C. Jebb, 'Sir C. T. Newton', *Journal of Hellenic Studies*, XIV (1894) xlix-liv

Jenkins, *Archaeologists* Ian Jenkins, *Archaeologists and Aesthetes* (London 1992)

Jenkins, 'Classical Antiquities' Ian Jenkins, 'Classical Antiquities', *Sir Hans Sloane. Collector, Scientist, Antiquary. Founding Father of the British Museum* ed. Arthur MacGregor (London 1994), 167–73

Jennings, 'Earth Surface' J. Jennings, 'Changes in the Earth Surface', *Mon. Mag.*, 41 (1816), 217–18

Jennings, 'Geology' J. Jennings, 'On Geology', *Mon. Mag.*, 42 (1817), 518–9

Jocelini de Brakelonda *Chronica Jocelini de Brakelonda de rebus gestis Samsonis Abbatis Monasterii Sancti Edmundi*, ed: John Gage Rokewode, Camden Soc. (London 1840)

Kendrick, 'BM' T. D. Kendrick, 'The British Museum and British Antiquities', *Museums Journal*, LI (1951), 139

Kidd, 'Roach Smith' Dafydd Kidd, 'Charles Roach Smith and his Museum of London Antiquities', *British Museum Yearbook*, II (London 1977), 105–35

Knights, *Clerisy* B. Knights, *The Idea of the Clerisy in the Nineteenth Century* (Cambridge 1978)

Konig, 'Guadaloupe'   C. Konig, 'On a fossile human skeleton from Guadaloupe', *Philosophical Transactions of the Royal Society* (1814), 107–20

Labarte, *Constantinople*   J. Labarte, *Le Palais Imperial de Constantinople* (Paris 1861)

Lawson, *Neale*   M. S. Lawson, *Letters of John Mason Neale, Selected and Edited by His Daughter* (London 1910)

Layard, *Nineveh*   A. H. Layard, *Nineveh and Its Remains* (London 1849), 2 vols

Lethaby, *Webb*   W. R. Lethaby, *Philip Webb and His Art* (London 1935)

Levine, *Amateur*   Philippa Levine, *The Amateur and the Professional: Antiquarians, Historians and Archaeologists in Victorian England, 1838–1886* (Cambridge 1986)

Levy, 'Camden'   F. J. Levy, 'The Founding of the Camden Society', *Victorian Studies* 7 (1963/4), 295–305

Llwyd, 'Parochialia'   E. Llwyd, 'Parochialia, Being a Summary of Answers to Parochial Queries', *Archaeologia Cambrensis*, 6th Ser., IX (1909)

Long, 'Sarsen Stones'   W. Long, 'The Sarsen Stones', *Wiltshire Archaeological and Natural History Magazine*, 4 (1858), 334

Lyell, *Life*   *Life, Letters and Journals of Sir Charles Lyell Bart*, ed. K. M. Lyell, 2 vols (London 1881)

Lyell, [Review]   C. Lyell, review of provincial societies' publications, *Quarterly Review*, 34 (1826), 153–79

Lysons, *Woodchester*   S. Lysons, *Account of Roman antiquities discovered at Woodchester in the county of Gloucester*, (London 1797)

Maas, *Gambart*   J. Maas, *Gambart. Prince of the Victorian Art World* (London 1975)

Macaulay, *History*   Thomas Babington Macaulay, *The History of England from the Accession of James II*, 5 vols (London 1849–61), vol. 5, ed. Lady Trevelyan (1858–61)

Macauley, *Introductory Address*   J. Macauley, *Introductory Address read before the Cuverian Natural History Society...November 1837* (Edinburgh 1837)

MacGregor and Bolick, *Ashmolean*   Arthur MacGregor and Ellen Bolick, *Ashmolean Museum, Oxford: A Summary Catalogue of the Anglo-Saxon Collections (Non-Ferrous Metals)* (British Archaeol. Repts., British Ser. 230) (Oxford 1993)

Macleod and Collins, *Science*   R. Macleod and P Collins (eds), *The Parliament of Science* (Northwood 1981)

Mantell, 'Bignor'   G. A. Mantell, 'Fine Roman Pavement discovered at Bignor', *Gentleman's Magazine*, 81 (2) (1811), 514–6.

Mantell, 'Rocks and Strata'   G. A. Mantell, 'The remains of Man, and works of Art imbedded in Rocks and Strata', *Archaeol. J.* (1850), 327–46

Mantell, 'Tilgate Forest'   G. A. Mantell, 'Remarks on the Geological Position of the Strata of the Tilgate Forest', *Edinburgh New Philosophical Journal*, 1 (1826), 262–5

Martin, *Herculaneum and Pompeii*   J. Martin, *Descriptive Catalogue of 'The Destruction of Herculaneum and Pompeii'* (London 1822)

Masfen, *Views*   J. Masfen, *Views of the Church of St Mary at Stafford...with an Account of it Restoration and Materials for Its History* (London 1852)

Mayer   *Joseph Mayer of Liverpool 1803–1886*, ed. M. Gibson and S.M. Wright (Soc. of Antiquaries of London Occ. Papers, ns XI) (London 1988)

Maxwell Scott, *Abbotsford*   M. M. Maxwell Scott, *Abbotsford: The Personal Relics and Antiquarian Treasures of Sir Walter Scott* (London 1893)

Metcalf, *Knowles*   Priscilla Metcalfe, *James Knowles. Victorian Editor and Architect* (Oxford 1980)

Michaelis, *Century*   A. Michaelis, *A Century of Archaeological Discoveries* (London 1908)

Middleton, 'Fluorine'   J. Middleton, 'On Fluorine in Bones, its source and its application to

	the determination of the geological age of Fossil Bones', *Proceedings of the Geological Society of London*, 4 (1845), 431–3
Middleton, 'Gradual Rise of Ocean'	J. Middleton, 'On the Gradual Rise of the Ocean', *Mon. Mag.*, 42 (1816), 290–2
Middleton, 'Planet'	J. Middleton, 'Theory of a Planet', *Mon. Mag.*, 36 (1813), 17–19
Middleton, 'Rise of Ocean',	J. Middleton, 'On the Rise of the Ocean', *Mon. Mag.*, 41 (1816), 1–3
Miele, *Gothic*	C. Miele, *The Gothic Revival and Gothic Architecture: The Restoration of Medieval Churches in Victorian Britain* (Ph.D. Thesis, Institute of Fine Arts, New York University 1992))
Miele, 'Victorian'	C. Miele, '"Their Interest and Habit." The Architectural Profession and Church Restoration', *Building the Victorian Church*, ed. C. Brooks and A. Saint (Manchester 1995)
Miller, *Cabinet*	Edward Miller, *That Noble Cabinet* (London 1973)
Miller, *Impressions*	H. Miller, *First Impressions of England and its People* (Edinburgh 1889)
Miller, *Sandstone*	H. Miller, *The Old Red Sandstone*, 11th thousand (Edinburgh 1869)
Milner, *Dissertation*	J. Milner, *Dissertation on the Modern Style of Altering Cathedrals* (London 1811)
Milner, 'Ecclesiastical'	J. Milner, 'The Means Necessary for Further Illustrating the Ecclesiastical Architecture of the Middle Ages', *Essays on Gothic Architecture by the Revd T. Warton, Revd J. Bentham, Captain Grose and the Revd J. Milner*, ed. J. Taylor (London 1800)
Milner, *Treatise*	J. Milner, *Treatise on the Ecclesiastical Architecture of England* (London 1836)
Momigliano, 'History'	A. Momigliano, 'Ancient History and the Antiquarian', *Journal of the Warburg and Courtauld Institutes*, 1950, 286–307
Mordaunt Crook, 'Architecture and History'	J. Mordaunt Crook, 'Architecture and History', *Architectural History* XXVII (1984), 555–78
Mordaunt Crook, 'Beresford Hope'	J. Mordaunt Crook, 'Progressive Eclecticism: the Case of Beresford Hope', *Architectural Design* LIII (1983), 56–63
Mordaunt Crook, *Burges*	J. Mordaunt Crook, *William Burges and the High Victorian Dream* (1981)
Mordaunt Crook, *Dilemma*	J. Mordaunt Crook, *The Dilemma of Style: Architectural Ideas from the Picturesque to the Post-Modern* (1987; 2nd edn 1989)
Mordaunt Crook, Emmett, *Essays*	J. Mordaunt Crook, introduction to J. T. Emmett, *Six Essays* (New York 1972)
Mordaunt Crook, 'Jackson'	J. Mordaunt Crook, 'T. G. Jackson and the Cult of Eclecticism', *In Search of Modern Architecture*, ed. H. Searing (1982), 102–20
Mordaunt Crook, Kerr, *House*	J. Mordaunt Crook introduction to R. Kerr, *The Gentleman's House* (New York 1972)
Mordaunt Crook, 'Pre-Victorian'	J. Mordaunt Crook, 'The Pre-Victorian Architect: Professionalism and Patronage', *Architectural History*, XII (1969), 62–78
Mordaunt Crook, 'Smirke'	J. Mordaunt Crook, 'Sydney Smirke and the Architecture of Compromise', *Seven Victorian Architects*, ed. J. Fawcett and N. Pevsner (1976)
Morrell, 'Perpetual Excitement'	J. Morrell, 'Perpetual Excitement: The Heroic Age of British Geology', *Geological Curator*, 5 (1993), 311–17
Morrell and Thackray, *Gentlemen*	J. Morrell and A. Thackray, *Gentlemen of Science* (Oxford 1981)
Morris, *News from Nowhere*	William Morris, *News from Nowhere: or, an Epoch of Rest, being some chapters from a Utopian Romance* (London 1891)
Mushet, 'Geologists'	D. Mushet, 'Our Globe and the Geologists', *Mining Magazine*, 26 (22 Nov. 1856), 798
Neale, *Hierologus*	J. M. Neale, *Hierologus, or the Church Tourist* (London 1844)
Neale and Webb, *Durandus*	John Mason Neale and Benjamin Webb, *The Symbolism of Churches and*

Church Ornaments: a translation from the first book of the Rationale Divinorum Officiorum, written by William Durandus, sometime Bishop of Mende (Leeds 1843)

Newton, 'Archaeology'   C. T. Newton, 'On the Study of Archaeology,' *Archaeol. J.*, VIII (1851), 1–26, reprinted in *Memoirs chiefly illustrative of the history and antiquities of the city and county of Oxford, Communicated to the annual meeting of the Archaeological Institute of Great Britain and Ireland held at Oxford, June 1850* (London 1854), 1–26, republished in Newton, *Essays in Art and Archaeology* (London 1880), 1–38

Newton, 'Calymnos'   C. T. Newton, 'Excavations and Discoveries at Calymnos, made, in November, 1854, by direction of Lord Stratford de Redcliffe, H. B. M. Ambassador at Constantinople', *Archaeol. J.*, XIII (1856), 14–37 (the paper had been read to Archaeological Institute of Great Britain and Ireland, Section of Antiquities, at the Shrewsbury meeting in August 1855); published separately, paginated 1–24

Newton, *Discoveries*   C. T. Newton, *A History of Discoveries at Halicarnassus, Cnidus, and Branchidae* (London 1862–3)

Newton, *Map*   C. T. Newton, *Map of British and Roman Yorkshire*, prepared under the direction of the Central Committee of the Archaeological Institute for the Annual Meeting at York in 1846 by Charles Newton. Drawn and engraved by W. Hughes (London 1847)

Newton, *Travels*   C. T. Newton, *Travels and Discoveries in the Levant*, 2 vols (London 1865)

Newton, 'Wilton'   C. T. Newton, *Notes on the Sculptures at Wilton House* (privately printed 1849), reprinted in *Memoirs illustrative of the history and antiquities of Wiltshire and the City of Salisbury, Communicated to the annual meeting of the Archaeological Institute of Great Britain and Ireland held at Salisbury, July 1849* (London 1851), 248–78

Nicholson, 'Increase or Decrease' William Nicholson, 'Increase or Decrease of the Ocean', *Mon. Mag.*, 41 (1816), 310

North, 'Paviland'   F. J. North, 'Paviland Cave, The "Red Lady", the Deluge, and William Buckland', *Annals of Science*, 5 (1942), 91–128

North, 'Centenary'   F. J. North, 'Centenary of the Glacial Theory', *Proceedings of the Geologists Association*, 54 (1943), 1–28

Orange, 'BAAS'   A. D. Orange, 'The Origins of the British Association for the Advancement of Science', *The British Journal for the History of Science* 6 (1972), 152–176

Oxford Arch. Soc., Rules   *Rules and Proceedings of the Oxford Architectural Society*, 1841–2 and 1844

Page, 'Diluvialism'   L. E. Page, 'Diluvialism and its Critics in Great Britain in the Early Nineteenth Century', *Toward a History of Geology*, ed. C. J. Schneer (Cambridge, Mass. 1969), 257–71

Paley, *Guide*   F. A. Paley, *The Ecclesiologist's Guide to Churches within a Seven Mile Circuit around Cambridge* (Cambridge 1844)

Paley, *Restorers*   F. A. Paley, *The Church Restorers: A Tale Treating Ancient and Modern Architecture and Church Decoration* (London 1844)

Petit, *Restorations*   J. L. Petit, *On Proposed Restorations of St Mary Stafford*, Privately published pamphlet 1842 (British Architectural Library, RIBA pam.018)

Pettigrew, 'Antiquarian'   T. J. Pettigrew, 'On the Objects and Pursuit of Antiquarian Researches', *British Archaeological Association Conference Transactions BAA, Winchester* (1845)

Pettigrew, 'Archaeology'   T. J. Pettigrew, 'On the Study of Archaeology, and the Objects of the British Archaeological Association', *JBAA* 6 (1851), 163–77

Pevsner,	N. Pevsner, *Architectural Review* LXXXVI, 1939, 55
Pevsner, 'Whewell'	N. Pevsner, 'William Whewell and his Architectural Notes on German Churches', *German Life and Letters*, ns 22, (1968–9), 39–48
Pevsner, 'Willis'	N. Pevsner, 'Robert Willis', *Smith College Studies in History*, XLVI (1970), 1–27
Pevsner, *Writers*	N. Pevsner, *Some Architectural Writers of the Nineteenth Century* (Oxford 1972)
Pevsner and Cherry, *Wiltshire*	N. Pevsner and B. Cherry, *The Buildings of England: Wiltshire*, rev. ed. (London 1975), first published 1963
Phillips, 'Diluvial Currents'	J. Phillips, 'The Direction of Diluvial Currents in Yorkshire', *Phil. Mag.*, ns 2 (1827), 138–41
Phillips, *Manual of Geology*	J. Phillips, *A Manual of Geology* (London and Glasgow 1855)
Picnic	*Picnic: the Illustrated Guide to Ilfracombe and North Devon, with notes on Lynmouth, Clovelly, Lundy, and adjacent resorts*, 3rd edn (Bristol 1891)
Piggott, 'Antiquarian'	S. Piggott, 'Antiquarian Thought in the Sixteenth and Seventeenth Centuries', *English Historical Scholarship in the Sixteenth and Seventeenth Centuries*, ed. L. Fox (Dugdale Society; Oxford 1956), 93–114
Piggott, 'Camden'	S. Piggott, 'William Camden and the *Britannia*', *Proceedings of the British Academy*, XXXVII (1951), 199–217
Piggott, 'Origins of Arch. Socs'	S. Piggott, 'The Origins of the English County Archaeological Societies', *Transactions of the Birmingham and Warwickshire Archaeological Society*, LXXXVI (1974), 1–15; and in *Ruins in a Landscape, essays in Antiquarianism* (Edinburgh 1976), 171–95
Piggott, 'Prehistory'	S. Piggott, 'Prehistory and the Romantic Movement', *Antiquity*, XI (1937), 31–8
Piggott, *Stukeley*	S. Piggott, *William Stukeley* (London 1954)
Popper, *Economica*	Popper, *Economica* (1944–5)
Popper, *Historicism*	K. Popper, *The Poverty of Historicism* (1957)
Prevost, 'Schistes calcaires'	C. Prevost, 'Observations sur les Schistes calcaires oolitiques de Stonesfield en Angleterre', *Annales des Sciences*, 4 (1825), 389–417
Pugin, *Contrasts*	A. W. N. Pugin, *Contrasts: or, a parallel between the noble edifices of the Middle Ages, and the corresponding buildings of the present day; shewing the present decay of taste* (London 1836); 2nd edn (London 1841)
Rapp, 'Geoarchaeology'	G. Rapp jr, 'Geoarchaeology', *Annual Reviews in Earth and Planetary Science*, 15 (1987), 97–113
Reed, *Why Not?*	C. Reed, *Why Not? A plea for a free public library and museum in the City of London* (London 1885)
Reynolds, *Discourses*	Sir Joshua Reynolds, *Discourses of Art*, 1778–90, ed. R.Wark (San Marino, California 1959)
Rhodes, 'Faussett'	Michael Rhodes, 'Faussett Rediscovered: Charles Roach Smith, Joseph Mayer, and the Publication of *Inventorium Sepulchrale*', *Anglo-Saxon Cemeteries: A Reappraisal*, ed. Edmund Southworth (Stroud 1990), 25–64
Rickman, *Attempt*	T. Rickman, *Attempt to Discriminate the Styles of English Architecture from the Conquest to the Reformation* (1817)
T. M. Rickman, *Rickman*	T. M. Rickman, *Notes on the Life of Thomas Rickman* (London 1901)
Riegl, 'Monuments'	A. Riegl, 'The Modern Cult of Monuments', *Oppositions*, XXV (1982)
Rodden, 'Development'	J. Rodden, 'The Development of the Three-Age System: Archaeology's First Paradigm', *Towards a History of Archaeology*, ed. G. Daniel (London 1981), 51–65
Roger, *Buffon*	J. Roger, *Buffon – Les époques de la nature – édition critique* (Paris 1988)

Ross, *Reisen*   Ludwig Ross, *Reisen nach Kos, Halikarnassos, Rhodos und der Insel Cypern* (Halle 1852)

Rowe, 'Character'   C. Rowe, 'Character and Composition: Or Some Vicissitudes of Architectural Vocabulary in the Nineteenth Century', *The Mathematics of the Ideal Villa and Other Essays* (Cambridge 1976)

Rudwick, *Deep Time*   M. J. S. Rudwick, *Scenes from Deep Time* (Chicago 1992)
Rudwick, *Fossils*   M. J. S. Rudwick, *The Meaning of Fossils* (London 1972)
Rudwick, 'Foundation'   M. J. S. Rudwick, 'The Foundation of the Geological Society of London. Its Scheme for Cooperative Research and Its Struggle for Independence', *British Journal for the History of Science*, I (December 1963), 325–55

Rudwick, 'Lyell'   M. J. S. Rudwick, 'Charles Lyell's Dream of a Statistical Palaeontology', *Palaeontology*, 21 (1978), 225–44

Rupke, *Chain*   N. A. Rupke, *The Great Chain of History* (Oxford 1983)
Ruskin, *Gothic*   John Ruskin, *The Nature of Gothic. A chapter of 'The Stones of Venice'* (Hammersmith 1892)

Ruskin, *Stones*   John Ruskin, *The Stones of Venice*, 3 vols (London 1851–3)
Ruskin 'Traffic'   John Ruskin, 'Traffic', *The Crown of Wild Olive, Three Lectures on Work, Traffic, and War* (London 1866)

Ruskin, *Works*   *Complete Works*, ed. E. T. Cook and A. Wedderburn, 39 vols (London 1903–12)

Scamuzzi, 'Fossile'   E. Scamuzzi, 'Fossile Eocenico con Iscrizione Geroglifica rinvenuto in Eliopoli', *Bolletino della Societa Piemontese di Archeologia e di Belle Arti*, ns 1 (1947), 1–4

G. G. Scott, *Recollections*   G. G. Scott, *Personal and Professional Recollections* (London 1879)
Scott, *Waverley*   W. Scott, *Waverley Novels* (Edinburgh 1842–6) ['Abbotsford Edition' published by R. Cadell]

Scrope, 'Lyell'   G. P. Scrope, 'Review of Lyell's *Principles of Geology* third edition', *Quarterly Review*, 53 (1835), 406–48

Secord, 'Survey'   J. Secord, 'The Geological Survey of Great Britain as a research school', *History of Science*, 24 (1986), 223–75

Sedgwick, 'Origin'   A. Sedgwick, 'On the Origin of Alluvial and Diluvial Formations', *Annals of Philosophy*, ns 9 (1825), 241–57

Shapin and Thackray,   S. Shapin and A. Thackray, 'Prosopography as a Research Tool in
  'Prosopography'   History of Science', *History of Science*, 12 (1974)
Sharp, 'Local Museums'   W. Sharp, 'On the Formation of Local Museums', *Reports of the British Association for the Advancement of Science*, 9th meeting Birmingham 1839 (1840), Transactions of the Sections, 65

Shortland, 'Darkness Visible'   M. Shortland, 'Darkness Visible: Underground Culture in the Golden Age of Geology', *History of Science*, 32 (1994), 1–61

Simpson, *Fonts*   F. Simpson, *A Series of Baptismal Fonts, Chronologically Arranged* (London 1828)

Simpson, *Yorkshire Lias*   M. Simpson, *The Fossils of the Yorkshire Lias described from nature*, 2nd edn (Whitby 1884)

Smith, *Coll.*   C. Roach Smith, *Collectanea Antiqua, etchings and notices of antient remains, illustrative of the habits, customs, and history of past ages*, 7 vols (London 1848–80)

Smith, *Retrospections*   C. Roach Smith, *Retrospections, Social and Archaeological*, 3 vols (London 1883, 1886, 1891)

Smith and Porcher, *Cyrene*   Captain R. Murdoch Smith, RE, and Commander E. A. Porcher, RN,

| | *History of the Recent Discoveries at Cyrene, made during an Expedition to the Cyrenaica in 1860–61, under the Auspices of Her Majesty's Government* (London 1864) |

Socin, 'Fossile' — C. Socin, 'Fossile eocenico con iscrizione geroglifica rinvenuto in Eliopoli', *Atti della Societa Toscana di Scienze Naturale, Memorie*, 53 (1947), 3–11

St Clair, *Elgin* — William St Clair, *Lord Elgin and the Marbles* (London 1967), 2nd edn (Oxford 1983)

Steer, 'Hawkins and Lysons' — F. W. Steer, *The Letters of John Hawkins and Samuel and Daniel Lysons 1812–1830* (Chichester 1966)

Stevenson, 'Museum' — R. B. K. Stevenson, 'The Museum, its Beginnings and Development', *The Scottish Antiquarian Tradition: Essays to mark the Bicentenary of the Society of Antiquaries of Scotland*, ed. A.S. Bell (Edinburgh 1981), 31–85, 142–211

Strange, 'Glamorganshire' — J. Strange, 'An account of some curious Remains of Antiquity in Glamorganshire', *Archaeologia*, 6 (1782), 6–38

Texier & Pullan, *Byzantine Architecture* — C. E. M. Texier and R. P. Pullan, *Byzantine Architecture* (1864)

Thompson, *Surtees* — A. H. Thompson, *The Surtees Society 1834–1934* (Durham 1939)

Thompson, *Cambridge Antiquarian* — M. W. Thompson, *The Cambridge Antiquarian Society 1840–1990* (Cambridge 1990)

Thorson and Holliday, 'Geoarchaeology' — R. M. Thorson and V. T. Holliday, 'Just what is Geoarchaeology', *Geotimes*, 35 n.7 (1990), 19–20

Tite, *Excavations* — W. Tite, *A Descriptive Catalogue of the Antiquities found in the Excavations at the New Royal Exchange preserved in the Museum of the Corporation of London* (London 1848)

Torrens, 'Bath' — H. S. Torrens, 'The Four Bath Philosophical Societies 1779–1959', *A Pox on the Provinces*, ed. R. Rolls and J. & J. R. Guy (Bath 1990), 180–8

Torrens, 'Cirencester' — H. S. Torrens, 'The Geology of Cirencester and District', *Early Roman Occupation at Cirencester* ed. J. Wacher and A. McWhirr (Cirencester 1982), 72–8

Torrens, 'Fryer' — H. S. Torrens, 'Joseph Harrison Fryer (1777–1855): geologist and mining engineer, in England 1803–1825 and South America 1826–1828', A Study in 'failure', *Geological Sciences in Latin America* ed. S. Figueiroa and M. Lopes (Campinas, Brazil 1994)

Torrens, 'Shorto' — H. S. Torrens, 'A Wiltshire Pioneer in Geology and his Legacy – Henry Shorto III...', *Wiltshire Archaeological and Natural History Magazine*, 83 (1990), 170–89

Torrens and Cooper, 'Richardson' — H. S. Torrens and J. A. Cooper, 'George Fleming Richardson (1796–1848) – man of letters, lecturer and geological curator', *Geological Curator*, 4 (1986), 249–72

Torrens and Ford, 'Farey' — H. S. Torrens and T. D. Ford, 'John Farey (1766–1826) an unrecognised Polymath' in J. Farey, *General View of the Agriculture and Minerals of Derbyshire* (1811) vol. 1 reprinted (Matlock 1989), 1–28

Torrens and Getty, 'Hunton' — H. S. Torrens and T. A. Getty, 'Louis Hunton (1814–1838) – English pioneer in Ammonite Biostratigraphy', *Earth Sciences History*, 3 (1984), 58–68

Torrens and Taylor, 'Cheltenham' — H. S. Torrens and M. A. Taylor, 'Geological Collectors and Museums in Cheltenham 1810–1988: a case history and its lessons', *Geological Curator*, 5 (1990), 175–213

Townsend, *Moses* — J. Townsend, *The Character of Moses established for veracity as an Historian* (Bath and London 1813)

Townson, *Natural History* R. Townson, *Tracts and Observations in Natural History*, (London 1799).

Tyler, 'Guadeloupe' D. Tyler, 'The Guadeloupe Skeletons: in the Steps of Cuvier', *Biblical Creation (special issue)*, 18 (1984), 36 and 43–52

Vaux, *BM* W. Vaux, *Handbook to the Antiquities in the British Museum* (London 1851)

Viollet-le-Duc, 'Voute' 'Voute', *Dictionnaire Raisonné de l'Architecture Française du xie au xvie siècle*, ed. E. E. Viollet-le-Duc, 10 vols (Paris 1854–68), IX (1868)

Waagen, *Kunstwerke* Gustav Friedrich Waagen, *Kunstwerke und Kunstler in England und Paris* (Berlin 1837–9) 3 vols

Wade, *Black Book* John Wade, *The Black Book; or Corruption Unmasked!* (London 1820)

Wade, *Middle and Working Classes* [John Wade], *History of the Middle and Working Classes; with a popular exposition of the economical and political principles which have influenced the past and present condition of the industrious orders* (London 1833)

Warren and Rose, *Pengelly* C. N. Warren and S. Rose, *William Pengelly's Techniques of Archaeological Excavation*, Torquay Natural History Society Publication, no. 5 (1994)

Watkin, 'Pevsner' D. Watkin, 'Sir Nikolaus Pevsner: a Study in Historicism', *Apollo*, Sep. 1992, 169–71

Watkin, *Rise* D. Watkin, *The Rise of Architectural History* (London 1980)

Waywell, *Free-Standing* G. B. Waywell, *The Free-standing Sculptures from the Mausoleum at Halicarnassus* (London 1978)

Weston, 'The Ark' S. Weston, 'A view of the opinions of various writers on the identical place where the Ark of Noah rested', *Archaeologia*, 18 (1817), 302–5

Wetherall, 'Foundation' D. M. Wetherall 'From Canterbury to Winchester: the Foundation of the Institute', *Building on the Past: Celebrating 150 Years of the Royal Archaeological Institute* (London 1994)

Wetherall, BAA (thesis) D. M. Wetherall, 'The British Archaeological Association: Its Foundation and Split' (Durham MA thesis, 1991)

Whewell, *German Churches* W. Whewell, *Architectural Notes on German Churches* (Cambridge 1830)

White, *Cambridge Movement* J. F. White, *The Cambridge Movement* (Cambridge 1962)

Williamson, *Reminiscences* W. C. Williamson, *Reminiscences of a Yorkshire Naturalist* (London 1896)

Willis, *Canterbury* R. Willis, The Architectural History of Canterbury Cathedral (London 1845)

Willis, *Middle Ages* R. Willis, *Architecture of the Middle Ages* (London 1844)

Willis, [review] Anon, Review of Willis's *The Architectural Nomenclature of the Middle Ages*, *Ecclesiologist*, III (1843), 146

Willis and Clark, *Cambridge* R. Willis and J. W. Clark, *Architectural History of the University of Cambridge* (Cambridge 1886)

Wilson, *Franks* D. M. Wilson, *The Forgotten Collector. Augustus Wollaston Franks of the British Museum* (London 1984)

Wood, *Ephesus* J. T. Wood, *Discoveries at Ephesus* (London 1877)

Woodbridge, *Landscape* K. Woodbridge, *Landscape and Antiquity* (Oxford 1970)

Worsaae, *Denmark* J. J. A. Worsaae, *The Primeval Antiquities of Denmark, translated and applied to the illustration of similar remains in England*, trans. and ed. W.J. Thoms (London 1849)

Wright, *Album* Thomas Wright, *The Archaeological Album; or, Museum of National Antiquities* (London 1845)

Young, *Scriptural Geology* G. Young, *Scriptural Geology*, 2nd edn (London 1840), (1982)

Young, 'Greatest Victorian' G. M. Young, 'The Greatest Victorian', *Today and Yesterday* (1948), 237–43, reprinted in *Victorian Essays*, ed. W. D. H. Handcock (1962), 123–8.

Zola, *Belly* E. Zola, *The Belly of Paris* (1873)

Zola, *Masterpiece* E. Zola, *The Masterpiece* (1886), trans. T. Walton and R. Pearson (1993).

Index of Persons and Places

NB. All societies and clubs are listed under that heading.